ADVANCE PRAISE FOR

# PEDAGOGIES OF WITH-NESS: STUDENTS, TEACHERS, VOICE, AND AGENCY

"Brilliant stories of oppression, marginalization, and power. Stories of schooling, sometimes angry and pain-filled - always honest and powerful. This collection brings us voices of passion, voices we have silenced and ignored at our own peril. We need the wisdom in this book, especially its powerful and empowering strategies for deep listening and collaboration. Impossible to read without gaining insight and compassion."

Mara Sapon-Shevin
Professor of Education, Syracuse University

"This book offers rich description of how we can help young people to learn how to make a difference in their lives and their community. It provides important examples of the conditions and contexts in which young people learn how to develop agency."

Dana Mitra
Professor of Education, Penn State University
Founding editor of the *International Journal of Student Voice*

"The chapters in this book collectively invite the reader to re-examine personal conceptualizations of child and adolescent growth and development, the purpose of schooling, and the individual and societal impact of specific pedagogies. Emphasis is placed on centering student voice as an imperative for reciprocal development in teaching and learning."

Etta R. Hollins
Professor Emerita and Kauffman Endowed Chair,
University of Missouri, Kansas City

# PEDAGOGIES OF WITH-NESS

# PEDAGOGIES OF WITH-NESS

## Students, Teachers, Voice, and Agency

EDITED BY LINDA HOGG,

KEVIN STOCKBRIDGE,

CHARLOTTE ACHIENG-EVENSEN,

AND SUZANNE SOOHOO

*Gorham, Maine*

Published by Myers Education Press, LLC
P.O. Box 424
Gorham, ME 04038



**Myers Education Press** is an academic publisher specializing in books, e-books, and digital content in the field of education. All of our books are subjected to a rigorous peer review process and produced in compliance with the standards of the Council on Library and Information Resources.

Library of Congress Cataloging-in-Publication Data available from Library of Congress.

13-digit ISBN 978-1-9755-0308-6 (paperback)
13-digit ISBN 978-1-9755-0307-9 (hard cover)
13-digit ISBN 978-1-9755-0309-3 (library networkable e-edition)
13-digit ISBN 978-1-9755-0310-9 (consumer e-edition)

Printed in the United States of America.

All first editions printed on acid-free paper that meets the American National Standards Institute Z39-48 standard.

Books published by Myers Education Press may be purchased at special quantity discount rates for groups, workshops, training organizations, and classroom usage. Please call our customer service department at 1-800-232-0223 for details.

*Cover design by Teresa Lagrange*

Visit us on the web at **www.myersedpress.com** to browse our complete list of titles.

## Contents

*Acknowledgments* *xi*

*Foreword* *xiii*

*Preface* *xv*

INTRODUCTION Student Voice and Agency: Introducing Three Galleries of Work xvii
*Linda Hogg (with) Kevin Stockbridge (with) Charlotte Achieng-Evensen (with) Suzanne SooHoo*

ONE Who Is Listening to Students? 1
*Christopher Lewis*

PART I The Identity and Voice Gallery

TWO The Identity and Voice Gallery 15
*Charlotte Achieng-Evensen*

THREE "The Unnecessary Gendering of Everything": Gender-Diverse Adults Speak Back to Their K–12 Schools 17
*Katherine Lewis*

FOUR Truancy: Young People Walk Away From Negative School Factors 27
*Delia Baskerville*

FIVE Rooted and Rising: The Self-Liberation of African American Female Students 37
*Michelle Flowers-Taylor*

SIX Voices of Scholars: Academically Successful Black Males and Their Stories of Culturally Relevant Pedagogies 49
*Quaylan Allen*

SEVEN Empowering Students With Emotional and Behavioral Disorders 59
*Gabrielle Popp*

EIGHT Into the Future by, With, and for Indigenous Youth: Rangatahi Māori Leading Youth Conversations 69
*Huia Tomlins-Jahnke, Joanna Kidman, and Adreanne Ormond*

PART II The Pedagogy Gallery

NINE The Pedagogy Gallery 81
*Linda Hogg*

TEN Making Music Grow: Student Perspectives on Culturally Responsive Music Education 83
*Tracy Rohan*

ELEVEN "People Don't Understand": Children Learning Through Drama as a Way to Develop Student Voice 93
*Delia Baskerville and Dayle Anderson*

TWELVE Student Voices in the Digital Hubbub 103
*Chris Proctor and Antero Garcia*

THIRTEEN "Multiple Perspectives and Many Connections": Systems Thinking and Student Voice 117
*Amy Lassiter Ardell and Margaret Sauceda Curwen*

FOURTEEN Finding Hope Through Dystopian Novels 129
*Christopher Lewis*

PART III The Youth–Adult Partnerships Gallery

FIFTEEN The Youth–Adult Partnerships Gallery 141
*Kevin Stockbridge*

SIXTEEN We're the Bosses: Youth Action Council Designs an Equitable Makerspace 143
*Day Greenberg, Micaela Balzar, Angela Calabrese Barton, Edna Tan, and YAC Youth*

SEVENTEEN Repurposing the Master's Tools: Leveraging Business Education to Build a Better World 153
*Linda Hogg and Anne Yates*

EIGHTEEN Applying Gentleness Against the Force: The Dojo as a Site of Liberation for Autistic People 165
*Erin McCloskey*

NINETEEN "It Was Time for Us to Take a Stand": An Ethnic Studies Classroom and the Power of Student Voice 175
*Jorge F. Rodriguez, Carah Reed, and Karen Garcia*

TWENTY Collaborative Leadership: A Story of Student–Principal School Transformation 187
*Susanne Jungersen*

TWENTY-ONE Angeles Workshop School: An Experiment in Student Voice 197
*Ndindi Kitonga*

PART IV Pedagogies of With-ness

TWENTY-TWO Pedagogies of With-ness: Reflecting on and Beyond the Exhibition 211
*Linda Hogg (with) Charlotte Achieng-Evensen (with) Kevin Stockbridge (with) Suzanne SooHoo*

*Contributors* *217*

*Index* *221*

# *Acknowledgments*

GRETA THUNBERG FOR YOUR INSPIRATION and activism, which taught us to reframe impossibility as a dare rather than a fact. You were our muse. We offer this book as a small contribution, in solidarity with you and other youth activists.

Students represented within these pages, whose voices gift us with their wisdom and vision for new possibilities.

Our community of authors, whose passion and work are the heart of this book. We are grateful for your positive responsiveness to several rounds of review.

Chris Myers for giving us this opportunity to feature scholars from two countries as a path to global solidarity of teachers for and with students.

Eddy Emilien for interpreting our words and creating artwork for our book cover.

Professor Joanna Higgins and Emeritus Professor Cedric Hall (Victoria University of Wellington) for their support and feedback to Linda on very early drafts of the book proposal.

Emerita Professor Christine Sleeter (California State University, Monterey Bay), who insightfully brought Suzi and Linda together.

# *Foreword*

*Kevin Kumashiro*, author of *Against Common Sense: Teaching and Learning toward Social Justice*

WHILE GROWING UP, ART GALLERIES were never my favorite spaces. Even when taking a summer art class, I would look at our projects, the displays all around us of projects in progress by local artists and teachers, or the next-door public exhibits and I would find myself bored, somehow blind to what I was "supposed" to be seeing, or doubting my ability to appreciate what so many others apparently could.

That there would be one right way to (re)view art was a notion rattled in my head when, as a young adult, I heard a lecture about the pedagogy of museums and the many ways that museums teach through not only the content but also the structure, design, and framing of that content, particularly when reminding viewers that any exhibit is partial, perspectival, and will always be mediated in meaning-making by the lenses through which each viewer gazes. Experiencing museums can be far more interactive through the questions that they demand that viewers ask of the content, and they can be far more discomforting and/or stirring (emotionally and politically) when those questions implicate the viewers themselves. So, too, with art galleries—they can be viewed voyeuristically and apolitically, but they can also be experienced as interventions in meaning-making, self-reflexivity, and leveraging the creative endeavor to remake the here and now.

Educational scholars and advocates often hold up student voice as art—and here, what I find deeply problematic is when such use of voice verges on showcasing, on merely amplifying their voices as if their unmediated voices are, in and of themselves, pedagogical. Ironically, what is intended or implied to respect student voice ends up as far more patronizing and condescending because missing in such exhibiting of voice is any critical engagement as partners, comrades in shared struggle, and worthy of the collective preparation that any of us require when speaking in ways that we hope will be held, heard, and taken to heart. No, just as their voice should not be taken as apparent of truth, neither should our listening be taken as merely absorbing from a distance. To be working toward justice in solidarity with youth is to engage, challenge and be challenged, and be with.

This is precisely what we have with this important new book. Rather than the too-common trend among scholars to exalt student voice uncritically, Hogg, Stockbridge, Achieng-Evensen, SooHoo, and colleagues highlight students-with-teachers engaging in critical pedagogy and shared struggle—a pedagogy of "with-ness." In so doing, they amplify their original insights and collective interventions that are at once humbling yet demanding of hope. From understanding the identities, experiences, and diversities among youth to imagining the pedagogical possibilities in and out of classrooms to forging community partnerships with classrooms and schools, the various chapters are presented like artwork in galleries, including docents to each gallery that offer questions to guide and invite open-ended ways of reading, reflecting, applying, and questioning what we see, hear, feel, remember, and imagine with each chapter.

In this moment, when widespread youth mobilizing is reshaping the landscape of education, we need precisely this book and its galleries of voice to help us make sense of the power of collectivization, of young people working with one another and working with adults across vast differences but toward unifying goals of justice. Let's dive into that struggle, not just for our youth but also with them.

# *Preface*

WE BEGAN THIS BOOK PROJECT prior to the COVID-19 pandemic. However, its relevance has been heightened by the new and emergent challenges for schooling. The pandemic has created enormous upheaval, and schools have not been immune. A move to online teaching and learning calls for teacher and students to imagine new ways to be *with* each other.

COVID-19 freshly exposes not only societal inequities (e.g., Bhala et al., 2020; Raifman & Raifman, 2020) but also educational ones. Its impacts are much more severe in vulnerable populations (e.g., Flentje et al., 2020; Zhang et al., 2020). In the United States, thousands of students have slipped out of teachers' vision because they have not been able to engage in the new forms of learning instigated by the pandemic. Brought to the forefront, also, is the reality that many students suffer mental health issues, including loneliness, anxiety, and depression (Racine et al., 2020). We realize that this suffering and inequity is not new, but it has been exacerbated and intensified by our current circumstances.

In their discussion of ways to build student resilience in the face of COVID-19, Dvorsky et al. (2020) reiterate Masten's insight that "resilience does not come from rare or special qualities, but from the everyday magic of the ordinary, normative human resources in . . . children, in their families and relationships, and in their communities" (Masten, 2001, cited in Dvorsky et al., 2020, p. 1). As teachers and schools adapt in response to the pandemic, the role of schools as protective communities is even more important (Courtney et al., 2020). Within our upended way of life, awareness of and respect for students as individuals, and attention to caring relationships—with-ness—is more important than ever.

## References

Bhala, N., Curry, G., Martineau, A. R., Agyemang, C., & Bhopal, R. (2020). Sharpening the global focus on ethnicity and race in the time of COVID-19. *The Lancet*, 395(10238), 1673–1676. doi:10.1016/SO140-6736(20)31102-8

Courtney, D., Watson, P., Battaglia, M., Mulsant, B. H., & Szatmari, P. (2020). COVID-19 impacts on child and youth anxiety and depression: Challenges and opportunities. *The Canadian Journal of Psychiatry*, 1–4. doi:10.1177/0706743720935646

Dvorsky, M. R., Breaux, R., & Becker, S. P. (2020). Finding ordinary magic in extraordinary times: Child and adolescent resilience during the COVID-19 pandemic. *European Child and Adolescent Psychiatry*. doi:10.1007/s00787-020-01583-8

Flentje, A., Obedin-Maliver, J., Lubensky, M. E., Dastur, Z., Neilands, T., & Lunn, M. R. (2020). Depression and anxiety changes among sexual and gender minority people coinciding with onset of COVID-19 pandemic. *Journal of General Internal Medicine*. doi:10.1007/s11606-020-05970-4

Racine, N., Cooke, J. E., Eirich, R., Korczak, D. J., McArthur, B-A., & Madigan, S. (2020). Child and adolescent mental illness during COVID-19: A rapid review. *Psychiatry Research*. doi:10.1016/j.psychiatryres.2020.113307

Raifman, M. A., & Raifman, J. R. (2020). Disparities in the population at risk of severe illness from COVID-19 by race/ethnicity and income. *American Journal of Preventive Medicine*, *59*(1), 137-139. doi:10.1016/j.amepre.2020.04.003

Zhang, J., Lu, H., Zeng, H., Zhang, S., Du, Q., Jiang, T., & Du, B. (2020). The differential psychological stress of populations affected by the COVID-19 pandemic. *Brain, Behavior, and Immunity*, *87*, 49-50. doi:10.1016/j.bbi.2020.04.031

INTRODUCTION

# Student Voice and Agency: Introducing Three Galleries of Work

*Linda Hogg (with) Kevin Stockbridge (with) Charlotte Achieng-Evensen (with) Suzanne Soohoo*

ART IS THE MEDIUM OF prophecy. Jazz singer Nina Simone famously said that art must address the times. This book is a curated exhibition of pieces, possibilities presented by educators and scholars who, in solidarity with students, stand for an ethic of commitment to student voice, agency, and student–educator partnerships. Permeating this collection is an ethic of *with-ness*—a way of knowing, being, and acting that imagines pedagogy in a new frame. It is a prophetic response to what plagues our times and we speak more about it in our final chapter. In this hyper-networked, post-truth era of global challenges, contradictions, and upheaval, youth are raising their voices and exercising agency in new ways. This collection responds to their clarion call.

## Why Is This Book Important Right Now?

Recently, many images of student voice and agency have graced our screens. Across the globe, youth activists demonstrate the transformative potential of student voices in education and the world. Students around the globe are demanding this right. We have seen K–12 students in United States speaking up, walking out, and marching for social justice. The "March For Our Lives" group, co-founded by David Hogg, published a gun-control proposal hoping to galvanize debate and draw out youth voters in the 2020 federal elections. In New Zealand, Okirano Tilaia organized the *Students Uniting in Love* vigil attended by thousands after a terrorist attack on Muslims. In Sweden, Greta Thunberg inspired international school walkouts to promote climate justice. In a speech to the United Nations, Greta admonished adults: "You are not mature enough to tell it like it is. You are failing us. But the young people are starting to understand your betrayal" (Thunberg, cited by Milman, 2019, para. 2).

This exhibition of work offers artforms of possibilities organized into three galleries. Our intention is for readers to wander through, making their own pathways. While exploring, readers will discover facets of possibility envisioning what classrooms could be. At each entrance, the section introduction includes questions acting as docents, and questions are posed at the conclusion of each chapter. They beckon readers to engage in mental dialogue with the artists as a way of knowing. It is in walking and talking "with" that readers establish relational solidarity (Horton & Freire, 1990). We hope that wandering through these galleries offers views of some ways that educators can support student voice and agency by being in relational solidarity with students and teacher allies.

Being in relational solidarity with students to support their voices and agency demands intentionality and commitment to action (Gaztambide-Fernandez, 2012), especially within today's neoliberal environment, where deficit ideas of youth are causing student voices to be suppressed. Deficit views see youth as those who are "to be feared, controlled, contained, and . . . kept in" (Steinberg, 2011, p. 269). Increasingly popular "penal pedagogies" (Giroux, 2009), such as zero-tolerance policies, and criminalization of students through use of handcuffs and tasers are indicative of a "war on youth" (Giroux, 2016). Ageism and deficit thinking about youth disallows students' development as active and empowered citizens, rendering them incapable of exercising power and agency in their communities for the betterment of society.

## What Do We Mean by Student Voice?

Student voice reveals, through articulation, silence, and expression, youth consciousness about the world. It also echoes a "wide-awakeness" (Greene, 1995, p. 35) in students about their selfhood and their position in that world. For students, it means "to voice what it is I am." It precedes and accompanies the beginning of critical consciousness by "naming the world" (Freire, 1998).

Student voice is sacred. It is the utterances of valuable human beings sharing their wisdom as experts of their own experiences. As such, it creates an ethical and epistemological obligation for teachers to cultivate spaces that are open and responsive to student voices and student knowing. Not only are teachers obliged to be listeners but also to be artists in the crafting of equitable educational spaces. When student voices are gathered, listening and taking action in response is an ethical responsibility (Groundwater-Smith, 2007). This process is teaching and learning, and it is dynamic—a process of becoming for both students and teachers.

We believe that consideration of student voice, and its impact on education, cannot end with a discussion of the contradictory poles of speaker and listener. Rather, we imagine that student voice, as an expression of critical consciousness, necessitates more than simply hearing. It compels us to move into action. When teachers and students come together to change realities problematized by these voices, they engage a new kind of solidarity in action. We define this as "*with-ness*."

## The Three Galleries of Work

Here, we unpack facets of student voice shown in each of the three galleries.

### *The Identity and Voice Gallery*

Within the Identity and Voice Gallery, readers will find works that provide living vignettes of minoritized students' school lives. Looking around this gallery reminds us of who is in classrooms and asserts their right to belong. Through the art emerge voices of students who are often silenced and invisible. Hearing these voices is a first step toward "know[ing] enough about the people around [you] to enter into dialogue with them" (Stanley, 2003, p. 38).

In artworks in the Identity and Voice Gallery, students speak about what is happening in their classrooms for them, describing impacts and consequences that their educational experiences have had on them personally. They share advice for schools and readers, based on their shared experiences *with* teachers.

In Katherine Lewis's art, we see schooling through the eyes of gender-diverse students. Delia Baskerville introduces us to long-term truants and their stories about what led them to decide that remaining outside the classroom was safer than being in it. Michelle Flowers-Taylor shares insights that ground academically successful African American females in education. Quaylan Allen's piece introduces voices of Black male scholars reflecting on effective teacher practices. In Gabrielle Popp's work, students who are excluded from mainstream education due to emotional and behavioral disorders paint a picture of schooling that enables them to be their best selves. Huia Tomlins-Jahnke, Joanna Kidman, and Adreanne Ormond illustrate the importance of cultural liaisons in their vignette of Maori youth. The works in this gallery reveal what students say about schooling and the possible actions they would like to see undertaken.

### *The Pedagogy Gallery*

In the Pedagogy Gallery, artwork offers vignettes of pedagogical performances in which teachers deliberately engage, integrate, and develop opportunities for student voice—thus developing students' agency. This pedagogy avoids the trap of imposing teacher ideas upon students (Fleming, 2015). These teacher-artists are working on doing less teaching as preaching. We invite you into the Pedagogy Gallery, to examine ways that airspace is reserved for students and how voices can be drawn out, nurtured, and centralized in classrooms.

The canvases and art materials are diverse. Tracy Rohan's students assert the importance of culturally inclusive music education. Delia Baskerville and Dayle Anderson's work gives a view of drama conventions in action in New Zealand elementary classrooms. Chris Proctor and Antero Garcia project readers into the virtual world of a student author's digital interactive storytelling project. Amy Ardell and Margie Curwen show us two classes which fostered development of student voice through a systems thinking program. Chris Lewis shapes a montage of how reading dystopian novels in a book club helped U.S. high school seniors to critically examine the realities and possibilities of their own world.

### *The Youth–Adult Partnerships Gallery*

Transformative student voice work is dialogic, collective and inclusive, intergenerational, and transgressive (Pearce & Wood, 2016). The work requires mutual reciprocity. It is cultivated in spaces where adults and students undertake a co-generative approach to learning. This gallery showcases youth–adult partnerships propelled by student voices. The artwork maintains a focus on students enacting their truth to power, which means movement from problem-posing to possibility-making.

Come into this gallery to witness the movement of students and teachers as co-actors in "radical collegiality" (Fielding, 1999, p. 3). In the chapter by Day Greenberg, Micaela Balzer, Angela Calabrese Barton, Edna Tan, and the Youth Action Council, readers are welcomed to encounter a youth–adult partnership that centers student agency in the construction of makerspace. Linda Hogg and Anne Yates describe how student passion led to innovative outcomes in business education when teachers nurtured youth vision of ecological justice. Erin McCloskey welcomes us into a dojo where neuro-diverse youth and their sensei construct an inclusive space of learning. Jorge Rodriguez, Carah Reed, and Karen Garcia highlight the transformative power of student voice addressing injustice in schools when in partnership with teachers. Susanne Jungersen's work considers the possibility of democratic educational leadership through a description of youth–adult decision-making processes and their transformative effects. Ndindi Kitonga provides readers a view into an alternative school committed to student voice and democracy, including some tensions and challenges of enacting this ethical stance.

*Historical Archives and Pedagogy of With-ness*

Alongside the galleries are a literature review and concluding chapter. The literature review, by Chris Lewis, describes our contemporary educational landscape and provides an overview of levels of student involvement. We stand on the shoulders of scholars whose theoretical work, research, and practice illuminate higher levels of student agency and voice. The concluding chapter highlights the conceptual framework of the book: *pedagogies of with-ness*. With-ness is the unifying, reverberating motif which we have identified as the essence of all the artworks. Join us, the book editors, as you come out of the galleries. This is the space where we collectively make sense of our experiences from this art exhibition. Let the viewing begin.

## References

Fielding, M. (1999). Radical collegiality: Affirming teaching as an inclusive professional practice. *Australian Educational Researcher, 26*(2), 1–34.

Fleming, D. (2015). Student voice: An emerging discourse in Irish education policy. *International Electronic Journal of Elementary Education, 8*(2), 223–242.

Freire, P. (1998). *Pedagogy of freedom: Ethics, democracy, and civic courage*. Oxford, England: Rowman & Littlefield.

Gaztambide-Fernandez, R. (2012). Decolonization and the pedagogy of solidarity. *Decolonization: Indigeneity, Education and Society, 1*(1), 41–67.

Giroux, H. A. (2009). *Youth in a suspect society: Democracy or disability?* Hampshire, England: Palgrave Macmillan.

Giroux, H. A. (2016, 19 October). *The United States war on youth: From schools to debtors' prisons*. Truthout. Retrieved from https://truthout.org/articles/america-s-war-on-youth-from-schools-to-debtors-prisons/

Greene, M. (1995). *Releasing the imagination: Essays on education, the arts, and social change.* San Francisco, CA: Jossey-Bass.

Groundwater-Smith, S. (2007). Student voice: Essential testimony for intelligent schools. In A. Campbell & S. Groundwater-Smith (Eds.), *An ethical approach to practitioner research: Dealing with issues and dilemmas in action research* (pp. 113–128). New York, NY: Routledge.

Horton, M. & Freire, P. (1990). *We make the road by walking: Conversations on education and social change*. Philadelphia, PA: Temple University Press.

Milman, O. (2019, September 23). Greta Thunberg condemns world leaders in emotional speech at UN. *The Guardian*. https://www.theguardian.com/environment/2019/sep/23/greta-thunberg-speech-un-2019-address

Pearce, T. C. & Wood, B. E. (2016). Education for transformation: An evaluative framework to guide student voice work in schools. *Critical Studies in Education, 60*(1), 113–130. doi:10.1080/17508487.2016.1219959

Stanley, T. (2003). Creating the 'space' for civic dialogue. *Phi Delta Kappan, 85*(1), 38–39.

Steinberg, S. R. (2011). Redefining the notion of youth: Contextualizing the possible for transformative youth leadership. *Counterpoints, 409*, 267–275.

ONE

# Who Is Listening to Students?

*Christopher Lewis*

DANA MITRA (2008) ASKED, "WHAT might happen if we viewed youth as part of the solution, rather than as part of the problem?" (p. 1). The philosophical and ideological implications of Mitra's question reposition youth as knowledgeable problem-solvers in a world that often ignores their experiences.

Systemic inequality and power structures in education make the inclusion of youth voice challenging because empowering student voice means dismantling the hierarchy of dialogic space between teachers and students. It involves building reciprocal relationships which emphasize shared construction of knowledge in democratic spaces. Teachers who constantly reflect on their practices and the theories that inform their pedagogy exemplify Freire's (1970/2000) vision of praxis: "Only human beings *are* praxis—praxis which, as the reflection and action which truly transform reality, is the source of knowledge and creation" (pp. 100–101). Through a problem-posing model of education, "individuals develop their power to perceive *the way they exist* in the world *with which* and *in which* they find themselves; they come to see the world not as a static reality, but as reality in process, in transformation" (Freire, 1970/2000, p. 83). Transforming schools, and, more broadly, society, cannot occur if youth are not viewed as equal stakeholders capable of imagining a world they will soon lead. However, Rudduck and Fielding (2006) argue that the popularity of youth voice is dangerous if the *why* and *how* are not addressed; schools must anticipate how student perspectives will affect institutional systems and what role students will play as stakeholders who work *with* adults. If youth are consulted to only reflect on traditional schooling practices, then the positivistic model of education is reinforced, and voice becomes mere tokenism.

Reviewing the history of education in the United States helps explain the passive role students often embody in classrooms (Freire 1970/2000; Giroux, 1997). Some researchers have attempted to question and destabilize hegemonic power through the study of voice as a tool for liberation (Giroux, 1997;

McLaren, 2007; Shor & Freire, 1987). More recent research interrogates how adult privilege undermines authentic student participation (Alcoff, 1991; Cook-Sather, 2007; Fielding, 2004, 2007). What does the inclusion of youth voice sound like today? How do political contexts shape the way youth are viewed? The shifting political landscape has opened spaces, physical and digital, where youth feel empowered and are speaking out.

In this review, I first provide a brief overview of shifts in education policy and an examination of power structures within schools. Second, I use Adam Fletcher's (2017) "Ladder of Student Involvement" to describe examples of student voice in schools. Finally, I conclude by looking forward. Youth are positioned to offer unique, timely, and relevant commentary on their experiences. More important, empowering student agency can elevate their perspectives, make schools more equitable, and improve a school's culture.

## Our Contemporary Context

At the institutional level, schools function within a narrative controlled by those in power: politicians who decide policy, administrators who oversee policy implementation, and teachers who implement shifting education paradigms in classrooms. Missing from the education narrative are the experiences and perspectives of youth. In the current neoliberal environment, schools function as bureaucracies where financial solvency and test scores are paramount. This comes at the expense of developing creativity, problem-solving, and compassion in youth. Giroux (2013) says, "Welcome to the dystopian world of corporate education in which learning how to think, be informed by public values, and become engaged critical citizens are viewed as a failure rather than a mark of success" (para. 4) and "privatization, commodification, militarization, and deregulation" are guiding principles (para. 16). Attaining the "American Dream" is hopeless for the marginalized and disenfranchised despite the democratic foundations upon which U.S. public education has been built (Miguel & Gargano, 2017).

Giroux (2003) called contemporary youth the "abandoned generation" who are affected by governments that instill fear instead of building hope. The application of market principles to education results in policies that remove protections for youth and increases the likelihood that inclusion falls to the wayside. For example, billionaire and current U.S. secretary of education

Betsy DeVos is committed to deregulating student rights policies associated with Title IX, transgender protections, students with disabilities, for-profit academic institutions, campus sexual assault, and faulty student loans (Bloomfield & Aja, 2017).

Since the 1980s, in line with the global rise of neoliberalism, public education has undergone significant overhauls and accountability has become ubiquitous. In 1983, *A Nation at Risk* was published, decreasing the public's faith in educators and increasing the demand for more federal involvement in determining curriculum and accountability (Willis et al., 1993). This report fuelled the Reagan presidency and the conservative right to propose a business-like model of fixing education problems (Giroux, 2003; Macedo, 2006). No Child Left Behind (NCLB) (2001) increased school accountability to close the achievement gap for racial and economic minority groups through the content standards movement and use of high-stakes testing to encourage academic proficiency (Darling-Hammond, 2010; Giroux, 2003). However, increased high-stakes testing negatively affects how students are treated in classrooms and how teachers make pedagogical choices (Fecho, Mallozzi, & Schultz, 2007). Teachers work within a system where they are deskilled and face curriculum that fails to engage counternarratives critical of sociopolitical conditions reproduced in many schools (Giroux, 1989; Giroux & McLaren, 1987; Kumashiro, 2010; Sleeter, 2008). To encourage accountability and efficiency, a push for corporate takeovers of schools and districts has integrated free-market capitalism into education.

Increasing access to technology in the age of social media has shaped public perception of Millennials and Generation Z (born in or after 1996; Dimock, 2019). Those in power negatively depict youth as lacking an attention span and constantly demanding positive reinforcement (Gray, 2014; Havig, 2013; Taylor & Keeter, 2010). Much of the discussion about shifting values between the two generations is situated in schools and workspaces where youth identities are forming (Mohr & Mohr, 2017; Selingo, 2018). However, the Pew Research Center notes the unique experience of Generation Z because they grew up in an already connected, technology-rich environment amid economic turmoil during a recession (Dimock, 2019). Naturally, these contextual factors influence Generation Z's interconnectedness and how they communicate and advocate on large-scale issues. The rapidly changing world, in which youth are leading the way, continues to evolve—but will schools remain stuck in the past? Will society reject youth who were enculturated in the environment that it created?

Schools are failing at their stated purpose—to educate students to become global citizens—but Giroux (2003) notes that they are succeeding at their hidden purpose. Discrimination and oppression are often reinforced dysconsciously through the "hidden curriculum," which can be seen in "the total physical and instructional environment, governance structures, teachers' expectations, and grading procedures" (McLaren, 2009, p. 75). Youth often feel alienated from education when politicians and teachers choose curricula where youth do not see themselves represented (Apple, 2006; Delpit, 1995; Gay, 2010; hooks, 1994; Nieto, 2002). Additionally, students are negatively affected by institutional policies and teachers' pedagogical choices that silence or devalue their perspectives (Fecho et al., 2007; Fielding, 2004; Freire, 1970/2000, 1998; Giroux, 1997; Mitra, 2006). Political control over curricula, pedagogy, and assessment affects all aspects of students' educational experiences. These conditions teach educators and youth that compliance within the system means you get by without harm. But what happens when stakeholders ask questions? Problematizing an institution's hidden curriculum requires trust and reciprocity between adults and students.

## Levels of Youth Involvement

To further youth voice work, the process of schooling must be contextualized within systems of power that define the youth experience. If youth are limited to commentary about school environments and pedagogy, then the transformation and liberation discussed by Freire (1970/2000) is not possible. Naming and problematizing more complex systems of power related to issues of race, class, gender, sexuality, or ability enable youth to participate in broader discussions about their world. Too often students are limited to topics like discipline policies, grading procedures, or cafeteria food, and nothing is done after they contribute to the discussion. When evaluating the extent to which youth are heard, we must focus on the content and the subsequent actions taken by those in positions of power.

Fletcher's (2017) "Ladder of Student Involvement" represents the ways in which youth knowledge and participation are evident in educational settings. This is one possible model that can be used to evaluate the range of ways student voice is employed in schools. The model is useful because, as Fletcher explains, the ladder is not meant to evaluate schools as a whole but discrete instances of student involvement. The ladder was developed using Roger Hart's (1992) research on alliances between students and adults and shared decision-making. What differentiates each level of the ladder is the way students provide information and the extent to which their feedback is used to change observed conditions (Fielding, 2001; Fletcher, 2005, 2017; Hart, 1992; Mitra & Gross, 2009). Additionally, when comparing levels of participation, there are differences in how the adult community frames the validity of students' experiences and ideas. At lower levels (1–3), labelled *nonparticipation* by Hart (1992), students are viewed as subjects and remain passive or even manipulated (Cook-Sather, 2007; Fielding; 2007; Fletcher, 2005, 2017). Youths might be heard, but there is little guarantee that adults are listening. In this case, voice does not necessitate a listener; instead, the power structure is maintained and students' views are not validated.

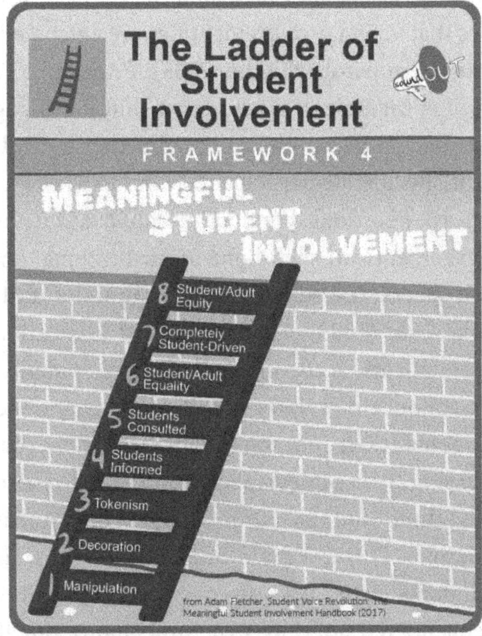


**Figure 1.1.** Ladder of Student Involvement. Adapted by Adam Fletcher (2017). Reprinted with permission.

Fletcher (2005, 2017) describes the higher rungs (7–8) as *student/adult partnerships* where students and adults actively co-create meaningful change. *Completely student-driven* includes classroom projects, student-initiated inquiry, participatory action research (PAR), and youth participatory action research (YPAR). These processes position students as active participants with agency. By placing students in the role of researcher, traditional sources of knowledge are challenged by legitimizing students' experiences (Cahill, 2007; Duncan-Andrade & Reyes, 2008; Fielding, 2004; Mitra, 2003, 2008; O'Brien, 2010). Fine (Cammarota & Fine, 2008) defines PAR as "a radical epistemological challenge to the traditions of social science, most critically on the topic of where knowledge resides" (p. 215). By giving power to students' views, adults may gain access to new perspectives of the world.

To elaborate more on a couple of ways to achieve completely student-driven involvement, Mirra, Filipiak, and Garcia (2015) argue that YPAR redefines youth voice through agency, which "represents the power that derives from the pursuit of those questions that matter most to students . . . It is contextually bound, always in negotiation, and mediated by the histories, social interactions, and cultures that young people's identities are entangled within" (p. 53). According to Fine (Cammarota & Fine, 2008), PAR and YPAR are not just methodologies but epistemological views that shift knowledge sources from the adult to adults *and* students. Thus, critical pedagogy and youth research projects can potentially liberate participants from oppressive structures.

When students ask questions, conduct research, and determine findings, their level of engagement can shed light on institutional and environmental issues within a school, the surrounding community, and potentially the world. For example, Lee's (1999) ethnography includes Latina/o and African American students with low academic performance; students were trained to be co-researchers, conduct interviews, and identify major trends in the data. In these projects, students asked questions about institutional barriers that were obstacles to increasing their achievement. Student-led research is also present in courses like Ethnic Studies (Cammarota, 2016; Cammarota & Romero, 2014). In Cammarota's (2016) Ethnic Studies course in Tucson, Arizona, YPAR allowed students to be "both the researcher and the researched" (p. 239). Students "engendered not only structural change but also transformation of themselves" (Cammarota, 2016, p. 239) because the intersection of YPAR and Ethnic Studies provides "dual-subjectivity" that generates agency for students (Lozenski, 2019). Students in Cammarota's courses raised concerns about the physical conditions of their school and later about the importance of ethnic studies when the course was banned by the legislature and Arizona governor Jan Brewer. In these classrooms, students are positioned as stakeholders actively contributing to school reform efforts.

Fletcher's (2015) highest level of student involvement (rungs 7–8), *student/adult equity*, is evident when adults and youth build reciprocity and trustworthiness to minimize hierarchical power. In collaboration, youth and adults share the responsibility of increasing academic success and improving school culture (Bolstad, 2011; Mitra, 2006, 2008; Yonezawa & Jones, 2007). Most of these partnerships focus on school reform where students are honored as stakeholders and participate in some form of action research (AR) or forum for discussing school-related issues (Fielding, 2001; Jones & Yonezawa, 2009; Mitra, 2005, 2006; O'Brien, 2010; Oldfather, 1995; SooHoo, 1993; Yonezawa & Jones, 2007).

Establishing forums or steering committees is one way to provide an opportunity for students to voice their opinions about particular issues at school; however, the challenge is for adults to avoid manipulating students by listening with no resulting action (Cook-Sather, Cohen, & Alter, 2010; Mitra, 2006, 2008; Yonezawa & Jones, 2007). Student forums go beyond focusing on social events; they provide spaces for youth to openly discuss academic and school culture issues. Educators, in turn, must be open to the recommendations and listen for the purpose of understanding. Mitra (2008), Cook-Sather et al., (2010), and Fielding (2001) describe successful examples, noting how teachers and students viewed themselves as collective groups and how they viewed each other as a community. Significant outcomes vary depending on the time commitment and frequency of forum meetings. These examples do not completely meet the criteria Fletcher (2005) describes because students might still be seen as contributors to the discussion and not change agents. As adults and youth more frequently coordinate reform efforts together, schools will benefit from the inclusivity.

## Now What?

As neoliberalism maintains its stronghold on education and marginalizes youth voice, democratic ideals dissipate, knowledge is commodified, and civic engagement wanes (Baltodano, 2012; Diera, 2016). However, might schools be places where youth could learn about civic participation and actually become engaged in democracy? As more youth-led resistances occur and youth voices ring out on social media, educators have a responsibility to creates spaces for their students to analyze controversial issues. To do so, there are three areas educators must attend to in their development of systems that empower youth. First, educators have a responsibility to engage youth in discussions about the complexity of identity and the systems that shape individual and collective experiences both in and beyond schools. Second, we must continue to interrogate the purpose of education and embrace humanizing pedagogies. Third, in a world where youth feel alienated and disempowered, empathy is an essential critical tool needed to build collective efficacy. Mirra (2018) argues that critical civic empathy will help youth move beyond tolerance and instead make them agents of change.

Perhaps the most important challenge educators must face is learning how to truly listen, not just so youth are heard but also so their opinions inspire action. When adults work intentionally *with* youth, power structures will be reduced and the collective can work toward building more democratic and inclusive schools. If Mitra's (2008) ideas about viewing students as part of the solution are taken up, and adults and students work *with* each other, what new possibilities might blossom in our schools and communities? How might such a change in worldview affect our world?

## References

Alcoff, L. (1991, Winter). The problem of speaking for others. *Cultural Critique*, pp. 5–32.

Apple, M. W. (2006). *Educating the "right" way: Markets, standards, God, and inequality* (2nd ed.). New York, NY: Routledge.

Baltodano, M. (2012). Neoliberalism and the demise of public education: The corporatization of schools of education. *International Journal of Qualitative Studies in Education, 25*(4), 487–507. doi:10.1080/09518398.2012.673025

Bloomfield, D. C., & Aja, A. A. (2017, December 4). Betsy Devos is undermining students' rights under the guise of deregulation. *Education Week*. Retrieved at https://www.edweek.org/ew/articles/ 2017/12/04/what-will-betsy-devos-do-next.html

Bolstad, R. (2011). From "student voice" to "youth-partnership." *set: Research Information for Teachers, 1*, 31–33.

Cahill, C. (2007). Doing research *with* young people: Participatory research and the rituals of collective work. *Children's Geographies, 5*(3), 297–312. doi:10.1080/14733280701445895

Cammarota, J. (2016). The praxis of ethnic studies: Transforming second sight into critical consciousness. *Race Ethnicity and Education, 19*(2), 233–251.

Cammarota, J., & Fine, M. (2008). *Revolutionizing education: Youth participatory action research in motion*. New York, NY: Routledge.

Cammarota, J., & Romero, A. (Eds.) (2014). *Raza studies: The public option for educational revolution*. Tucson, AR: University of Arizona Press.

Cook-Sather, A. (2007). Resisting the impositional potential of student voice work: Lessons for liberatory educational research from poststructuralist feminist critiques of critical pedagogy. *Discourse: Studies in the Cultural Politics of Education, 28*(3), 389–403. doi:10.1080/01596300701458962

Cook-Sather, A., Cohen, J., & Alter, Z. (2010). Students leading the way toward social justice within and beyond classrooms. *Equity & Excellence in Education, 43*(2), 155–172. doi:10.1177/0192636507309810

Darling-Hammond, L. (2010). *The flat world and education: How America's commitment to equity will determine our future*. New York, NY: Teachers College Press.

Delpit, L. (1995). *Other people's children: Cultural conflict in the classroom*. New York, NY: The New Press.

Diera, C. (2016). Democratic possibilities for student voice within schools undergoing reform: A student counterpublic case study. *Journal for Critical Education Policy Studies, 14*(2), 217–235.

Dimock, M. (2019, January 17). *Defining generations: Where Millennials end and Generation Z begins*. Pew Research Center. Retrieved from https://www.pewresearch.org/fact-tank/2019/01/17/where-millennials-end-and-generation-z-begins/

Duncan-Andrade, J., & Reyes, J.M. (2008). *The art of critical pedagogy: Possibilities for moving from theory to practice in urban schools*. New York, NY: Peter Lang.

Fecho, B., Mallozzi, C. A., & Schultz, K. (2007). Policy and adolescent literacy. In B. J. Guzzetti (Ed.), *Literacy for the new millennium, vol. 3* (pp. 37–52). Westport, CT: Praeger Perspectives.

Fielding, M. (2001). Students as radical agents of change. *Journal of Educational Change, 2*(2), 123–141.

Fielding, M. (2004). Transformative approaches to student voice: Theoretical underpinnings, recalcitrant realities. *British Educational Journal, 30*(2), 295–311.

Fielding, M. (2007). Beyond "voice": New roles, relations, and contexts in researching with young people. *Discourse, 28*(3), 301–310.

Fletcher, A. (2005). *Meaningful student involvement guide to students as partners in school change*. Seattle, WA: HumanLinks Foundation. Retrieved from https://soundout.org/wp-content/uploads/2015/06/MSIGuide.pdf

Fletcher, A. F. C. (2017). *Student voice revolution: The meaningful student involvement handbook*. Olympia, WA: CommonAction Publishing. Retrieved from https://soundout.org/student-voice-revolution/

Freire, P. (2000). *Pedagogy of the oppressed* (M. B. Ramos, Trans.). New York, NY: Continuum. (Original work published 1970)

Freire, P. (1998). *Pedagogy of freedom: Ethics, democracy, and civic courage*. Lanham, MD: Rowan & Littlefield.

Gay, G. (2010). *Cultural responsive teaching: Theory, research, and practice*. New York, NY: Teachers College Press.

Giroux, H. A. (1989). Schooling as a form of cultural politics: Towards a pedagogy of and for difference. In H. A. Giroux & P. McLaren (Eds.), *Critical pedagogy, the state, and cultural struggle* (pp. 125–151). Albany, NY: SUNY Press.

Giroux, H. A. (1997). *Pedagogy and the politics of hope: Theory, culture, and schooling: A critical reader*. Boulder, CO: Westview.

Giroux, H. A. (2003). *The abandoned generation: Democracy beyond the culture of fear*. New York, NY: Palgrave Macmillan.

Giroux, H. A. (2013). Beyond dystopian education in a neoliberal society. *Fast Capitalism*. Retrieved from http://www.uta.edu/huma/agger/fastcapitalism/10_1/giroux10_1.html

Giroux, H. A., & McLaren, P. (1987). Teacher education as a counterpublic sphere: Radical pedagogy as a form of cultural politics. *Philosophy & Social Criticism, 12*(1), 51–69.

Gray, S. (2014, April 30). Even more proof that the "lazy millennial" stereotype is dead wrong [Blog entry]. *Salon*. Retrieved from http://www.salon.com/2014/04/30/over_one_third_of_millennials_say_new_tech_increases_their_work_hours/

Hart, R. (1992). *Children's participation: From tokenism to citizenship*. Florence, Italy: UNICEF International Child Development Centre.

Havig, B. (2013, November 4). Millennials vs. boomers: 5 stereotypes that aren't true (mostly) [Blog entry]. *Forbes*. Retrieved from: http://www.forbes.com/sites/gyro/2013/11/04/5-millennial-stereotypes-that-arent-true-mostly/

hooks, b. (1994). *Teaching to transgress: Education as the practice of freedom*. New York, NY: Routledge.

Jones, M., & Yonezawa, S. (2009). Student-driven research. *Educational Leadership, 66*(4), 65–69.

Kumashiro, K. (2010). Seeing the bigger picture: Troubling movements to end teacher education. *Journal of Teacher Education, 61*(1–2), 56–65.

Lee, P. W. (1999). In their own voices: An ethnographic study of low-achieving students within the context of school reform. *Urban Education, 34*(2), 214–244. doi:10.1177/0042085999342005

Lozenski, B. D. (2019). Constructing a dual-subjectivity: Understanding the intersection of ethnic studies and YPAR. *Global Journal of Transformative Education, 1*(1), 26–37.

Macedo, D. (2006). *Literacies of power: What Americans are not allowed to know*. Boulder, CO: Westview.

McLaren, P. (2007). *Life in schools: An introduction to critical pedagogy in the foundations of education* (5th ed.). Boston, MA: Pearson.

McLaren, P. (2009). Critical pedagogy: A look at the major concepts. In A. Darder, M. P. Baltodano, & R. D. Torres (Eds.), *The critical pedagogy reader* (2nd ed., pp. 61–83). New York, NY: Routledge.

Miguel, C., & Gargano, J. (2017). Moving beyond retribution: Alternatives to punishment in a society dominated by the school-to-prison pipeline. *Humanities, 6*(2), 15. doi:10.3390/h6020015

Mirra, N. (2018). *Educating for empathy: Literacy learning and civic engagement.* New York, NY: Teachers College Press.

Mirra, N., Filipiak, D., & Garcia, A. (2015). Revolutionizing inquiry in urban English classrooms: Pursuing voice and justice through youth participatory action research. *English Journal, 105*(2), 49–57.

Mitra, D. L. (2003). Student voice in school reform: Re-framing student-teacher relationships. *McGill Journal of Education, 30*(2), 289–304.

Mitra, D. L. (2005). Adults advising youth: Leading while getting out of the way. *Educational Administration Quarterly 41*(3), 520–553.

Mitra, D. L. (2006). Student voice from the inside and outside: The positioning of challengers. *International Journal of Leadership in Education, 9*(4), 315–328.

Mitra, D. L. (2008). *Student voice in school reform: Building youth-adult partnerships that strengthen schools and empower youth.* New York, NY: SUNY Press.

Mitra, D. L., & Gross, S. (2009). Increasing student voice in high school reform. *Educational Management Administration & Leadership, 37*(4), 522–543.

Mohr, K. A. J. & Mohr, E. S. (2017) Understanding Generation Z students to promote a contemporary learning environment. *Journal on Empowering Teaching Excellence, 1*(1), 84–94.

Nieto, S. (2002). *Language, culture, and teaching: Critical perspectives for a new century.* Mahwah, NJ: Lawrence Erlbaum Associates.

O'Brien, E. L. (2010). Should a student in school be seen and not heard? An examination of student participation in U.S. schools. *Law, Social Justice, & Global Development Journal, 2*, 1–17.

Oldfather, P. (1995). Songs "come back most to them": Students' experiences as researchers. *Theory Into Practice, 34*(2), 131–137.

Rudduck, J., & Fielding, M. (2006). Student voice and the perils of popularity. *Educational Review, 58*(2), 219–231.

Selingo, J. J. (2018). *The new generation of students: How colleges can recruit, teach, and serve Gen Z.* Washington, DC: Chronicle of Higher Education.

Shor, I., & Freire, P. (1987). *A pedagogy for liberation: Dialogues on transforming education.* South Hadley, MA: Bergin & Garvey.

Sleeter, C. (2008). Equity, democracy, and neoliberal assaults on teacher education. *Teaching and Teacher Education, 24*(8), 1947–1957.

SooHoo, S. (1993). Students as partners in research and restructuring school. *The Educational Forum, 57*(4), 386–393.

Taylor, P., & Keeter, S. (Eds.). (2010). *Millennials: Confident. Connected. Open to change.* Pew Research Center. Retrieved from http://www.pewsocialtrends.org/files/2010/10/millennials-confident-connected-open-to-change.pdf

Willis, G., Schubert, W. H., Bullough, R. V. Jr., Kridel, C., & Holton, J. T. (1993). *The American curriculum: A documentary history.* Westport, CT: Greenwood.

Yonezawa, S., & Jones, M. (2007). Student co-researchers: How principals can recruit, train, and enlist the help of students to examine what works and does not work in their schools. *National Association of Secondary Schools Principals Bulletin, 91*(4), 322–342.

PART I

# THE IDENTITY AND VOICE GALLERY

TWO

# The Identity and Voice Gallery

*Charlotte Achieng-Evensen*

WELCOME TO THE IDENTITY AND Voice Gallery. Here we encounter youth identity as the proclamation of a "self" defined both autonomously and within the context of a specific society. Youth voices, in this collection, exhibit selves who are transformative and critical change agents. By presenting their self-conceptualizations to the world, their determined voices contest current limit situations (Freire, 1970/2000, p. 95) within classroom and educative spaces. Thus, they resist the idea that who they are is wholly defined by who others say they are. Furthermore, they challenge systems and practices reifying accepted norms of schooling. Students display what it means to be inclusive, holistic, and attentive to the needs of learners. Bhabha (1994) conceives of types of contestations mounted by students as the "right to narrate" (p. xx). As students testify to conditions that have marginalized them, as youth identify labels that have dehumanized them, as young people recount spaces that have alienated and forced them to conform to narratives of less than, they resist narratives of dominance. They enact, claim, and negotiate their rights to full personhood. As Bhabha (2004) notes, "we hear a right to narrate, a desire for 'a collective, ethical right to difference in equality'" (Balibar, cited in Bhabha, p. 56). In this gallery, we invite you to consider ways youth uphold their definitions of selves.

## References

Bhabha, H. K. (2004). *The location of culture.* London, England: Routledge.

Freire, P. (2000). *Pedagogy of the oppressed* (M. B. Ramos, Trans.). New York, NY: Continuum. (Original work published 1970)

THREE

# "The Unnecessary Gendering of Everything": Gender-Diverse Adults Speak Back to Their K–12 Schools

*Katherine Lewis*

As we all settled in for our discussion, Blaine set down their backpack, pulled up a chair, and volunteered to go first. "My name is Blaine. My pronouns are they/them and what I want to say back to schools is, 'Just stop it; stop gendering everything!'"

Blaine was one of eight gender-diverse people talking to me about their experiences in K–12 schools (Lewis, 2017). As the researcher facilitating the focus group, I asked each person to introduce themselves by sharing their name and pronouns and briefly answering the question, "What do you want to say back to your K–12 schools about your experiences related to gender?" Blaine's response set the tone for the discussion and, by the end of the session, the classroom walls were covered in posters that featured suggestions for creating gender-inclusive schools and outlined what the group called *gendered microaggressions*.

As I listened to these experiences of school life, I wondered about gender-diverse students I may have overlooked in my own classrooms over the years. I had a lot of questions for myself: *Who* had I not seen and heard? In what ways did *I* "gender everything"? What could I have done differently to build a gender-inclusive learning environment? I knew my educator colleagues would have similar questions and realized that hearing these gender-diverse voices helps us see *who* and *what* we have missed in schools. This chapter illuminates some of these perspectives and experiences that many educators do not see or hear.

## Whose Voices?

Eight people who identified as gender diverse shared their experiences and insights with me: Blaine, Onyx, Kirk, Sky, Steve, Harper, Nix, and Nikki. I individually interviewed each person prior to the focus group discussion. These interviews focused on understanding each person's gender identity and listening to their memories of attending K–12 schools in the United States. Although every person may have a gender, it can be a difficult concept to define. Considering that our gender identities are both *personal*—inherently and deeply felt (American Psychological Association, 2015)—and *social*—behaviors and roles we are expected to follow (Lugg, 2003), I asked each person I interviewed to describe their identities in their own words.

Blaine and Onyx described themselves as *agender*; Kirk and Sky used the term *genderqueer*; Steve and Harper both wrote *nonbinary*; Nix described themself[1] as *gender nonconforming*; and Nikki said they were *genderfluid*. Table 3.1 outlines these terms and their descriptions (including a citation and an explanation heard during interviews).

**Table 3.1.** Gender-diverse terms and descriptions

| Term | Description |
|---|---|
| Agender | "Does not identify as having a gender identity that can be categorized as male or female" (Green & Maurer, 2015, p. 8) or, as Onyx puts it, "I am neither a boy nor a girl; I'm nothing on the binary. I'm just floating around the binary as my individual self." |
| Genderqueer | "Redefine gender or decline to define themselves as gendered altogether" (American Psychological Association, 2015, p. 862); Kirk said genderqueer means: "When I wear clothes, I try to separate what society thinks a gender should wear versus what I feel like wearing." |
| Nonbinary | Rejects the idea that gender is either man/masculine/male or woman/feminine/female (Green & Maurer, 2015) and, instead, expresses gender along a continuum of masculinity and femininity (Meyer & Pullen Sansfaçon, 2014); Steve explained, "I realized that my masculine identity was more than just a female person that was masculine; To me, I define it as . . . I feel 60% masculine and 40% feminine, so instead of being on a binary of man and woman, it's on a spectrum of masculine and feminine." |
| Gender nonconforming | "Differs from gender norms associated with their assigned birth sex" (American Psychological Association, 2015, p. 862); in explaining nonconformity, Nix said, "I always wanted to wear more feminine clothing and makeup, but it wasn't allowed for boys." |
| Genderfluid | "Moving between genders" (American Psychological Association, 2015, p. 862); Harper explained, "I was playing around with the ideas of gender, switching up names and pronouns—seeing what really kind of fit me." |

In this chapter, *gender diversity* is used as an umbrella term to describe a wide variety of gender identities (including those listed earlier). *Gender diversity* can be used to talk about gender along a spectrum, in recognition that a person can be a woman, a man, both a man and a woman, neither woman nor man, or genderless.

Although all interviews were recorded on a university campus in Central Texas, only four of the people interviewed attended K–12 schools located solely in Texas (Onyx, Steve, Harper, and Nikki). Kirk attended schools in Massachusetts, Virginia, and Maryland; some of Nix's schooling was in Colorado; and Sky and Blaine shared memories from California schools.

### What Did We Talk About?

During our initial conversations, each person talked about their general experiences in K–12 schools, their gender-related experiences, and any messages they received about gender in these settings. Later in the interview, they recalled moments in which they were excluded from activities organized around gender and then explored how these experiences affected their relationship to school. Several weeks later, we came together as a focus group to revisit these topics and make suggestions back to K–12 schools.

### What Was Learned?

"I just never felt like I belonged in school," explained Kirk. Kirk was not alone in this feeling. As I listened to each person share stories about school life, I kept hearing comments related to safety and belonging. Unfortunately, school was not a safe place for Onyx, Sky, and Nix—they shared painful memories of being verbally (and sometimes physically) harassed by others and explained that these experiences made them dislike going to school altogether. Although Blaine, Kirk, Steve, Harper, and Nikki said they felt relatively safe in these settings, it was clear that each person I spoke with felt little to no sense of belonging in their K–12 schools.

Weird. Different. Disconnected. Distant. Other. Outsider. These are some of the one-word answers I heard when asking about each person's relationship to their K–12 schools. In follow-up conversations, I asked them to explore not only why school was not a place of belonging for them but also how they responded to these environments.

In reply to the prompt about why school was not a place of belonging, Blaine seemed frustrated, quickly and fervently stating, "Everything was gendered, everything you did—getting in line, playing sports, the way people talk to you, all that sort of stuff." Blaine was not the only person to make comments about the gendered nature of schooling. During both individual and group conversations, I heard each person talking about schools as highly "gendered" places. Nikki said that "*everything* was boy and girl; it's very she/he, pink/blue; the girls' team and the boys' team and the girls on the left and the boys on the right . . . it's just super separated." As I talked with Blaine and Steve, they said schools were preoccupied with what they termed the "unnecessary gendering of everything." Blaine explained:

> It's just the little things . . . guys on this side of the room, girls on this side of the room. It's how the conversations flow, with the added assumption that all guys act a certain way and all girls act a certain way.

As I listened, I realized that gender plays a strong role in these settings and began thinking about how we carry out schooling in ways that exclude gender-diverse students. What was the point of separating people into two gender categories? *Unnecessary* may be an apt description for these common practices, but the consequences are more than unnecessary; they are exclusionary.

While their schools were "super separated" by gender, each person shared that gender was, typically, not a topic for discussion. Kirk explained, "conversations about gender were rare and talking about gender diversity was *nonexistent*." Within the focus group, everyone agreed that many gender-related messages in schools tell people how to be a *normal* girl or boy. They decided to list some of these messages on a poster:

> Boys will be boys.
> Man up.
> That's not ladylike.
> Stop running like a girl.
> Girls don't say words like that.

The list goes on, but this brief example gives us an idea of the gendered language commonly heard in these settings. It is clear that schools are highly gendered spaces in which we receive messages about what it means to be a *normal* girl or boy. What happens, however, if someone does not fit neatly within these norms?

Some of the people I interviewed either attempted to conform or hid aspects of their personalities in schools. Both Kirk and Steve attempted to conform to their schools' strict gender norms. Kirk was continuously teased about having a disability and not being "girly enough." In response, Kirk said they tried "dressing really feminine and wearing makeup" and explained that this was "one way to minimize bullying." In my conversations with Steve, they talked about attempting to conform to femininity norms so they "could fit in and make friends." When Onyx and I discussed their relationship to school, Onyx simply said, "I always knew how to keep things hidden." When asked to elaborate, they explained, "I loved pretty things and makeup, but other kids teased me about being *girly*." Onyx reacted by hiding their genuine interests from peers and reluctantly mirroring masculine behaviors and interests to avoid being teased. Hearing each person talk about constantly feeling pressure to conform to strict norms and/or hide aspects of their personalities made me realize how gender-separating practices in schools can lead to a limited sense of belonging for many students and especially gender-diverse people.

During individual interviews, I also asked each person to recall activities organized around gender and share how they participated in and felt about these moments. As I listened, I was surprised that each narrative took place outside general classrooms and focused on physical education, recess, sports, choir, and school dances.

Onyx started telling their story by saying, "Ugh . . . sports, in general, are weird and gendered . . . *extremely*!" Nikki, Blaine, Onyx, and Sky shared memories about games during recess and physical education classes. Nikki explained that, in these settings, "they would separate us in boys and girls, and girls could only play certain games and guys could only play certain games." Although expected to play "girl games," Nikki preferred activities intended for boys and wondered, "Why can't I play boy games? Why can't we all just be playing the same games?" Blaine, Onyx, and Sky echoed this frustration: "Regardless of which side I was on, I'd be uncomfortable. I'm not supposed to be with the guys and I'm not supposed to be with the girls" (Blaine). "I didn't want to be in either group; I always felt like I was the outsider, so I was just by myself most of the time" (Onyx). "It was always, 'Girls will do this, and boys will do this.' There was no option" (Sky).

In sharing these memories, each person talked about feeling "uncomfortable," sometimes to the point of refusing to participate. Blaine said they always participated but "hated going to gym." On the other hand, Onyx would often respond by sitting on the sidelines in lieu of participating because they could not "decide which side to join." Sky also refused to participate on several occasions: "I would just sit down in the middle of the field and not play the game."

Harper, Kirk, Steve, and Nix shared memories about choir and school dances. In high school, for example, Harper enjoyed and successfully sang the "boys' parts" of songs but was only *allowed* to sing the "girls' parts" in choir. Although they participated (sang the "girls' parts"), Harper felt "frustrated" about the lack of choice for musical expression in choir. Nix shared a memory about refusing to attend school dances: "We weren't allowed to take same-gender partners to prom, so I didn't go," they explained. At the time, they responded with anger; now, Nix explained, "I feel like I missed out on something, missed an experience." Many students look forward to these experiences, but sometimes gender-segregating policies get in the way.

Steve began telling their story by referring to such policies: "I would have loved to go in pants and a vest and a button-down with a tie; I would've looked dope!" Steve and Kirk talked about attending school dances with strict dress codes. They both wanted to wear a suit and tie to prom, but school policies required them to wear dresses. Although they attended their school dances while adhering to the dress codes ("I was wearing a dress, getting my hair done, going all out" [Steve]), Kirk remembers feeling "terrible and uncomfortable" and was "jealous of the boys wearing suits." Steve said, "I didn't enjoy myself; I kept trying to cover myself up." Although they tried to participate, both Kirk and Steve left their respective events quite early. As Steve shared this memory, they expressed some regret: "There was all these things I wanted to do to express myself that were being denied . . . I really should've done it the way that I wanted to."

Through multiple conversations, I had the opportunity to listen closely to these memories of school life and consider the roles educators played in those moments. Overall, these discussions illuminated much about the gendered nature of K–12 schools. It was clear that a combination of highly gendered structures, practices, and policies created environments that exclude many (especially gender-diverse) people. Several people I interviewed felt unsafe and every person felt little to no sense of belonging in schools. The prevalence of gender-separating activities and policies that reinforce roles and stereotypes seemed to create an unwelcoming environment for any person who did not fit neatly into the strict categories and norms in place.

Listening to each person's memories about being excluded from activities (organized by gender) left me wondering about the ways in which schools structure physical education, recess, sports, choir, dance, and related events. Although they were present as members of the community, these students were not authentically included. In other words, schools overlooked them. *Why* were these students missed, and how might we reorganize activities to be inclusive of gender diversity?

## What Does This Mean for Educators?

To better serve our gender-diverse students, we must *first* listen to them. Considering the K–12 experiences and perspectives of gender-diverse people helps us to engage in cycles of reflection and action (Freire, 1970/2000) as we work toward building gender-inclusive schools. Listening is a first (and necessary) step. I encourage my colleagues to continuously ask, *Who am I missing and what is school life like for them?*

Perhaps you were not surprised to learn that each person felt little sense of belonging in schools. Climate reports consistently show that gender-diverse students experience negative school environments and those who resist gender norms are often targets of discrimination (Greytak, Kosciw, Villegas, & Giga, 2016). Maybe, like me, you found yourself nodding along to the list of gender-related messages generated by the focus group and then thought about the times *you* organized activities around gender. As reflective educators, we may already be positioned to notice (and change) some of these gender-separating practices in our own classrooms. This is important work. The way we organize our classrooms matters. The words we use matter.

At the same time, the voices guiding this chapter illuminate the need for a schoolwide approach to addressing the exclusionary and "unnecessary gendering of everything," with particular attention given to common gender-separating activities (including physical education, recess, and dance events). Within our school communities, we may be in conversation about proactively and deliberately building inclusive, welcoming spaces. Gender (and gender diversity) should be included in these conversations.

School leaders have an important role to play here; they help set the tone, communicate goals, inform policies, and organize members of the school community. Considering the need for a schoolwide approach, I suggest intentionally addressing gender (and gender diversity) during school employee training, especially when discussing what is meant by *best practices*. Using gender-neutral language, challenging gender roles and stereotypes, addressing (and changing) exclusionary policies, and restructuring activities that separate students into gender groups are best practices that improve school life for all people, including gender-diverse students. These changes make a difference for any student who, like Blaine, wants schools to "stop gendering everything." Perhaps we can start with a simple question about the gendered structures of schooling, *Was that necessary?*

## Reflection Questions

Reflect on your own K–12 schooling experiences related to gender and list examples of gender-separating activities and policies. Then, list examples of similar activities and policies you have observed (either as a preservice or inservice teacher) in today's schools. How does what you are observing now compare with your own experiences? What, if anything, has changed?

List specific examples of boy/girl groupings in schools and discuss with a partner while considering Nikki's statement that schools were "super separated" and that "everything was boy/girl, he/she . . . " Then, collaborate to create a list of ways to sort students into groups that do not rely on separating into two gender categories.

Imagine that your school's principal wants to take a campus-wide approach to gender inclusive schooling and has asked you to share resources for the upcoming employee training session. Explore one of the sites listed at the end of the chapter (under "Other Recommended Resources") and prepare a brief list of examples (which may include book recommendations, lesson plans, policy ideas, etc.) for your principal. If helpful, organize the list into the following categories: gender-neutral language, challenging roles and stereotypes, addressing exclusionary policies, and restructuring gender-separating activities. Which of the examples you listed could be implemented immediately? Which gender-inclusive actions require a longer timeline for implementation?

## Other Recommended Resources

Gender Spectrum
GLSEN
Gender Diversity

## Note

1. Blaine, Onyx, Kirk, Sky, Steve, Harper, Nix, and Nikki are pseudonyms, and each person uses gender-neutral pronouns *they/them*; in this chapter, *they/them/themself* refers to an individual gender-diverse person.

## References

American Psychological Association. (2015). Guidelines for psychological practice with transgender and gender nonconforming people. *American Psychologist, 70*(9), 832–864.

Freire, P. (2000). *Pedagogy of the oppressed* (M. B. Ramos, Trans.). New York, NY: Continuum. (Original work published 1970)

Green, E. R., & Maurer, L. M. (2015). *The teaching transgender toolkit: A facilitator's guide to increasing knowledge, reducing prejudice & building skills*. Morristown, NJ: Center for Sexuality Education.

Greytak, E. A., Kosciw, J. G., Villenas, C., & Giga, N. M. (2016). *From teasing to torment: School climate revisited: A survey of U.S. secondary school students and teachers*. New York, NY: GLSEN.

Lewis, K. M. (2017). *Toward transformative gender justice: Listening to gender non-binary individuals' experiences of school* (Unpublished doctoral dissertation), Texas State University, San Marcos, Texas. Retrieved from https://digital.library.txstate.edu/bitstream/handle/10877/6761/LEWIS-DISSERTATION-2017.pdf?sequence=1&isAllowed=y

Lugg, C. A. (2003). Sissies, faggots, lezzies, and dykes: Gender, sexual orientation, and a new politics of education? *Educational Administration Quarterly, 39*(1), 95–134.

Meyer, E. J., & Pullen Sansfaçon, A. (Eds.). (2014). *Supporting transgender and gender creative youth: Schools, families, and communities in action*. New York, NY: Peter Lang.

FOUR

# Truancy: Young People Walk Away From Negative School Factors

*Delia Baskerville*

## Historical Attribution of Blame

THE STORY OF THE TRUANT child began in the United States pre–World War I. Historically, the use of deficit labelling identified children who truant as: "incorrigibles," "abnormal boy," "recalcitrant lads" (Trustees of Boston University, 1907, p. 348); "chronically troublesome," "delinquent" (Richman, 1906, p. 237); "bad," "stubborn," "contrary" (Williams, 1927, p. 284); "unadjusted" (Brown, 1934, p. 194); "difficult," "awful," and "dull" (Norton, 1934, pp. 435, 439, & 444, respectively); and failures with "peculiar mental characteristics" (Williams, 1927, p. 284), implying some form of psychological disorder. Psychological examinations of 110 truancy court cases heard between 1929 and 1930 identified half of the truants as being borderline in intelligence and showing "grade retardation" (McElwee, 1931, p. 210).

Peers of children who truant were labelled by doctors and researchers as "vicarious associates" (Richman, 1906, p. 238), "idle wanderers" (Richman, 1906, p. 239), and "bad companions" (Williams, 1927, p. 285). Truant children, who associated with "loafers and juvenile criminals" involved in "vice and crime" (Kuser, 1916, p. 366), were also assigned a negative, bad student identity—it was claimed that "bad associates" contributed to truancy (Broadwin, 1932, p. 253).

Broadwin (1932) was the first to attribute truancy to personality difficulties. His close study of six children, two in depth, all truanting school, identified truancy as symptomatic and part of personality difficulties, obsessions, and anxiety. Truant children were located in discussions associated with disorders and maladjustment, which identified the individual child as flawed. By the early 1940s, truancy was seen as a symptom associated with a range of causal factors requiring diagnosis and treatment (Geiger, 1941). Youth who Truant (YwT) were positioned as "phobic." By the 1960s, personality abnormalities of these children (phobias or neurosis) were suggested as a cause of truancy (Kahn & Nursten, 1962), and by the late 1970s, perceived abnormalities were subjected to close scrutiny.

The use of these various forms of deficit labelling implies that adults have perceived YwT as deviant and susceptible to failure due to flawed, defiant identities. The categorising of children in this way has several limitations. It associates individual problems of YwT with an identifiable group of rebellious children, it stigmatizes them as less valuable than their attending peers, and it attributes failure to individual weaknesses and deficiencies within the child, which identifies and demeans them as the problem. The underlying assumption here is that school structures do not contribute to the dynamic of truancy. However, listening to the voices of YwT offers us insights into the experiences that they perceived as socially unjust in classrooms and illuminates ways that YwT can be supported to develop a positive academic identity and remain in classrooms.

## A New Story

Although school truancy is a significant issue in the United States, youth perspectives about causes and ways to solve the problem were missing until the second decade of the 21st century (Gase, DeFossett, Perry, & Kuo, 2016). This chapter draws on data from a doctoral thesis that used a grounded theory approach, concurrently gathering and analysing data generated through 20 interviews with 13 students from four secondary schools in New Zealand (Baskerville, 2019). In keeping with grounded theory, the study was designed to construct a theory about the basic social process that accounted for most of the similarities and differences in the reported participant behaviour. The focus was on the collective experience, not the individual. The research focused on students' perspectives to understand their truancy experiences in the New Zealand social and educational context.

These voices highlight and identify several factors as contributing to their perceived tenuous and deteriorating bond with teachers. As we see in the following quotes, YwT professed that opportunities to learn in the classroom were inequitable:

> I was somewhat jealous; she [teacher] made me feel like I wasn't good enough and it wasn't fair because I needed help and [student name] didn't. Some teachers

> can be quite biased. Like have their favourites or they like boys more than girls or something. [Name] was like that, so was [name] the [subject] teacher. (Rose)

> My teacher's unfair and unreasonable, she treats all us kids differently. It's usually just me that gets told off. If I don't understand, I don't get help. She just says I'm dumb. It's one of the times that I felt like the teachers were taking people's sides. (Becky)

> He is too busy trying to get these girls on this side of the room to actually at least do something. He is too busy helping someone else, giving them so much attention that he barely notices that your hand goes up, so you are there for 20 minutes and your hand gets tired so you just put it down and give up. (Amy)

> I used to have to do it all on my own and I just wanted a helping hand and I never got it. So, it kind of made me give up hope. Everyone asks [for help] but it is up to the teacher if they are busy or what they are doing so it's kind of like, you are the last option for them. (Christina)

YwT experience prejudice in the classroom. They struggle to understand the work set by teachers and need help from their teachers to engage with learning. When teachers do not help them, YwT think it unreasonable. They find it unsettling to be neglected, labelled, minoritized and invisible in class. Resentment builds as some teachers attend to others, who YwT perceive to be unmotivated anyway. They also observe that inattention is a teacher choice. Consequently, YwT identify themselves as not being as important as others. They feel undervalued despite their attempts to get their teacher's attention. When YwT perceive injustices as contributing to their positioning as inferior, and outsiders in class, they choose to truant class.

At times, the lack of teacher support evokes a strong emotional response:

> That work was too hard; or like you do not want to do it. The teacher will be teaching, like helping everyone but like if I put my hand up and I don't get attention I was like oh no I'm going to walk out the door. (Decity)

> Sometimes I am challenged, but sometimes it's too much challenge and I can't finish it. That makes me sad, 'cause the teacher doesn't help. I found school depressing and just wanted to be alone. (Tyrone)

YwT are ready and want to learn, but classroom events affect them emotionally, diminish their motivation and cause them to detach from the teacher and the task. YwT are troubled by the challenges of hard work; they feel disempowered and unable to do anything to change the situation. They do not feel part of the class, which influences their decision to truant.

Experiences of exclusion, unmet learning needs, and consequent surfacing emotions are barriers to participation in class:

> When I wasn't getting any attention [from the teacher] in music, I would be overly sad with maybe over thinking about, because I didn't used to get noticed that well. (Christina)

> Sometimes in class I wouldn't get attention and if I don't get attention like no one's listening to me, I want to do something, like leave. (Decity)

> I get scared, like if I am not good at work. Others are usually quite clever at work and teachers talk to them. It's embarrassing. Makes me feel kind of mad. (Courtney)

YwT observe teachers as being selective, providing care to those they perceive as already advantaged in the classroom. In contrast, they perceive that they are left to struggle alone and do not have sufficient support to learn. The pressure this positioning imposes results in YwT taking perceived teacher behaviours personally, leading to surfacing emotions, heightened insecurity, diminished motivation to learn, and an emerging desire to leave.

YwT claim that the attention they receive from some teachers is unpleasant:

> Some of them [teachers] were a bit harsh and they'd pick out all the like little things I'd do: like what I'm wearing, like if I had correct shoes. (Decity)

> The [subject name] teacher was rude, everybody hated her. I am not the only one—she was nasty to me. We just had a massive personality clash and she just didn't want to help me at all. (Rose)

> She [the teacher] called me helicopter all the time, took my hat off me, never gave it back and that's why I hated her. I never went to her classes. (TM)

Perceived teacher rudeness, disrespect, meanness, and unsupportive behaviours evoke a strong negative response. When teachers discipline YwT for off-task behavior, while not necessarily giving academic assistance to attempt set tasks, YwT perceive them as hostile and unkind. They resent disrespect from teachers, so much so that they truant their classes.

Youth who truant identify instances when perceived unfair treatment contributes to their sense of being ostracised. Teasing and labelling influence their ability to feel at ease, or safe, in class:

> He never told me I needed to fix the errors; I didn't know they were there. Or he would lose my work and then I just stopped going after a while. (Rose)

> She [the teacher] was mean, just standing there and being really like, telling you full on what is what, usually growling at you. (Christina)

> When I was new to class, they [peers] teased me, they swore at me and called me names. I didn't want to go. They just, they're mean. (Courtney)

> I was just seen as a loser pretty much, the little druggie who everyone looked down their noses at and no one took seriously. They wrote me off as a loser and that was it. No one really cared [enough to know my partner had committed suicide] so there was no point going to school. (Julie)

YwT interpret judgmental approaches and disrespect from both teachers and peers as a lack of care; most of them perceive school as a negative experience. When youth feel that their status is lower than their teacher and peers, they interpret unmet learning needs as unacceptable and choose to leave class to avoid continued disrespect.

## What Are Youth Who Truant Telling Us?

According to YwT, their experiences of learning processes in classrooms are unjust. YwT claim that some teachers' choices contribute to dysfunctional interactions in classrooms. They perceive that teachers have power over their learning, and because—as YwT report—they do not receive support to learn, school is depressing. YwT are troubled by two aspects of dynamics in classrooms: (1) exclusion from learning and (2) inferior status. School is a place where YwT lack academic support and experience invisibility and persecution. These factors, along with their diminished motivation, sense of being undervalued, and increased isolation, contribute to a feeling of exclusion from learning. Likewise, their perceived inferior status is due to unfair treatment, a lack of care, and peer discrimination. YwT perceive they experience neglect and a sense of failure and are assigned a negative academic identity that informs their decisions to be truant.

Research provides further insight about the crucial role that teachers play in students' growing disengagement (Tarabini, Jacovkis, & Montes, 2017). In Tarabini et al.'s (2017) study in Catalonia, six focus groups of young people 14 to 16 years of age, currently attending "second-chance schools" (p. 841), reported that teachers' lack of academic, social, and emotional support to achieve academic success translated to students' lack of motivation, increased feelings of anger, and a sense of frustration. Like New Zealand YwT, they want help to complete their work and learn. However, they are not receiving it. YwT perceive that they require support and care from teachers and respect from peers in order to develop a positive academic identity. As noted by Berryman, Nevin, SooHoo, and Ford (2015), social justice in education must be concerned with recognizing, respecting, including, and valuing all students for their potential. However, many students are pushed out rather than wanting to leave (Fine, 1991). When YwT experience negative school factors, they choose to walk away from the injustice. This decision to truant may be motivated by their need to protect themselves. Gase et al. (2016) concur. Students in their study suggested that fighting and bullying contributed to a "dangerous school environment which resulted in school avoidance" (Gase et al., 2016, p. 310). Teachers and negative school factors influence YwT decisions to stop attending class.

These voices show that as ongoing classroom experiences diminish their sense of self-worth, a critical moment is reached when the importance of attending school wanes. YwT want respect as individuals, not to be labelled as failures. This finding is consistent with the more general view of recent reports by the Children's Commissioner Office (2018a, 2018b), which claim negative stereotyping leads students to feel burdened and to be treated differently from classmates. Students wanted school to change so their learning needs were met; they wanted to be fairly treated, encouraged, respected, and involved—behaviors that the Children's Commissioner Office (2018a, 2018b) emphasizes as important for giving students a sense of inclusion.

These students' voices suggest that, for them, inclusion in action means feeling connected with their teachers, being confident that they (the students) are visible, and being able to trust teachers to help them. Teacher kindness is also important to YwT. There is a body of research identifying recognition, helpfulness, care, and academic support as evidence of teacher kindness and claiming that positive teacher-student relationships promote student well-being and attendance (Bishop, Berryman, Tiakiwai, & Richardson, 2003; Hawk & Hill, 2000; Krane, Ness, Holter-Sorensen, Karlsson, & Binder, 2017). Teacher kindness therefore appears to be a factor in student well-being, which then minimizes the risk of YwT having to remove themselves from class as a way to protect their well-being.

## The Story Continues: What Next?

As highlighted by YwT, several everyday intentional actions by teachers and other adults in schools have the potential to strengthen relationships and improve students' participation in class activities so that they develop a sense of belonging and connect to class and school. These include (1) focusing on improving the social climate in classrooms so that students feel visible and respected, (2) addressing deficit thinking toward these students by focusing on teacher agency to improve students' willingness to attend, and (3) analyzing each learner's strengths and barriers to learning in order to provide relevant academic and social support.

Strengthening student well-being and success are worthy of consideration in relation to the previously mentioned actions. Student well-being, mental health, and learning are connected. Positive feelings, optimism, and satisfaction with learning characterise students' well-being in school (Ministry of Education, 2017). In addition, effective pastoral care, guidance, and counseling promote students' well-being and success by reducing psychological discomfort and stress. These in turn improve students' engagement, retention, and achievement (Ministry of Education, 2017). Transformational change can occur when adults in schools show an openness to listen, learn, and understand the nature of change required for the marginalized group to be more self-determining and receive structural support to make these changes (Berryman, Ford, Nevin, & SooHoo, 2015).

Compulsory schooling is often understood from government and educational professionals' perspectives (Thompson & Bell, 2011), but in order to achieve democratic education and make schools accountable for the success of the most marginalized students, students must be recognized as stakeholders in the learning process (Cook-Sather, 2010; Ferguson, Hanreddy, & Draxton, 2011). Students themselves must be consulted about their lived experiences, family backgrounds, cultures, hopes, and dreams (Smyth, 2006). Therefore, in order to understand and change the dynamics of a phenomenon like truancy, the problem must be tackled from an insider student perspective. It is from this standpoint that we will begin to understand aspects of conditions from which students feel the need to withdraw themselves.

YwT can identify what is dysfunctional about power interactions in their relationships with school staff and peers regarding their decision to truant. Listening to stories of YwT may inform teachers, educators and policy makers to move toward preventative teacher actions, which will aim to have fewer students truanting class.

## Concluding the Story

Given the evidence of YwT student voice, the historical attribution of blame is simplistic and unhelpful. YwT perceived classroom climate to be prohibitive for regular attendance. As schools are accountable for marginalized students' success, there are implications for school leaders and teachers relating to intentional inclusive teaching and social practices that support and promote student well-being. Change is required.

Strict and comprehensive school policy on inclusion is important. This provides structure for school leaders to support teachers and other staff to enhance their ability to listen and see problems when they arise, to intentionally establish and maintain safe learning environments, and to set expectations for respectful interactions in their classrooms. When such policies are implemented, YwT will be able to receive social and academic support and be noticed so that they experience a safe school environment, emotionally, socially, and physically.

Finally, it is important to consider how adults and YwT collaboratively apply a critical lens to, first, identify necessary actions that will strengthen YwT participation in class; second, to develop a truancy plan that shows where and when identified support is required; and, third, to implement identified solutions-focused strategies to diminish truancy. Additionally, teachers can reflect on (1) what strategies they could use to see all students; (2) how they distribute their time between all their students; (3) how they will facilitate building positive, equitable relationships with, and between, students; and (4) how they might show respect and care for students so all students know they matter. Only then will school be a place where all youth can belong, have a positive experience, engage in learning and increase the likelihood of their well-being and achievement.

## Reflection Questions

In what ways did teachers contribute to students truanting class?

What strategies would you use as an educator/teacher to reduce labelling, build positive relationships, and diminish truancy in your classroom?

How would you support students with a history of truancy to attend and participate in your class?

## References

Baskerville, D. J. (2019). *Under the skin of truancy in Aotearoa (New Zealand): A grounded theory study of young people's perspectives* (Unpublished doctoral dissertation). Victoria University of Wellington, Wellington, New Zealand.

Berryman, M., Ford, T., Nevin, A., & SooHoo, S. (2015). Culturally responsive contexts: Establishing relationships for inclusion. *International Journal of Special Education, 30*(3), 39–51.

Berryman, M., Nevin, A., SooHoo, S., & Ford, T. (2015). *Relational and responsive inclusion: Contexts for becoming and belonging*. New York, NY: Peter Lang.

Bishop, R., Berryman, M., Tiakiwai, S., & Richardson, C. (2003). *Te Kotahitanga: The experiences of year 9 and 10 Māori students in mainstream classrooms*. Wellington, NZ: Ministry of Education.

Broadwin, I. T. (1932). A contribution to the study of truancy. *American Journal of Orthopsychiatry, 2*, 253–259.

Brown, F. (1934). The truant child. *School and Society, 6*(40), 772–773.

Cook-Sather, A. (2010). Students as learners and teachers: Taking responsibility, transforming education and reducing accountability. *Curriculum Inquiry, 40*(4), 555–575.

Children's Commissioner. (2018a). *He manu kai matauranga: He tirohanga Māori: Education matters to me; Experiences of tamariki and rangatahi Māori*. Wellington, New Zealand: NZSTA.

Children's Commissioner. (2018b). *Education matters to me: Progress and achievement*. Wellington, New Zealand: NZSTA.

Ferguson, D. L., Hanreddy, A., & Draxton, S. (2011). Giving students voice as a strategy for improving teacher practice. *London Review of Education, 9*(1), 55–70.

Fine, M. (1991). Invisible flood. *Equity and Choice, 8*(1), 30–37.

Gase, L. N., DeFosset, A., Perry, R., & Kuo, T. (2016). Youths' perspectives on the reasons underlying school truancy and opportunities to improve school attendance. *The Qualitative Report, 21*(2), 299–320.

Geiger, S. G. (1941). Truancy: A symptom of a conflict between the child and his environment. *Federal Probation, 5*(2), 22.

Hawk, K., & Hill, J. (2000). *Making a difference in the classroom: Effective teaching practice in low decile, multicultural schools* (Report prepared for the Ministry of Education and the AIMHI Forum). Retrieved from https://www.educationcounts.govt.nz/publications/maori_education/english-medium-education/5459

Kahn, J, H., & Nursten, J, P. (1962). School refusal: A comprehensive view of school phobia and other failures of school attendance. *American Journal of Orthopsychiatry, 32*, 707–718.

Krane, V., Ness, O., Holter-Sorensen, N., Karlsson, B., & Binder, P. (2017). You notice that there is something positive about going to school: How teachers' kindness can promote positive teacher-student relationships in upper secondary school. *International Journal of Adolescence and Youth, 22*(4), 377–389.

Kuser, W. L. (1916). Truant children. *The Survey, 37*(13), 366.

McElwee, E. W. (1931). A study of truants and retardation. *Journal of Juvenile Research, 15*, 209–214.

Ministry of Education. (2017). *The Ministry of Education annual report for year ended 30 June*. Wellington: The New Zealand Government.

Norton, P. L. (1934). Team work for the wayward child. *Journal of Criminal Law and Criminology, 25*(3), 434–437.

Richman, J. (1906, May). The incorrigible child. *Educational Review, 31*, 484–506.

Smyth, J. (2006). 'When students have power': Student engagement, student voice, and the possibilities for school reform around 'dropping out' of school. *International Journal of Leadership in Education, 9*(4), 285–298.

Tarabini, A., Jacovkis, J., & Montes, A. (2017). Factors in educational exclusion: Including the voice of youth. *Journal of Youth Studies, 21*(6), 836–851.

Thompson, G., & Bell, J. (2011). Mired in the shadows: Quiet students in secondary schools. *Discourse Studies in the Cultural Politics of Education, 32*(3), 399–413.

Trustees of Boston University. (1907). The root of truancy. *The Journal of Education, 65*(13), 348.

Williams, H, D. (1927). Truancy and delinquency. *Journal of Applied Psychology, 11*(4), 276.

FIVE

# Rooted and Rising: The Self-Liberation of African American Female Students

*Michelle Flowers-Taylor*

As an African American woman who has been academically successful, I wrote this chapter because I had grown tired of hearing about what was not working in education for young African American women and girls. I wanted to hear from students themselves to capture their success stories and key factors of achievement. By shifting focus to discern the points of proof from individual female college students, I hoped that these young women's stories would reveal key aspects of their identity development that helped them advance academic outcomes.

Engaging in this research was both a personal and political effort grounded in the belief that, as Houle (1995) states, "common sense [is] a specific form of knowledge" (p. 1); it rejected the notion that "expert knowledge" is more legitimate than lived experience or emotional response. The latter fueled my ability to detect intersectionalities of race and gender in this chapter. I asked myself the question:

> If you were to talk to an African American woman who is younger than you to share with her how to develop a sense of her own identity in light of stereotypes in the world, what advice would you give her?

My research question was, What factors help successful African American female students to develop a positive academic identity? My hope in seeking to answer this question was to address negative misconceptions regarding African American female students and their ability to succeed academically based on a self-conception of achievement. Despite stereotypes and misrepresentations, African American women and girls are succeeding academically, and their voices and experiences are worthy of considerably more attention in education.

## Hearing It Directly From the Students

In seeking to hear from African American women and girls, I employed narrative analysis to arrive at the unstated, implicit understandings that underlie their personal stories. Over a 6-month period, academically high-achieving African American female freshmen college students shared factors contributing to their successes, and I used narrative analysis to reveal similarities in the meaning of each person's story. As a result of data collected via surveys, one-on-one interviews, and focus groups, three key themes emerged: sacred space, multicultural worldviews, and possible/oppositional selves (Taylor, 2015). In this chapter, I expand upon these themes as I reflect on my own identity story as an African American female.

Students Dana and Maria helped contextualize the importance of feeling confident and secure in their identity, as a foundation for them as students.

> Dana: So with my friends . . . talking about our insecurities, ourselves, or how you feel. Being able to empower each other. Once you have this confidence, motivation or inspiration and you know what you want from talking to other people . . . it's a driving force. I think the main thing is confidence in yourself. That is what has helped me continue to be good in school. When you don't feel secure, then I feel like all the bricks at the bottom are going to fall . . . and you're going to lose yourself.

> Maria: If you have that foundation you still have those people who you know at all times will be there for you, help you, and support you. Then you can develop your identity by those other things on that foundation.

Dana and Maria are academically high-achieving African American freshmen female university students attending historically Black colleges and universities (HBCUs). To develop a complete picture of factors that contribute to female African American students' academic success, some other students I interviewed were from Ivy League, private, and state universities in the United States.

## Sacred Space

Students discussed the significance of "sacred spaces," which for them were locations for safety where they could be themselves among supportive peers.

Through developing supportive relationships in sacred spaces such as social clubs and school-based groups, as well as with family and friends, they were able to develop coping tools to address racial microaggressions, acquire the means to enhance positive messages about themselves, and trust themselves as a source of their own empowerment. In these sacred spaces, they could feel safe to "just be" and to use expressive styles of communication commonly found in African American culture. They could vent frustrations and develop tools to negotiate their biculturation because of commonalities shared with their fellow members.

In sacred spaces, the students felt empowered to learn about other people and other experiences in the global community (Cofield, 2012). The balance between these identities—one who grounds herself within a safe community composed of trusted allies who are like her, where she can "just be" herself in a safe, nurturing environment, and one who is open to rising up to experience the world at large—affirmed and supported their positive sense of selfhood. For these students, to "just be" meant to exist without trying to acculturate in order to be accepted. T'Nique stated, "[I need to just be] where I can get a point across" without having to say it in Standard American English. For Katrina, to "just be" was the main reason that she chose an HBCU:

> At an HBCU, you're just yourself. You know when you're around Black people, you're just more comfortable in the way you talk. I feel like if you're around White people, you have to adjust to what they like, make sure that you're accepted by them.

Katrina's recognition of sacred spaces for African American females underlines the social context of how students' race and gender influence how others—including their teachers—perceive them, and how they develop self hood and identity for themselves (Sue, 2010). These women and girls found sacred spaces in their lives where they were able to "develop their voice through opportunities to enter into dialogue and engage in a critical process of reflection from which they can share their thoughts, ideas, and lived experiences with others in an open and free manner" (Darder, 2011, p. 62). The sacred spaces allowed them to express themselves because the process of interpretation was safe and interaction was encouraging and supportive. Building self-confidence was integral to boosting a positive sense of selfhood and identity that empowered their ability to excel academically. Within sacred spaces, self-confidence flourished.

While Katrina found her sacred space at an HBCU, several other students felt safe among more diverse student groups. They shared that they felt secure in the company of people with whom they shared commonalities other than race and gender, and they were excited to expand their social circles and exert style-shifting skills in multicultural environments. This speaks to the students' ability to maintain bicultural identity of which a major component is the use of language. Based upon their academic performance, it is safe to assume that students performed the dominant culture's style of communication even as they were able to code-switch/style-shift in participation of their own cultural groups. To this end, they negotiated their biculturalism through communication and engaged in biculturation, where they "learn[ed] and practice[d] both mainstream culture and ethnic culture at the same time" (Darder, 2011, p. 47). They successfully negotiated their biculturation through social clubs and recreational groups—church organizations, mentorship programs, and school-based clubs—they found comfort and safety in these sacred spaces where they shared commonalities with their fellow members (Brown, 2013).

Self-confidence formed in sacred spaces, and, for these successful Black girls, feeling grounded within sacred space was a foundation which allowed them to expand a multicultural worldview.

## Multicultural Worldview

A multicultural worldview is a lens with which to view oneself within a multicultural world.

Within the narrative discourses, Dana, Shelly, and T'nique demonstrated that a "multicultural worldview" influenced their identity formation by enabling them to engage in dialogue in a way that presupposed social equality among its participants and expanding their social circles by exerting style-shifting communication skills in multicultural environments. These multicultural environments consisted of people from other cultural and ethnic identities and sometimes also people from their own cultural background.

There is a link between peer relationships and children's social and emotional intelligence (Hudley, 2008). Peers also play an essential role in the development of a person's "multicultural worldview." Each of the students expressed the importance of experiencing diverse communities and being involved with people from different social and ethnic backgrounds as a means to promote personal growth. For example, Dana cited her semester abroad in Spain and how she felt she grew so much from her time there:

> When I went abroad for the summer, and my roommate—she's from Poland—we were in Spain and it was a Spanish program. I learned so much about her, her life in Poland and then what it's like there. I got to teach her a lot about America. It was just from these little connections and being able to communicate with somebody, and in Spanish as well, having a whole 'nother world of people that you can communicate with, it's allowed me to learn so much about other people and it helped me learn more about myself and learning from other people.

The positive impact of having a multicultural worldview was echoed by Shelly in another conversation:

> I think that dialogues make your perspective either stronger or they make you just think about why you believe what you believe or why you think how you think. I think that's one of my favorite things about speaking to other people, especially speaking to people who have a different perspective.

Shelly's comment mirrors Paulo Freire's sentiments about the importance of dialoguing with other people. He states that a person who is committed to undertaking dialogue with other people

> enters into reality so that, knowing it better, he or she can better transform it. This individual is not afraid to confront, to listen, to see the world unveiled. This person is not afraid to meet the people or to enter into dialogue with them. (Freire, 1970/2000, p. 39)

Dialogue often causes one to examine the rationale and root cause driving their actions. For these Black girls, feeling grounded within the sacred space allowed them to expand a multicultural worldview.

The support of allies was another factor that emboldened the students to navigate effectively within multicultural environments and clarify their ideas about avoiding potential pitfalls that some saw their peers succumb to in school. T'Nique made this point clear when she talked about how allies in her church influenced her identity development:

> If I didn't have Karen, if I didn't have the people at my church who are from different backgrounds—there's people who just, who just were in my life for short spurts of time. If I did not have those people, I just would not be the same kid. I would be that typical teenager: drugs, sex, alcohol—anything else that could just help me pretty much cope with my emotional issues.

Trusted allies enabled the students to develop their individual identities. With them, the students could express themselves freely and gain a sense of wholeness and liberation. Furthermore, these experiences helped them to cultivate dreams of a possible life they might live—visions of life that included high expectations regarding future success.

## Possible Self/Oppositional Self

Students had clear ideas about their possible self—who they wanted to be. Katrina illustrated the importance of a multicultural worldview as she talked about what kind of person her "possible self" was and how her possible self shows up in the world. She stated:

> [My possible self] can hold her own with a bunch of White guys in Congress and in the government. But at the end of the day, she always knows where she has come from. She knows how to talk for all types of people: just not White people, just not African American—every culture, creed.

As well as a possible self, the girls' stories also illustrated their "oppositional self," or persona and qualities that they are purposefully hoping to avoid as they navigate their daily lives. Students tend to excel academically when they have clearly defined concepts of "possible self" (Markus & Nurius, 1986) and an equivalently, clearly defined "oppositional self." T'Nique described her "possible self," embodied in her mentor, as well as her "oppositional self," personified in a family relative whom she did not wish to emulate. Talking about her mentor, T'Nique said:

> I know that I can count on Sue. I can call her whether its day or night, morning, evening, whenever. I can call her and just talk to her no matter what's going on, and she can listen, and she can help me process. She can remain humble and selfless. She doesn't crack under pressure. She's consistent. That's the big thing. She's a very consistent person.

T'Nique emphasized that Sue is "never just *almost there* [with her support]. And, I never want to be that *almost there* person. I want to be that person that if something needs to be done. Boom! It's done." T'Nique's oppositional self is an "almost there" person—someone who is inconsistent in their support and ability to dialogue with other people. Describing her oppositional self, T'Nique highlighted the importance of listening and respecting the perspectives of others:

> The person who doesn't really have that ability to stop to listen and hear and process and then go forth without having to just know it's my way or the highway. 'Cause you may not know it the way that I do and end up being wrong.

Through her mentorship relationship with Sue, T'Nique was able to follow in the footsteps of someone who models behaviors that she aspires to achieve. The other girls echoed similar stories regarding aspirational characteristics of individuals whom they followed to help shape their own identities.

## The Transformative Experience of Listening

As I sought to capture success stories and key factors of achievement of academically successful female African American students, I found myself challenged by my own narrative. While conducting my research, I had a focus on protocols, tools, and "expert knowledge" developed by other researchers to assess the veracity of students' interview responses rather than accepting the truth of their remarks. I had distanced myself and forgotten that 20 years ago, I was an academically high-achieving African American female student who needed to overcome some of the very same challenges these students discussed and were overcoming. I had a vantage point and voice that were valid. My mentor, Dr. Antonia Darder, called out my lapse in judgment. She urged me to have faith in the students and to accept them as masters of their thinking so that I could wholeheartedly and openly dialogue with them. Dr. Darder's guidance was in alignment with Paulo Freire, who states, "Faith in man [and woman] is an *a priori* requirement for dialogue" (Freire 1970/2000, p. 79). I eventually came to accept that operating in faith would help me to develop a critical understanding of students' reality.

Despite my stated goal to capture the success stories and key factors that supported achievement of female African American students, I caught myself using a mind-set where I was taking a deficit approach: seeking to identify negative factors in African American female students. Through a deep reflective process, I realized that my viewpoint was skewed in that I was projecting some of the limiting perceptions to which I had been subjected throughout my life as a student and later as an educator. Societal messages had permeated my consciousness so that now I was also re-creating the oppressed-oppressor dynamic. Sadly, my negative experiences were framing my research. They caused me to doubt the truth of the wisdom that students shared with me. I questioned my interpretations of that knowledge. However, I learned to dialogue with students to develop a critical awareness of their reality through reflection and action—what Freire called *conscientization*—and I was able to achieve a greater understanding and appreciation for their experience.

## Arriving at an Asset-Based Perspective

Realizing my biases, I drew on the critical pedagogy theoretical framework in order to arrive at an asset-based perspective of the African American students represented here. Critical pedagogy incorporates critique of society, raising consciousness, and valuing students' voices by honoring student individuality. As a framework, critical pedagogy enables students and educators to become fully participating members of society who are empowered to create and recreate continually increasing freedom for every person (Darder, 2014).

As a female African American student, I developed critical consciousness as a matter of survival. I always felt that I was responding to stereotypes about my academic abilities. For instance, I was nonverbal when I started school, and teachers assumed that I had a developmental disability. In reality, my mother had passed away shortly beforehand. I had to find ways to shift teachers' perspectives and help them learn about me and my experience rather than have them rely on inaccurate beliefs.

Now, as an educator, I have reinvigorated my approach. My goal continues to be to uncover truths about high-achieving African American students as a means of debunking myths surrounding this population.

I hope the findings in this chapter will inform African American students and educators who are struggling with "the manifestation of the oppressed-oppressor contradiction" (Darder, 2014, p. 129). I hope, too, that other educators will undertake similar journeys to not only uncover the stories of their students but also to reflect on their own evolution in the process.

## Conclusion

Students are the experts in their own experiences (Lang, 2007). The African American female voices presented here express the importance for them of having a foundation that fosters a feeling of groundedness with the mechanisms of sacred space, multicultural worldview, and possible/oppositional selves. By elevating student voices as the source of pedagogical solutions, educators, parents, and students themselves can help each other to navigate and overcome biased learning environments. These African American female students' stories demonstrate ebullience and hope for the future. They continue to carve out space in order to rise to become the leaders and thinkers they aspire to be. As educators, we have a call to action to support them and other students like them in this endeavor. By empowering their voices, we can help to transform the educational system.

On a deeply personal level, I have recently become a mother. At only one year of age, my daughter is already expressing her opinions and feelings in her baby-babble way. I know that it will be critical for me to listen and be receptive to her perspectives and ideas about herself and the world around her.

As a by-product of motherhood, I now see a little of my daughter in all the young African American female students with whom I have the pleasure to engage in dialogue in classrooms and other educational settings. I am invested in their future and thankful for the trust that their parents have bestowed upon me. As a parent, I know how important it is to have a caring and affirming community of caretakers and educators in a child's life. To that end, I have come to agree with Freire (1970/2000) that education should be, at its core, an act of love, which requires dialogue. Through dialogue with students, educators can hopefully appreciate "common sense as a specific form of knowledge" (Houle, 1995, p. 1), and beware of depending on "expert knowledge" to interpret voices of African American female students. Now more than ever, in this era of shifting power dynamics, it is critical to support these students as they demand agency in their personal and academic lives. As educators, school leaders, and parents, we have a duty to be responsive to their needs as we lift their voices above the fray.

## Reflection Questions

What can you do to create sacred space for minoritized students?

How can you support students to develop their possible selves and oppositional selves?

What reflective practices could help you think about students' identity development?

## References

Brown, R. N. (2013). *Hear our truths: The creative potential of Black girlhood.* Champaign: University of Illinois Press.

Cofield, W. B. (2012). *Learning circle—Sacred space: A case study of African-American women cultivating a self-loving attitude in the midst of systemic oppression.* San Francisco: California Institute of Integral Studies.

Darder, A. (2011). *Culture and power in the classroom: Educational foundations for the schooling of bicultural students.* Boulder, CO: Paradigm Publishers.

Darder, A. (2014). *Freire and education.* New York, NY: Routledge.

Freire, P. (2000). *Pedagogy of the oppressed* (M. B. Ramos, Trans.). New York, NY: Continuum. (Original work published 1970)

Houle, G. (1995). Common sense as a specific form of knowledge: Elements for a theory of otherness. *Current Sociology, 43*(2), 89–99.

Hudley, C. (2008). The influence of peers on the development of a multicultural worldview. In J. K. Asamen, M. L. Ellis, & G. L. Berry (Eds.), *The SAGE handbook of child development, multiculturalism, and media* (pp. 266–285). Thousand Oaks, CA: Sage.

Lang, J. M. (2007, March 9). Did you learn anything? Students are very accurate judges of the most important question we can ask them about their classroom experiences. *Chronicle of Higher Education, 53*, 27.

Markus, H., & Nurius, P. (1986). Possible selves. *American Psychologist, 41*(9), 954–969.

Sue, D. W. (2010). *Microaggressions in everyday life: Race, gender, and sexual orientation.* Hoboken, NJ: Wiley.

Taylor, M. F. (2015). *Sacred spaces: A narrative analysis of the influences of language and literacy experiences on the self- hood and identity of high-achieving African-American female college freshmen* (Unpublished doctoral dissertation). Loyola Marymount University, Los Angeles, California.

SIX

# Voices of Scholars: Academically Successful Black Males and Their Stories of Culturally Relevant Pedagogies

*Quaylan Allen*

DRAWING UPON ETHNOGRAPHIC DATA FROM a study of Black male students in a U.S. secondary school, this chapter presents the narratives of academically successful Black males. In particular, the chapter focuses on Black male students' reflections on race, schooling, and academic achievement and the role their teachers play in their academic success. The agency of students and culturally relevant pedagogies of their teachers within the context of schooling as a reproductive force is essential to our understanding of Black male educational progress.

## Introduction

Jamal, Jayson, Mark, and Sean were high school students who attended a racially integrated secondary school in the western United States. I met these young scholars, along with their parents and teachers, when they participated in an ethnographic study I conducted in a U.S. secondary school. During my time getting to know these young men, I learned that they were involved in a range of school activities such as academic clubs, sports teams, and student leadership and art programs and that they came from families who held high academic expectations for them. Their parents not only proactively racially socialized them to be proud of their racial identities but also prepared them to navigate a society in which race, gender, and class barriers are endemic and systemic. Positive racial socialization has been associated with academic achievement and psychological well-being, and these young men seemed prepared to navigate a school institution that generally reproduces social inequalities and reproduces Black males as deviant.

It might be obvious then that these young scholars were also academically successful and were seen as high achievers. There are many ways in which success can be defined, and I recognize the contentious nature of placing parameters around what "success" is. However, for the purpose of this chapter and based on the type of data collected in the study, academic success is generally defined by (a) having a grade point average at or above 3.0 on a 4.0 scale, (b) completing an advanced-level course, (c) being on track to meet standardized benchmarks, (d) intending to enroll in college, and (e) being identified as a high achiever by school personnel. Each of the young men met or exceeded this definition of success and the stories they shared regarding their achievement serve as a disruption to dominant narratives of Black academic failure.

Hunter and Davis (1994) note that the voices of Black men are rarely included in narratives about them. The exclusion of Black men's voices thus gives precedent to a dominant narrative that pathologizes Black boys and men as culturally and intellectually deficient while ignoring effects that economic, racial, and political conditions of Black communities have on educational and social outcomes for Black men. In particular, Black boys in the United States exist within highly segregated neighborhoods and schools, attend schools that are inequitably funded, and are tracked into lower ability and special education programs. They are over-policed in schools, subjecting them to what is widely known as the school-to-prison pipeline (Gregory, Skiba, & Noguera, 2010; Orfield, Ee, Frankenberg, & Siegel-Hawley, 2016). The complexity of the Black male experience in school is overshadowed by dominant discourses that downplay the impact of school and social policy and instead reproduce a popular narrative of Black male anti-intellectualism, deviance, and failure. Thus, notions of Black male success are rarely considered as a reality, although there is evidence that Black boys do succeed in schools despite structural barriers they might encounter (Harper, 2015; Warren, 2017; Wood & Palmer, 2015).

There is an emerging body of literature on Black males that pushes back against deficit discourses about Black boys and men and instead seeks to disrupt White patriarchal ideological hegemony by focusing on Black male success (Bonner, 2014; Harper & Wood, 2016; Wilson, Douglas, & Nganga, 2013; Wright, 2011). This chapter contributes to this emerging body of literature by centering the voices of academically successful Black males attending a secondary school in the United States. In particular, the chapter focuses on narratives of Black boys as they discuss what good teachers do that contribute to their success. The students describe teachers who engage in culturally relevant pedagogies and provide insight into the possibilities of how to better support Black male success.

## Conceptual Framework

Culturally relevant pedagogy is a pedagogy of resistance that contests the perpetuation of White middle-class knowledge by drawing upon the cultural knowledge, experiences, and strengths of Black male students to better meet their academic and social needs (Gay, 2002; Howard, 2003; Ladson-Billings, 1995b). According to Ladson-Billings (1995a), culturally relevant pedagogy consists of three propositions: (1) Students must experience academic success, (2) students must maintain cultural competence, and (3) students must develop a critical conscious in which they challenge social injustices and inequalities. Thus, when teachers scaffold using the prior academic and cultural knowledge of Black students, they create accessible learning opportunities and decrease potential school–home cultural dissonances.

For example, teachers employing culturally relevant pedagogies maintain high academic expectations for their culturally diverse students and might teach academic content areas by drawing upon multicultural texts, artistic performance, or popular music (Emdin & Lee, 2012; Lopez, 2011; Tate, 1995). Culturally relevant teachers might also have students bring in their cultural experiences and community concerns to provide context to the academic content (Esposito, Davis, & Swain, 2012; González et al., 1995). In doing so, teachers come to better understand their students' cultures and can make school curriculum relevant to students' lives (Howard, 2001; Lynn, 2006). Additionally, teachers can engage students in a critical understanding and problem-solving of social issues that their students identify as important (Esposito et al., 2012; Lopez, 2011).

## How Teachers Contribute to Success: Culturally Relevant Pedagogy

Like many schools around the United States, the secondary school I was studying did not provide Black boys equal educational opportunities. For instance, Mark describes his observation of how Black students are treated on campus:

> Some of the teachers don't know how to deal with the Black kids . . . so instead of teaching them or working with them, they send them to some other class and write them off as ADD. They send them to OCS, suspend them. They do what they can to get them out of their hair, not caring what happens in the long term.

Mark's narrative points out the problem of how poorly prepared teachers contribute to the disproportional discipline and academic tracking of Black boys (Gregory et al., 2010; Harry & Klingner, 2006). The students also describe teachers who drew upon larger stereotypes about Black men and assumed they were less intelligent or lowered their expectations of them. Mark goes on to explain his own personal experience with teachers' assumption of his intelligence:

> Some of the teachers, like new teachers, are kind of distant from me at first and then I think once they realize, if I'm in their class and they see my grades, then they're like, "This is a cool student," and that's when they start kind of warming up to me and having more of a relationship.

Young Black scholars like Mark are assumed to be unintelligent until proven otherwise, and assumptions of intelligence, anti-intellectualism, and deviance by school personnel create significant barriers for Black boys by limiting their opportunities for educational success. However, in addition to their own agency, resilience, and parental support, the academic achievers in this study also identify teachers who contributed to their success by supporting their learning. In sum, they identify teachers who engaged in culturally relevant pedagogies, which included holding high academic expectations and challenging their students academically, grounding their curriculum in real-world application, and demonstrating an ethic of care.

### *High Expectations and Academic Rigor*

Black male students often find themselves in classrooms where the curriculum is "dumbed down" or where academic rigor is sacrificed in favor of classroom management and the regulation of Black male bodies. The young scholars talk about teachers who saw them beyond racial stereotypes and started with the assumption that all students were capable of a rigorous academic experience. These teachers held high expectations for Black boys and challenged them in the classroom in ways the students feel prepared them for college and real-world readiness. Sean describes his appreciation for the rigor of his teacher's instructional approach:

> I had an English class last year . . . It was, the teacher you could tell he had a good background in English and so he challenged us, and his main goal was he was preparing us, he was trying to prepare us for college. He was one of those "looking ahead" kind of teachers. And the things he had us doing was like doing essays beyond like what we should normally be doing.

High academic expectations must also be accompanied with rigorous instructional practices that contribute to academic success. Like Sean's teacher, good teachers challenged their students by making clear connections between their instructional strategies and the students' future goals, and thus were able to shape student engagement and academic behaviors. It's also worth noting here that even young men in the study who were not as academically successful described their appreciation for teachers who challenged them. One student describes a teacher who challenged him in class and how much he values the experience even though he only earned a C grade. He explains, "But it was a worth it. I wasn't tripping off of it because of the fact that I actually learned. From that class, I can take that knowledge and I can use it in the real world." Having challenging teachers was of value to all the students in the study and was an important factor to student learning and Black male academic success.

### *Real-World Application*

In addition to supporting success, the young men described good teachers who made the curriculum relevant and grounded in real-world applications. Students provided examples of teachers who asked students to reinterpret, rewrite, or act out classic literature into modern localized contexts or who incorporated local youth cultural interests into their lesson designs. For instance, a business teacher understood that a common practice among the boys at the school was to buy and sell new and used Nike Air Jordan basketball shoes among each other. Many young men would even stand in line outside shoe stores all night to buy multiple boxes of the newest Jordan shoe when they were released. These students would then wait until the shoe was sold out and then sell their stock for significantly more than they paid for it. The business teacher would draw upon these youth practices as a scaffold in teaching about principles of the free-market system and situated student learning within the specific context of their everyday lived experiences. Similarly, Jamal, who found the subject of biology tiresome, discusses his appreciation for his teachers who supported his understanding by grounding content knowledge within accessible contexts:

> But like my biology teacher, it's like *biology*. And she still is able to make connections to the real world and give examples. So I was able to process it more because, you know, it's easier to learn it than to memorize it. So like if you're making those connections, you're really learning it.

High-stakes testing and increasing standardization in schools has significantly influenced the rigid and scripted nature of school curriculum. Black boys are more likely to attend schools with less qualified or novice teachers who rely heavily on curriculum scripts, and thus, they teach knowledge that is often devoid of any meaningful context for their students or ignore their students' lived realities altogether. The young scholars in this study praised teachers who did the opposite and invited students' localized interests and knowledge into classrooms as a way to scaffold. Grounding curriculum in students' lived realities and helping students experience academic success are critical toward a culturally relevant pedagogy (Gay, 2002; Ladson-Billings, 1995a). For the teachers in this study, this was enacted by holding high expectations for their Black male students, challenging them academically, and grounding their curriculum in real-world experiences.

### *Ethic of Care*

The teachers who engaged in culturally relevant practices were also described as the most caring about their teaching, their students, and student success. Mark explains that his teachers "really wanted you to get an education. Like the teachers are always showing me that they really want me to learn and become something." For the young men, caring teachers were those who kept students accountable, challenged them even when they didn't want to be challenged, and kept the focus on student learning with less concern about simply meeting mandated standards. Caring for students also meant helping them feel comfortable within the classroom environment and being available to provide academic support before, during, or after school. Jayson describes the caring practices of his teacher, explaining:

> She helped a lot because like the stuff I didn't understand, she would like stay after class or come in at lunch and she would give me guidance and she would help me do it. And so I liked her for that. She was a teacher who really wanted you to learn and be educated and stuff.

It's important to clarify here what type of care these young men experienced from their teachers as it relates to culturally relevant pedagogy. Ladson-Billings (1995b) explains how care practices of culturally relevant teachers not only involve relational interdependence with their students but also include a moral responsibility to the relationship between education and social justice (Ladson-Billings, 1995b). That is, an ethic of care is not just about relationship building but more importantly a recognition of and response to social injustices that Black boys face. As I have written elsewhere (Allen, 2015), the boys identify and value teachers who understood the ecology of factors that limit Black male opportunity and success, who were willing to suspend their judgment in their interactions with Black boys, and attempt to understand their students. Furthermore, these young scholars value care practices of their teachers who challenged their students academically and drew upon restorative and de-escalating practices when working with Black male youth. Most important, the students valued teachers who were advocates and allies for their Black male students, particularly around issues of educational access and school discipline (Allen, 2015). Care practices rooted in a commitment to social justice are essential to a culturally relevant pedagogy and are therefore essential for Black male success.

## Conclusion

Teachers and educators of Black boys and men can learn from the voices of their students. Teachers are powerful institutional agents and possess the ability to influence the academic and social trajectories of youth. Black boys can succeed in school but require teachers who are willing to listen to, learn from, and understand their Black male students. By focusing on the experiences of Black male achievers, we learn the importance of rigor, relevancy and care in the success of Black males and the ethical commitments needed for culturally relevant teaching.

## Reflection Questions

What can we learn by listening to the voices of our boys of color, and by attempting to understand how race, class, and gender intersect in their lived experiences? How can we draw upon their preexisting knowledge and experiences to inform the relevancy of our curriculum and pedagogical practices?

What biases might we have about the academic capabilities of Black male students? Where do you think these biases come from, and how might they influence the way we engage with and teach Black boys? How can we support Black male success using a growth mind-set?

How can we support student agency by connecting teaching and learning, and the educational achievement of Black boys, to a broader goal of Black liberation? In other words, how can we support young Black men's critical consciousness and use of educational attainment toward improving the social conditions that impact their everyday lives?

## Recommended Resources

Bonner, F. A. (2014). *Building on resilience: Models and frameworks of Black male success across the P–20 pipeline.* Sterling, VA: Stylus.

Milner, H. R. (2010). *Start where you are, but don't stay there: Understanding diversity, opportunity gaps, and teaching in today's classrooms.* Cambridge, MA: Harvard Education Press.

Howard, T. C. (2010). *Why race and culture matter in schools: Closing the achievement gap in America's classrooms.* New York, NY: Teachers College Press.

Warren, C. A. (2017). *Urban preparation: Young Black men moving from Chicago's South Side to success in higher education.* Cambridge, MA: Harvard Education Press.

Wood, J. L. (2018). *Black minds matter course.* Retrieved from https://jlukewood.com/black-minds-matter/

## References

Allen, Q. (2015). Race, culture and agency: Examining the ideologies and practices of U.S. teachers of Black male students. *Teaching and Teacher Education, 47*, 71–81.

Bonner, F. A. (2014). *Building on resilience: Models and frameworks of Black male success across the P–20 pipeline*. Sterling, VA: Stylus.

Emdin, C., & Lee, O. (2012). Hip-hop, the Obama effect, and urban science education. *Teachers College Record, 114*(2), 1–24.

Esposito, J., Davis, C. L., & Swain, A. N. (2012). Urban educators' perceptions of culturally relevant pedagogy and school reform mandates. *Journal of Educational Change, 13*(2), 235–258.

Gay, G. (2002). Preparing for culturally responsive teaching. *Journal of Teacher Education, 53*(2), 106–116.

González, N., Moll, L. C., Tenery, M. F., Rivera, A., Rendon, P., Gonzales, R., & Amanti, C. (1995). Funds of knowledge for teaching in Latino households. *Urban Education, 29*(4), 443–470.

Gregory, A., Skiba, R., & Noguera, P. (2010). The achievement gap and the discipline gap: Two sides of the same coin? *Educational Researcher, 39*(1), 59–68.

Harper, S. R. (2015). Success in these schools? Visual counternarratives of young men of color and urban high schools they attend. *Urban Education, 50*(2), 139–169.

Harper, S. R., & Wood, J. L. (Eds.). (2016). *Advancing Black male student success: From preschool through PhD*. Sterling, VA: Stylus.

Harry, B., & Klingner, J. (2006). *Why are so many minority students in special education? Understanding race and disability in schools*. New York, NY: Teachers College Press.

Howard, T. C. (2001). Powerful pedagogy for African-American students: A case of four teachers. *Urban Education, 36*(2), 179–202.

Howard, T. C. (2003). Culturally relevant pedagogy: Ingredients for critical teacher reflection. *Theory into Practice, 42*(3), 195–202.

Hunter, A., & Davis, J. E. (1994). Hidden voices of Black men: The meaning, structure, and complexity of manhood. *Journal of Black Studies, 25*(1), 20–40.

Ladson-Billings, G. (1995a). But that's just good teaching! The case for culturally relevant pedagogy. *Theory into Practice, 34*(3), 159–165.

Ladson-Billings, G. (1995b). Toward a theory of culturally relevant pedagogy. *American Educational Research Journal, 32*(3), 465–491.

Lopez, A. E. (2011). Culturally relevant pedagogy and critical literacy in diverse English classrooms: A case study of a secondary teacher's activism and agency. *English Teaching: Practice and Critique, 10*(4), 75–93.

Lynn, M. (2006). Education for the community: Exploring the culturally relevant practices of Black male teachers. *Teachers College Record, 108*(12), 2497–2522.

Orfield, G., Ee, J., Frankenberg, E., & Siegel-Hawley, G. (2016). Brown at 62: School segregation by race, poverty and state. *UCLA: The Civil Rights Project/Proyecto Derechos Civiles*.

Tate, W. F. (1995) Returning to the root: A culturally relevant approach to mathematics pedagogy. *Theory into Practice, 34*(3), 166–173.

Warren, C. A. (2017). *Urban preparation: Young Black men moving from Chicago's South Side to success in higher education*. Cambridge, MA: Harvard Education Press.

Wilson, C. M., Douglas, T.-R. M., & Nganga, C. W. (2013). Starting with African-American success: A strength-based approach to transformative educational leadership. In L. Tillman & J. J. Scheurich (Eds.), *Handbook of research on educational leadership for equity and diversity* (pp. 111–133). New York, NY: Routledge.

Wood, J. L., & Palmer, R. T. (2015). *Black men in higher education: A guide to ensuring student success*. New York, NY: Routledge.

Wright. B. L. (2011). I know who I am, do you? Identity and academic achievement of successful African-American male adolescents in an urban pilot high school in the United States. *Urban Education, 46*(4), 611–638.

SEVEN

# Empowering Students With Emotional and Behavioral Disorders

*Gabrielle Popp*

CHILDREN WITH EMOTIONAL AND BEHAVIORAL disorders are one of our most vulnerable populations in the United States. They have some of the lowest rates of postsecondary employment, enrollment in college, and home ownership, while making up a disproportionate amount of the incarcerated population. The Individuals with Disabilities Education Act (IDEA), 1990, defines an emotional and behavioral disorder (EBD) as an emotional disability characterized by one or more of the following over a long period to a marked degree that adversely effects the child's educational performance:

1. Inability to build or maintain satisfactory interpersonal relationships with peers and/or teachers. For preschool-age children, this would include other care providers.
2. Inability to learn which cannot be adequately explained by intellectual, sensory, or health factors
3. Consistent or chronic inappropriate type of behavior or feelings under normal conditions
4. Displayed pervasive mood of unhappiness or depression
5. Displayed tendency to develop physical symptoms, pains, or unreasonable fears associated with personal or school problems

These youth have the highest school dropout rate for any disability category—44%, and when they leave school, only 64% are employed. A mere 6.4% enroll in a 4-year college, and only 34% live independently (Wagner, Newman, Cameto, Garza, & Levine, 2005). It is even more alarming to look at the data for children and adults with EBD in juvenile detention centers and jails. The National Council on Disability (2015) estimates that anywhere between 30% and 85% of youth arrested have a disability. Due to the overrepresentation of children and adults with EBD in the justice system, some researchers argue that incarceration is the default system for this population

(Wagner et al., 2005). These statistics are deeply troubling. As a society, we are failing. It is imperative that we do better by this population. Having taught children with EBD for over 10 years, the research weighs heavy on me. I know we must do better.

## Wraparound Services in New Zealand

Looking for answers, I applied for a Fulbright Scholarship to New Zealand where I heard that something different was going on with wraparound services in schools. New Zealand has implemented a national wraparound service delivery model, Intensive Wraparound Services (IWS), for children with severe EBD. I wanted to see an approach that focuses on meaningful collaboration among the child's community, as opposed to the silo approach where schools, families, and community agencies are not truly working together. Recent research on New Zealand's IWS program has been promising. Students enrolled went from predominantly minimal to moderate ratings in self-control, social competencies, pro-social attitudes, and relationships with families. The impact for Māori (indigenous) youth has been especially positive.

In New Zealand, IWS is referred to as Te Kahu Tōī, a Māori metaphor related to the strength that community can provide. Te kahu tōī is a prestigious warrior korowai (cloak) constructed from the strong leaf fibre of the mountain cabbage tree; its high status arises from its strength and difficult construction (Museum of New Zealand Te Papa Tongarewa, n.d.). In IWS, the complex interweaving of collective information, ideas and skills from professionals, whānau (family) and community combine to form te kahu tōī. The heavy, waterproof cloak wraps around the student protectively, and its precious status is a source of pride, because it affirms the mana (precious spirit) of the wearer (Ministry of Education, 2012).

New Zealand's Ministry of Education (2012) states that the aim of IWS is to "encourage pro-social behavior, provide support to teachers, family/whanau and the community to achieve positive outcomes for the child or young person, and to improve learner engagement and achievement" (para. 3). IWSs are founded upon 10 principles: strengths, individualization, family voice and choice, natural supports, collaboration, teams, community, persistence, respect for culture, outcomes, and evidence. I observed wraparound programs in four different educational settings in New Zealand: a mainstream school, an activity center, an alternative school, and a residential school. Each school implements a slightly different wraparound program, but they all follow the IWS principles.

## Looking for Answers

I was excited to meet with students in these environments, to learn about their experiences at school. What did students think were the impact(s) of the evident partnership between themselves and school staff? How was their behavior being shaped from these experiences? I researched students' perceptions around wraparound services and what was meaningful to them. I interviewed students with noted behavioral challenges at four schools in New Zealand. The schools represented the continuum of placement options for students with severe behavioral needs: a mainstream school, an activity center, an alternative school, and a residential school. This research had human ethics (institutional review board) approval and student well-being was the foremost consideration. Pseudonyms are used in this chapter to protect the identity of students interviewed.

After developing a relationship with students and staff in the schools, I conducted one-on-one interviews with students in the wraparound programs. All the students had been enrolled in the wraparound program for at least 2 months and were identified as having severe behavioral challenges. I also interviewed the wraparound coordinator for each of the four programs. Across all environments, I learnt there were five features that made for a successful wraparound program: a support person, restorative practices, natural supports, student voice, and extracurricular activities.

### *Relationships*

Students in all four environments noted that relationships were the key to success in wraparound programs. One student told me, "[The Wraparound Program] makes me feel like I'm not alone, and I'm not the only one going through this kind of thing."

A crucial element of wraparound programs was each student being designated a support person who met with their student throughout each week to discuss how they were doing. This pivotal role involved integrating the students into the school community and ensuring that students felt supported. Assigned support people were all adults working in the school; some examples I saw were teachers, paraprofessionals, principals, community liaisons, social workers, and custodians. This was how one student described their weekly liaison meeting and what it meant to them:

> A liaison meeting is where once a week the teacher will meet up with each one of their students, and we'll just talk about our goals, and do they think that they're reaching them, and is there anything that you need help with, or are you okay—is your well-being okay? Just like how I said they help people that don't have lunch and stuff like that; they just ask, is everything okay at home—do you need any lunch—do you need anything? They tell you what you are doing right. So it's nice to be able to have that someone that says, look how far you've come—you've done so well. That just gives you the motivation to keep going.

During conversations with students, relationships were most consistently emphasized by students as important to their current success. Many students identified staff in their wraparound programs as "family" or "best friends." Jonah, a student at the alternative school, described his relationship with his support person as that of "an old married couple." When discussing relationships, several students indicated that it was important to be able to joke around with staff.

Trust was an element of relationships discussed by many students. Students expressed that it was important that staff in the programs say what they mean. These students have often been through several schools, which has created trust issues between themselves and schools. Students need to be able to trust that school staff will follow through on their word and not give up on them. When I probed about why they were able to develop strong relationships with staff in wraparound programs, some ideas that students shared were the staff encouraged students, understood where students were coming from, listened to students, and helped students understand their self-worth. Establishing a positive, trusting relationship with adults in the school helped students feel safer, more comfortable, and part of the school community.

### *Restorative Practices*

Restorative justice was integrated into New Zealand's youth justice system in 1989 as an effort to divert young people away from criminal prosecution (O'Driscoll, 2008). New Zealand's model is one of the first uses of restorative justice on a national scale. The four underpinnings of restorative justice are relationships, respect, responsibility, and repair (O'Driscoll, 2008). Restorative justice has seeped into New Zealand's educational system through restorative practices. Restorative practices promote inclusiveness, relationship building, and problem-solving, through such restorative methods as circles for teaching and conflict resolution and conferences that bring victims, offenders, and their supporters together to address wrongdoing (Porter, 2017). Instead of punishment, students are encouraged to reflect on and take responsibility for their actions and come up with plans to repair harm. The philosophy is that students are more likely to make positive behaviour changes when schools do things with them rather than to them or for them. Wraparound programs that included restorative practices were most successful in supporting students with changing their behavior. When I asked students whether their behavior has changed, some of their comments were the following:

> I never thought this program was going to help me, but I know—I can't feel it helping me, but it does on the inside it does, but I just can't feel it.

> Last year my grades were really bad. I didn't go to class often because I didn't like school, but now that I have these people to talk to, I go to class all of the time.

> I was a really bad student. I thought I was going to get kicked out of school, and then I came here, and it's just completely switched my whole lifestyle around.

Wraparound programs used restorative practices to remediate conflict and teach positive problem-solving skills. Brophy (2003) explains the importance of explicit instruction and opportunity for the practice of positive problem-solving skills and behavior. On his blog, Aaron Hogan (2015) encourages teachers to think about teaching behaviors as you would academic skills:

> Students who make academic mistakes are given time to review, relearn, and reassess until they master the content. But with students who fail to meet

> behaviour expectations, more often than not we respond by assuming wilful disobedience, removing students from the classroom, and assigning disciplinary consequences. (para. 2)

Students with EBD need time to review, relearn, and reassess their behavior. Restorative practices allow such opportunities.

### *Natural Supports*

Natural supports are students' support and assistance that naturally flow from associations and relationships typically developed in natural environments, such as family, school, work, and community. Natural supports are easily accessible by the child and family and create a wider support network. They are usually readily available in the community. These supports are particularly important for youth with EBD who tend to be isolated from their school and home communities. During wraparound meetings, I saw diverse natural supports. Some examples were: cousins, religious leaders, a sheep shearer (the child wanted to pursue sheep shearing, a common profession in their community), LGBTQ advocate, a community cultural representative, a friend, and community leaders. New Zealand's national curriculum has a community engagement principle, which defines community engagement as "meaningful, respectful partnerships between schools and their parents, whānau (family), and communities focused on improving the educational experiences and success of each child" (Ministry of Education, 2007, p. 11). The underlying principle of whānau relates to an environment rich in natural supports.

### *Student Voice*

Student voice is emphasized in the IWS process and in wraparound programs. One school had weekly student voice meetings. One student told me, "We do a thing called Student Voice. Do you do that? It is where we all come together as a group and talk. I can make suggestions to improve the school." The students felt their voices were valued and listened to. Attention to student voice was emphasized by nearly every student I spoke to. When I asked a student to define student voice, he said, "It's about us being heard." When a student's voice is heard, they are empowered to grow, take risks, and make changes.

The first student I met with was Alex. He was excited to tell me about himself and the school. Almost immediately he said, "Before I came here, I couldn't keep to my own thing; I couldn't deal with my own anger." Alex, like many other students at his residential school, had attended five schools prior to this one. I probed Alex about what makes the residential school different, what helped him change, and he immediately talked about relationships with staff: "The staff here do what they are going to say they will do. I can trust them." He said part of that trust comes from knowing that they will listen to him and really hear him when he talks. Attention to student voice was also emphasized by other students at the school. Thinking back to a weekly student voice meeting I attended, I recalled teachers treating students with great respect and really hearing their voices. Talking with students, it was obvious that they felt this respect.

Jerimiah was the last student I interviewed. The afternoon we talked, he was in isolation because of an incident with another student. The afternoon withdrawal had been agreed upon after discussion by everyone in a student voice meeting, which I had attended. Jeremiah described the residential school as "a place kids come to change, help others, and learn about what you're going to do when you go to mainstream." I asked him how his behavior had changed since attending the residential school. He quickly responded:

> Normally, if I was angry, all of these windows would be gone. In my old school there was a problem with this kid I never liked, and then something bad went down, like blood—and I got kicked out. My teachers were scared of me because of what I did. They didn't like me after that. I was angry this morning, but I knew that I could talk in the meeting. I could ask the staff stuff and they would give me a straight answer at the meeting. The staff here listen to the students.

The IWS process intentionally prioritizes and amplifies student voice and perspectives. Students involved in IWS have a leadership role in their meetings; they can invite who they would like attend, discuss the services that benefit them, and share their experiences with the plan so far. Subsequently, these students experienced success in their schools. Student voice is at the heart of IWS because it is individualized—focused on addressing each student's needs.

## Reimagining It in the U.S. Context

Improving life outcomes for children with EBD is something that both the United States and New Zealand educational systems are working to address to improve their school experiences and life trajectories. In U.S. schools, we often take a very structured, authoritative approach to educating this population. We use strict behavior management systems, which result in high rates of suspensions and expulsions. Students with disabilities are twice as likely to be suspended as their nondisabled peers, and preschool children with disabilities make up three quarters of all suspensions and expulsions (Perkes, 2018). Meanwhile, New Zealand utilizes an educational approach that is rooted in partnership and student voice. Teaching students skills and allowing them to practice is essential for transference of skills beyond high school. New Zealand's approach demonstrates possibilities that could arise from loosening the structure and rigidity of programs in the United States and making room for student agency.

## Conclusion

I left New Zealand hopeful. Across the country, I observed schools emphasizing students as leaders and partners in their education, moving students from the margins to the center of their own educational experiences. This was particularly evident regarding students with EBD. Student voice was used as a positive, proactive alternative to rigid, teacher-led behavior interventions. These were organized around key components and foundations of wraparound: support person, natural supports, restorative practices, and student voice. For me, it is hopeful because we see a model for what could happen in our schools. New Zealand made big changes to the way they service children with EBD, and these systematic changes could be adapted into what we do in the United States.

On my flight home to the United States, I imagined all the ways to apply the principles of wraparound to my own instructional practices and how I could support teachers in my district in changing their instructional practices. I'm working on integrating the tenets of wraparound into my classroom and each student's Individual Education Plan (IEP) process. I want to ensure that each student has a support person assigned to them, that natural supports of their choice are included in their IEP process, that discipline is managed restoratively in my classroom, and that student voice is emphasized in every lesson. This process has been a bit scary at first because I am relinquishing control of my classroom and working as a partner with my students, but I feel good about what I saw in New Zealand and the research around student voice and students with EBD. My long-term plan is to support my district in creating wraparound programs in each school to address all students' social and emotional needs. I look forward to continuing the journey to better serve students with emotional and behavioral disorders.

## Reflection Questions

How do wraparound services in New Zealand compare with what is happening in your school or district?

What are some effective ways to build relationships with students? Does this look different when students have EBD? Why or why not?

How can you utilize student voice to ensure that students (especially those with EBD) are advocated for and receiving the support they need?

## References

Brophy, J. E. (2003). *Teaching problem students*. New York, NY: Guilford Press.

Hogan, A. (2015, December 23). *Behavior expectations and how to teach them* [Web blog post]. Retrieved from https://www.edutopia.org/blog/behavior-expectations-how-to-teach-them-aaron-hogan

Ministry of Education. (2012). *Intensive wraparound service*. Wellington, New Zealand: Crown. Retrieved from https://www.education.govt.nz/assets/Documents/School/Supporting-students/Students-with-Special-Needs/IntensiveWraparoundServiceBrochure.pdf

Museum of New Zealand Te Papa Tongarewa. (n.d.). *Kahu tōī style of cloak*. https://collections.tepapa.govt.nz/topic/3635

National Council on Disability (2015, June). *Breaking the school to prison pipeline for youth with disabilities*. Washington, DC: National Council on Disability.

O'Driscoll, S. J. (2008). Youth justice in New Zealand: A restorative approach to reduce youth offending. In United Nations Asia and Far East Institute for the Prevention of Crime and Treatment of Offenders, *Annual report for 2007 and resource material series #75* (pp. 55–80). Toyko, Japan: UNAFEI.

Perkes, C. (2018, February 28). *Students with disabilities disciplined twice as often as peers.* Retrieved from https://www.disabilityscoop.com/2018/02/28/report-disciplined-twice/24783/

Porter, A. J. (2017, March 21). *Restorative practices in schools: Research reveals power of restorative approach: Part I.* Retrieved from https://www.iirp.edu/news/restorative-practices-in-schools-research-reveals-power-of-restorative-approach-part-i

Wagner, M., Newman, L., Cameto, R., Garza, N., & Levine, P. (2005). *After high school: A first look at the postschool experiences of youth with disabilities. A report from the National Longitudinal Transition Study-2 (NLTS2).* Menlo Park, CA: SRI International.

EIGHT

# Into the Future by, With, and for Indigenous Youth: Rangatahi Māori Leading Youth Conversations

*Huia Tomlins-Jahnke, Joanna Kidman, and Adreanne Ormond*

## Introduction

THIS CHAPTER DRAWS ON A project aimed at identifying how Māori youth (rangatahi) of Aotearoa New Zealand can be supported as they grapple with "big" questions, challenges and issues. Among these challenging global issues are the impacts of climate change and associated environmental damage; social dislocation and global economic crises; food and water insecurity; high youth suicide rates; rising levels of child poverty and preventable poverty-related diseases; interpersonal violence, armed conflict, and cultural and religious warfare between peoples and nations; and many other problems that are linked to overpopulation and consumption. By taking a kaupapa Māori strengths-based approach, we seek to open up spaces where Māori youth can articulate their own visions for the future well-being of their whanau/families and their communities. In this project, rangatahi mapped cultural and community assets that they considered significant.

For many rangatahi, in addition to global challenges, everyday life carries its own tensions and difficulties. For example, approximately one third of young Māori currently live in income poverty, twice the proportion of young non-Māori (Kawharu, 2015). Māori youth suicide rates are 2.4 times higher than for non-Māori youth (New Zealand Ministry of Health, 2015). Young Māori people have high unemployment rates and are more likely to be unemployed than non-Māori youth (Te Pou o Te Whakaaro Nui, 2015). Māori have a higher rate of incarceration than any other ethnic group in New Zealand (Statistics NZ, 2019) and report lower levels of life satisfaction than other population groups (Statistics NZ, 2019). In education, young Māori have a lower rate of attainment than non-Māori (New Zealand Ministry of Education, 2015). Similar social and cultural pathologies of indigenous youth are reflected globally among colonized peoples of First Nations Canada (e.g., Donald & Krahn, 2014); Native American communities in the United States (e.g., Lomawaima & McCarty, 2006; Schaeffer & Christensen, 2010) and Hawaii (e.g., Trask, 1999), and Aboriginal nations in Australia (Cunneen, 2001). Despite these formidable challenges, as rangatahi become adults, they will have to develop problem-solving strategies responsive to the unique needs and priorities of their communities, their whanau (family), hapū (subtribe) and iwi (tribe). The Kaupapa Māori strengths-based approach used here identifies ways that rangatahi can navigate the uncertainties ahead with confidence, poise, and hope. Our focus is on the power of rangatahi voices to determine what will work for them now and in the future in order to make a difference.

Local, regional and national conversations rarely include rangatahi in deliberations about future social, economic, and political challenges and opportunities. Furthermore, few opportunities exist where rangatahi Māori can articulate their hopes, fears, and aspirations. We take the position that it is vitally important to understand the role of hope and belonging in the lives of rangatahi and how this influences their aspirations and fears about the future. Our target group for our project were Māori youth 14 to 19 years of age. We selected this age group to reflect the concerns of young people in their teenage years who were more likely to be in the care of family or other adults and who had not yet reached the legal age of majority. Furthermore, they will also be responsible for finding solutions to the everyday global challenges facing iwi in the future.

An important consideration of engaging in these futuristic conversations included seeking permission in gaining access, particularly in tribal locations other than the authors' own. Access to tribal regions is more likely when tribal members with affiliations to those regions are involved (Soutar, 2008).

It is for this reason we enlisted Pat, a young and experienced youth worker, to assist us as the engagement facilitator. Over the years Pat has filled a range of roles as a full-time youth worker. From a Māori perspective Pat was considered a rangatahi. As a rangatahi, Pat's credibility among his tribe was measured by standards that apply to all whānau, hapū, and iwi. Pat was fluent in the Māori language and had knowledge of customs and cultural protocols. He possessed all-important skill sets to lead within traditional Māori contexts, such as on marae (traditional buildings), at hui (gatherings), and as kaikōrero (speaker) for the rituals of encounter associated with pōwhiri (welcoming process). Pat was certainly no stranger to tribal expectations. Therefore, he had the ability to lead rangatahi engagement activities and draw out their voices by bringing to the fore his experience, requisite skills, and demonstrated values.

Through Pat, we negotiated with the tribal leaders to gain access to rangatahi in the two tribal locations. In both cases, Pat's pedigree as the son of two well-known local families and his credibility as a "son and grandson of the people" were of enormous importance. In person, we travelled to meet the tribal governance body kānohi ki te kānohi (face-to-face) with the expressed aim of gaining permission and support from tribal leaders to carry out our project with rangatahi from their rohe (tribal districts). Rightfully, the tribe wanted to know who we were, how our project would benefit them, generally, and their rangatahi, in particular. As none of the research team were genealogically affiliated to this district (an important principle in kaupapa-a-iwi, tribally based research), Pat and his parents' involvement in the project and accompanying us at the governance meeting was a major factor in gaining the tribe's blessing and support.

## Rangatahi Marae-Based Hui (Meeting)

As the facilitator, Pat led a 3-day rangatahi engagement process in two tribal locations. The first was at his father's coastal marae, and the second was at a community facility in the small industrial town located in his mother's tribal area. Through family networks, young people (who would engage in discussions about future iwi challenges) were invited to the hui. This was the location where Pat arranged their on-site stay for the 3-day gathering. Within these 3 days, we sought to create spaces where rangatahi could build relationships with each other and with Pat. He led each gathering in accordance with tikanga Māori principles and informed by kaupapa-a-iwi, or tribally based action research (Baker, Pipi, & Cassidy, 2015).

Pat began the first day by leading us through pōwhiri (ritual of encounter) as the main kaikōrero (speaker) to welcome the rangatahi and their families in te reo Māori. Although most rangatahi present did not speak Māori, Pat conveyed a genuine warm, inclusive, and positive atmosphere. As a result of his facilitation, he succeeded in encouraging the rangatahi to stand and introduce themselves in either Māori or English. Pat's knowledge of the colonization process and its traumatic impacts, including intergenerational effects visited on every aspect of Māori lifeways (Walker, 2004), were important factors underpinning these initial encounters. He was able to navigate the trauma of language loss that has resulted in many rangatahi Māori who feel alienated from their culture. Pat's level of informed engagement was powerfully effective in gaining the young people's confidence and trust.

As is standard practice in marae settings, each day began and ended with karakia (akin to a prayer), which set the tone. The karakia is a formal action that encourages each person, for example, to respect and uphold the mana of others and to provide a spiritual link between the living and ancestors who have departed this world. To set the tone of the hui, Pat referred to a "garden metaphor" from his days growing up with his grandmother and helping her toil her gardens.

## Rangatahi Team Building

Pat used purposeful activities (those that stimulate and absorb young people) aimed at positive team building while simultaneously building self-confidence and trust in communicating with each other. The first team-building exercise involved rangatahi responding to a video about their local area and the District Council's plans to build a mussel farm near the town on land that included the skate park, a popular gathering place for local youth. As the District Council's community consultation process did not include voices of rangatahi, the possible loss of the skate park generated a lot of discussion among them. Year 11 student Ben considered that the mussel farm "will be good for [our area]. When they're building they're going to take out some of our land where the young people hang out . . . it'll be good for the people for jobs, a big opportunity for the employment rates." Tom, a recent school-leaver, said, "The skate park could be built somewhere else. It's the only place in [our town] where the young can hang out," while Year 12 student Puhi maintained that "the safest place for the skate park is where it is." Most of the students did not know each other prior to this hui, and there were obvious feelings of whakamā (shyness) apparent from the outset. Therefore, ensuring a safe space for rangatahi to speak confidently, to offer up their opinions freely, and to respect each other's contributions to the discussion was an important aspect of this team-building exercise.

Another team-building activity, called Utopia, involved rangatahi deciding in pairs how they would spend "$6 billion dollars lotto winnings" to benefit the community. Pat suggested each pair reflect on how easy or how hard the exercise was. Some rangatahi reported finding difficulty with the exercise. Specifically, they had difficulty when considering the meaning of being "rich" or "poor" because money was not necessarily the problem. Collective well-being of whānau, hapū, and iwi was considered more important than an emphasis on individual wealth. The Utopia activity was extended to small-group discussions and decisions about what their hapū and iwi would look like and what they would build for the iwi with lotto winnings.

This time, the discussion was wide-ranging. We heard what rangatahi considered their future aspirations in alignment with the interests of their whānau, hapū, and iwi. For example, rangatahi talked about a return to communal gardens by growing and sharing locally as well as maintaining healthy kaimoana (seafood) beds. Some rangatahi talked about the need to create more job opportunities through new business ventures, such as tourism, deer and pig hunting, and deep-sea fishing tours. Others advocated for environmental health and well-being and suggested recycling, a ban on plastic, and biodegradable composting. One student called Tai was particularly vocal about the environment and especially the impact of farming in the area:

> A few reasons why I think . . . people shouldn't farm . . . around our awa [river] is because way back our ancestors [tipuna] fought on these rivers . . . it's got a lot of history . . . this is where us kids . . . come to have a good time, to get to know each other and . . . that's a bit of a reason why we shouldn't do farming along rivers or anything. Just over there by the cows, you know it's not good . . . by the rivers. The mayor should put a ban on . . . farming near rivers . . . I'm not saying they're bad but cows and animals . . . we're finding some in the awa [river] and it's killing our fish.

## Rangatahi Communication

Pat had the ability to listen, to hear, to observe, and then to interpret how Rangatahi communicated with each other and with others outside their group. For example, he paid close attention to "youth talk"—particular turns of phrases, expressions, and language codes characteristic of Māori youth, as well as their attendant body language. Some examples include raised eyebrows, shoulder shrugs, deft hand signals, head turns, and eye movements signifying a familiar language immediately recognized and understood among peers. Pat's ability to communicate in and recognize both "youth talk" and body language as well as a particular brand of Māori humor (Te Momo & Jahnke, 2017) heightened his sensitivity to the rhythm and flow of rangatahi dispositions and frame of mind at any given time. This was particularly apparent after meals, when rangatahi were most lethargic, restless, or disinterested in carrying on with further activities. Typically in schools, we would have insisted activities start as planned, "rounding everyone up" with a no-nonsense, "ready or not" approach. In contrast, Pat patiently watched, listened, and observed the rangatahi, joining in from time to time as they expended restless energy by kicking a ball, strumming a ukulele, playing cards, or just hanging out—until they were ready to engage—at which time he simply reached for his guitar and began to sing a gentle, beautifully evocative, and effective signal that slowly drew the rangatahi together every time.

By the end of the second day, the effectiveness of Pat's measured approach to listening to what rangatahi had to say was apparent by their increased responsiveness to questions and to sharing ideas, including through creative expressions. By now, rangatahi were sufficiently comfortable with each other and confident enough for individuals to recite poetry they had written, sing waiata [song] they had crafted, and, in the case of Tama, spontaneously perform politically infused rap he made up on the spot—to the absolute delight of his peers. At this point, Pat's adroit facilitation steered rangatahi to a discussion of their hopes, aspirations, and fears for the future, which was the initial purpose of the project. In other words, it was only after the exercise in relationship building facilitated by Pat that we could begin to address the futuristic conversations regarding global challenges faced by iwi. Rangatahi were also able to formulate ideas about what they considered would be an "ideal" future for their communities.

In addition to community problem-posing and subsequent discussions, the opportunity for rangatahi to vocalize an ideal future for themselves relates to previous studies where young people were invited to articulate their "possible selves" within an imagined future (Hardgrove, Rootham, & McDowell, 2015). We extended the notion of "possible selves" as expressions of hopes and aspirations of individual young people. With Pat's help, we focused instead on how they might envisage collective "possible selves" that are produced by cultural and social relations now and in the future.

On the third and final day, we joined Pat in a strengths-based community asset mapping exercise (Pivik, 2012). Asset mapping involves considering the resources or assets that currently exist within their communities. At our gathering, groups of rangatahi made short video news clips about the current state of, and future aspirations for, various community sites or assets of their choice. They were first asked to consider resources that currently exist within their communities. Second, they were asked to identify which resources are missing or need to be developed in the years ahead. An excerpt from one video clip illustrates one group's aspirations for a derelict building that was once the town cinema, based on the strengths, abilities, and passion of many local rangatahi. Following is a dialogue from the transcript of a news clip led by rangatahi Hera and Rangi:

> Hera: Kia ora whanau, I'm here again with Rangi. Rangi tell me where are we right now?
>
> Rangi: So we're currently in the big auditorium part of the Deluxe Theatre and yeah we've got a vision for this place.
>
> Hera: Ae (yes), ae so we see on your bit of paper there's some of the korero (talk) that's been had around the future for this place. So we're looking at a Performing Arts studio and a school. Are you meaning one that operates out of this space?
>
> Rangi: That would be the dream. That would be the hope that this space would be more than capable of catering for a School of Performing Arts because obviously we have a lot of seats and also a lot of space . . . so yeah . . .
>
> Hera: Right so we've definitely got the resources here to be able to utilise this facility for this Performing Arts School so ka pai (that's good). Ok so again you've identified a recording studio, do you want to talk a little bit about that?
>
> Rangi: We have a lot of talented rangatahi that really love and are passionate about music so if we could have a recording studio for them to give them the opportunity to produce their own music . . .

Community asset mapping was a useful way of establishing resources that can be brought into play to transform dangerous, alienating, or confronting environments. This approach drew on the lived experiences of rangatahi and their intimate knowledge of their neighborhoods and communities as the beginning point for later analyzing the cultural, social, emotional, economic, and political assets and strengths that exist locally (Amsden & VanWynsberghe, 2005).

## Conclusion

Our project broke new ground by adapting and developing community asset mapping as a problem-solving tool to address the challenges and promises of indigenous futurity. This work would not have been possible without the guidance of a rangatahi, a kinsman and skilled specialist in youth development. Within the project, rangatahi voiced concerns about identity formation, the natural environment, and what costs current tribal economic development plans will have on their futures.

This project was designed to support and establish Māori youth leadership initiatives aimed at creating sustainable conditions for indigenous communities to flourish and thrive in the years ahead. We acknowledge the importance of indigenous youth of Aotearoa, and indeed indigenous youth of other colonized states in the world, developing meaningful ethical frameworks for decision-making. By enlisting a rangatahi to lead, spaces were built into the process for authentic conversations to take place.

## The Global Context

Indigenous peoples share similar experiences of colonial and imperial violence, terror, devastation, and oppression. We also share similar understandings about our relationship to the cosmos as familial, which suggests worldviews that are compatible and in harmony. Despite this, we cannot assume that the experiences of Māori youth in this study necessarily align with those of indigenous youth elsewhere such as in Canada, the United States, Hawaii, or Australia. What we found that may resonate with indigenous communities across the world, however, was that by enlisting the help and expertise of a rangatahi to lead and guide us, we were able to listen to the voices of rangatahi and learn about how young people might deal with indigenous aspirations in an era of scarcity and austerity.

## Reflection Questions

What are some of the determinants identified in this chapter of a strengths-based approach to engaging with rangatahi Māori?

In what ways was Pat able to mediate relationships with rangatahi in building their confidence to talk about their future aspirations?

How and why are Māori cultural values important factors in the empowerment of Māori youth?

Consider the context of your own teaching and learning community. What key ideas in this chapter could support your professional practice? What steps could you take to apply these concepts in your own context?

## References

Amsden, J., & VanWynsberghe, R. (2005). Community mapping as a research tool with youth. *Action Research, 3*(4), 357–381.

Baker, M., Pipi, K., & Cassidy, T. (2015). Kaupapa Māori action research in a Whānau Ora collective: An exemplar of Māori evaluative practice and the findings. *Evaluation Matters—He Take Tō te Aromatawai, 1*. Retrieved from http://www.nzcer.org.nz/nzcerpress/evaluation-matters/articles/kaupapa-maori-action-research-whanau-ora-collective-exemplar-maori-evaluative-practice-and-findings

Cunneen, C. (2001). *Conflict, Politics and Crime: Aboriginal Communities and the Police*. Sydney, Australia: Allen and Unwin.

Donald, D., & Krahn, M. (2014). Abandoning pathologization: Conceptualizing indigenous youth identity as flowing from communitarian understandings. In S. Steinberg & A. Ibrahim (Eds). *Critical Youth Studies Reader*, (pp. 114–129). New York, NY: Peter Lang.

Hardgrove, A., Rootham, E., & McDowell, L. (2015). Possible selves in a precarious labour market: Youth, imagined futures and transitions to work in the UK. *Geoforum, 60*, 163–171.

Kawharu, M. (2015). Aotearoa: Shine or shame? A critical examination of the sustainable development goals and the question of poverty and young Māori in New Zealand. *Journal of Global Ethics, 11*(1), 43–50.

Lomawaima, K. T., & McCarty, T. (2006). *"To remain an Indian:" Lessons in democracy from a century of Native American education*. New York, NY: Teachers College Press.

New Zealand Ministry of Education. (2015). *The Ministry of Education annual report*. Wellington, New Zealand: Author.

New Zealand Ministry of Health. (2015). *Understanding suicide in New Zealand*. Retrieved July 31, 2016, from http://www.health.govt.nz/our-work/mental-health-and-addictions/working-prevent-suicide/understanding-suicide-new-zealand

Pivik, J. R. (2012). Living on a rural island: Children identify assets, problems and solutions for health and well-being. *Children, Youth and Environments, 22*(2), 25–46.

Schaeffer, J., & Christensen, J. D. (2010). Inupiat ilitqusiat: To save our land and our people. In R. Barnhardt & A. C. Kawagley (Eds), *Alaska native education. Views from within* (pp. 59–95). Fairbanks: Alaska Native Knowledge Network Center for Cross-Cultural Studies, University of Alaska.

Soutar, M., Ngā Taonga ā Ngā Tama Toa Trust, & New Zealand Ministry for Culture and Heritage History Group. (2008). *Nga tama toa = The price of citizenship : C Company 28 (Māori) Battalion 1939-1945*. Auckland, New Zealand: David Bateman.

Statistics NZ. (2019). *Criminal conviction and sentencing statistics*. Wellington, New Zealand: Statistics NZ Govt.

Te Momo, F., & Jahnke, H. (2016). Katakata o te ngākau: Humour and laughter among a community of scholars. In M. Kepa & C. Stephens (Eds.), *Diversity in community: Indigenous scholars writing* (pp. 80–92). Wellington: New Zealand Council for Educational Research.

Te Pou o te Whakaaro Nui. (2015). *Taiohi Māori workforce participation and health: Experiences and statistics*. Retrieved May 1, 2017, from http://www.tepou.co.nz/uploads/files/resource-assets/taiohi-maori-workforce-participation-and-health-experiences-and-statistics.pdf

Trask, H. (1999). *From a native daughter. Colonialism and sovereignty in Hawaii* (Rev. ed.). Honolulu: University of Hawaii Press.

Walker, R. (2004). *Ka whawhai tonu matou: Struggle without end* (Rev. ed.). Auckland, New Zealand: Penguin Books.

PART II

# THE PEDAGOGY GALLERY

NINE

# The Pedagogy Gallery

*Linda Hogg*

WELCOME TO THE PEDAGOGY GALLERY, where we see living, embodied artforms of pedagogy with different shapes, colors, and textures of teachers and students. These artworks offer views of the hum of teacher–student interaction. Art pieces show different renditions of "withness" and organic community in solidarity with a bigger social movement of teacher–student activism. Here, we invite you to reflect with this artist community, whose focus is on honing their pedagogy—the art of teaching—to centralize and support student voice and agency.

Pedagogy is often described in terms of teaching models and strategies, but we focus on space for students in the human interaction within pedagogical models. Pedagogical decisions are ethical decisions, because "pedagogy is directed toward the relational and highlights the process by which we are made by others . . . Pedagogy takes place in an encounter between subjects, who are also made—and therefore transformed—in and through the encounter as subjects" (Gaztambide-Fernandez, 2012, p. 51). Educators intentionally elevating and centralizing student voices in classrooms to develop student agency is ethical and humanizing pedagogy. Through paying respectful attention to who is in the classroom and honoring and nurturing students' identities, needs, and aspirations within an ethos of fellowship, teachers and students are transformed. These artworks reflect each artist's unique palette. Which resonates most strongly for you? How will this visit inspire your own developing artistry?

## References

Gaztambide-Fernandez, R. (2012). Decolonization and the pedagogy of solidarity. *Decolonization: Indigeneity, Education and Society, 1*(1), 41–67.

TEN

# Making Music Grow: Student Perspectives on Culturally Responsive Music Education

*Tracy Rohan*

> As a senior student, now, learning and knowing music, I want to teach other people, like you sort of let them feel the way you feel about music, really passionate about music, and it's good to see other people, it's good to know that they feel the same way, and when they feel the same way it's really great to be in music, and to help others know about music to make music grow.

THIS IS SILESI TALKING ABOUT the pleasure of sharing his love of music with others. Silesi is a Year 12 student in Auckland, New Zealand. The chapter-opening quote captures a key theme that students talk about in this chapter: the potential of quality music education to be a foundation for inclusive practice and an opportunity to celebrate and promote diversity in the context of secondary schooling.

This chapter investigates student experiences of music learning within culturally diverse school communities. The voices of students are positioned as sources of rich and valid knowledge about schooling and the potential directions for change. Students explain their perceptions and beliefs with regard to content, pedagogy, and implicit values within secondary school music programs in New Zealand and the United States. Their words also highlight the important role of music education in the construction and cultivation of identity and values. The students' perceptions discussed in this chapter are evidence of the thoughtful and critical ways that young people can reflect on and address issues that are important to them when given space to do so. It is hoped that the experiences and issues illuminated by students will inspire a more co-constructed and critical approach to curriculum development and delivery.

Research in the area of student perspectives on music education is rather sparse, however, there are some interesting British findings regarding student views of school music learning and the importance of music in the lives of adolescents (Lamont, Hargreaves, Marshall, & Tarrant, 2003; North, Hargreaves, & O'Neill, 2000). The role of schools in providing fertile ground for students' identities to develop, connect, and multiply is well discussed by Thorsen (2002). He emphasizes the role of school music in the construction and cultivation of a person's cultural identity, facilitating the development of curiosity about others from a position of self-confidence and cultural competence (Thorsen, 2002, p. 6).

This chapter is concerned with students' views on the ways that music education may or may not respond to their cultural identities and interests and to the cultural diversity of local and global communities. British researcher Lucy Green proposes that the power of music to express social and cultural identities is a key challenge for teachers. She describes the way that music may be "worn" by young people in order to express cultural dimensions to others: "Particularly in the case of children and adolescents who are searching for identity as new adults in a changing society, music can offer a powerful cultural symbol, which aids in their adoption and presentation of a 'self'" (Green, 2002, p. 45).

The voices shared in this chapter are those of a small group of students from Auckland, New Zealand, and Seattle and Cleveland in the United States. These students were part of larger case studies in these settings that also included the perspectives of their teachers (Rohan, 2011). Each setting was selected for participation based on its reputation for demonstrating effective music education practice within a culturally diverse school community. The students were a diverse group of aspiring musicians, all enthusiastically engaged in music-making at home, in the community, and in the various opportunities available at school. For the purposes of this discussion I have chosen to "listen" more closely to the voices of four students in New Zealand and four students in the United States. I have chosen these students because they provided particularly thoughtful insight into their experience of music education, highlighting areas for improvement as they shared their views in relation to the following broad questions: In what ways is music education, as experienced by the students, informed by or responsive to cultural diversity? How might students and teachers co-construct a more responsive, inclusive music curriculum?

## Introducing the Students

Auckland is the largest city in New Zealand with a current population of over 1.5 million. It has large communities of indigenous Māori, Pacific, and Asian peoples, among other ethnic groups. The four students from Auckland are Sina and Silesi, who are Samoan New Zealanders, Michael, a Chinese New Zealander, and Seth, a Pākehā (of European descent) New Zealander. (Names have been changed to preserve the anonymity of the students.) Seattle, Washington, and Cleveland, Ohio, are both large cities with increasing ethnic diversity. More than half of the population in Cleveland is African American. The American students are Ayako, a Japanese American student; Elizabeth, a Chinese American student; Eryn, a Native American student; and Jasmine, who is African American. Ayako, Elizabeth, and Eryn attend school in Seattle, Washington, and Jasmine attends school in Cleveland, Ohio. All the students were in their final two years of schooling. All the students expressed bi- or multiple musical identities reflecting involvement in varied musical contexts at home and in the community.

## In What Ways Is Music Education, as Experienced by the Students, Informed by or Responsive to Cultural Diversity?

The majority view of the students was that school music education is dominated by Western music knowledge and practice. Most of the students had not considered that the cultural diversity of the student population or wider school community might inform their music programs and were largely unable to provide examples of ways that responsiveness to cultural diversity was evident in the programs. However, Sina and Silesi stood out from the other students in the way that social values and concern for others sat at the heart of their commentary. They were the most conscious of the ways that music education might marginalize or exclude particular groups of students through the privileging of one way of knowing about music. These students both demonstrated "social imagination" (Greene, 1995) in their ability to empathize with those students who may not feel that music education, as it is currently practiced, is for them. Their concern for the feelings and self-esteem of other students may reflect the collectivist nature of Samoan culture, which fosters interdependence and group success (Podsiadlowski & Fox, 2011; Tiatia,

2008) or it may simply highlight the fact that some students, for a variety of reasons, are more disposed to reflect on links between education and social justice than others. The most striking aspect of Silesi's comments was the immediacy of the link that he made between the diversity of people and what he believed should be the diversity of music program content. According to Silesi's worldview, people are diverse; therefore, music education should reflect that diversity. It is a relatively simple equation. Silesi, like other students, articulated cultural stereotypes: "Indians are more, like, sporty." However, this comment also provided a "face saving" explanation on behalf of Indian students, emphasizing his perception of their strength in sport as opposed to deficits in musicianship as likely reasons for their nonparticipation in music education. It also meant that Silesi did not have to address the possibility that the music program itself might be at fault, reflecting his respectful attitude toward authority. Sina articulated the view that, in the interests of a more inclusive approach, students should have the opportunity to influence music content choices. She called for a more student-negotiated approach. Sina also felt that student enjoyment of music learning is linked to identification with the music they are studying: "It's really important because if you can't identify then you probably won't enjoy it and so you won't try and understand it or enjoy learning about it."

All four of the New Zealand students saw music education as something that should be informed by and responsive to New Zealand's location in the Pacific, as well as needing to reflect the unique nature of the indigenous population, acknowledging, in particular, that Māori have particular ways of participating in music in their communities that teachers should understand and celebrate. However, Michael and Seth expressed the view, shared by others, that there is currently no room available in the curriculum for "world" musics.[1] This indicated that they, like others, did not view the curriculum as a flexible, negotiated process but rather a fixed document that was clearly currently "full." Seth and Michael argued that the marginal position of "world" musics is because non-Western musics lie beyond the main goals and content of music education programs. None of the students described "world" musics as having less intrinsic value than either classical or contemporary Western musics. However, there was a prevailing assumption that capture of the curriculum by Western classical music theory, practice, and history is a nonnegotiable norm in music education that is predetermined and immune to outside influence. According to Seth, students usually learn about "their own music" outside of school, due to the fact that the music program is largely driven by teacher preference and curriculum requirements. These, according to Seth, present a barrier to a more negotiated, flexible, and diverse approach to repertoire selection or teaching method.

Michael commented that there would be no time to specifically include the musical heritages of the students because learning in and about Western classical music is evidently the priority. However, he expressed a personal interest in all musics:

> We don't have enough time, and interest [to learn about the music of the particular cultural groups we have represented in the class]. It's not in the curriculum . . . I'm interested in everything . . . I don't know anything about [Chinese music]. I would like to learn about that, but there's no opportunity . . . It's just not in the curriculum. So, teachers don't teach it.

Like the New Zealand students, no students in the American case were able to comment on ways that the music education they were experiencing was informed by or responsive to the cultural diversity of the students or wider community. All four students felt that their cultural identities were important to them, and some felt that this should be more actively acknowledged and responded to in the context of their schooling. All four students expressed interest in other ways of knowing about music that might be held by culture bearers in their classrooms.

The four American students were all involved with the traditional and popular musics of their family cultural background through performance or listening for enjoyment. Elizabeth listened to all kinds of Asian pop music. She wanted to learn traditional Chinese instruments and wanted the opportunity to play contemporary compositions by Chinese composers for violin. Elizabeth believed that it is important that students understand that there are multiple music histories. She illustrated this with her experience of going to China and being told that she should be playing the work of Chinese composers. She had not known that there were Chinese composers because of what she perceived as the dominance of "Bach and Beethoven" in American high schools.

Ayako learned Japanese folk songs from her parents and was passionate about preserving her connection to Japan through participation in traditional

Japanese cultural activities. Ayako believed that students have musical identities linked to the ethnicity and culture of their families that they want to share and investigate in the context of school. For Ayako, the lack of diversity in the music offerings at school did not make sense given the very diverse nature of the student population: "I think exploring other kinds of music, other varieties is a really good way to experience music. We shouldn't always just stick to one topic and our class is very diverse, we have people from everywhere."

Ayako's family experience of enthusiastically maintaining Japanese cultural traditions and interests, including music, while living in America, influenced her feelings about this matter. Her friends, from other ethnic backgrounds, also enjoyed sharing their musical and cultural heritages and identities with each other. "My boyfriend's Korean, so his parents like to tell me about all these old traditional Korean songs. They'll ask me about Japanese songs."

Native American student Eryn believed that all music students in America should learn something about the first music of the land. He commented that his cultural heritage was very important to him particularly because "there are not many of us left and Native American music is not widely known about or accepted." While he liked the idea of having the opportunity to explore diverse musics, including the music of his own family background, he couldn't imagine how that could happen in the school setting, particularly given the minority position of non-White students in the school.

African American Jasmine believed that it is very important for the music program to be responsive to the cultural identities of the students. She agreed with the view held by the school race relations group that student achievement is promoted when students see people like themselves in leadership roles, for example, as the composers or performers of music considered worthy of study. She also thought it empowering for students to learn about the richness of their own musical heritage, including musics from aural/oral traditions.

## How Might Students and Teachers Co-Construct a More Responsive, Inclusive Music Curriculum?

Despite the enthusiasm of the students in both settings, it was clear the diversity of global musical expression, while a feature of their musical lives outside of schooling and understood from this personal perspective, was not a feature of the music education they experience at school. From their comments and espoused values, it was clear that they were ready for a school-facilitated critical interrogation of value-laden language such as "theory," "history," "rules," and "classical" as well as the notion that non-Western musics are "other" or "extra." They showed readiness to participate in the deconstruction of these terms to determine the hierarchies and unequal relationships that underpin their use. Given the time constraints and evident performance pressure, particularly in the American context, an integrated approach is clearly needed so that this critical tone can become a natural part of class discussion of any musics, rather than being artificially separated into a one-off unit of work.

We know from research (Bishop & Glynn, 1999; Gay, 2000) that academic achievement is raised when the students' cultural values and knowledge are clearly part of the teaching and learning process and when the curriculum is co-constructed according to student interests and aspirations. As Sina identified, it would be good if students had the opportunity to evaluate their courses and negotiate some of the content. Currently, many of the students believe that music program content is largely dictated by teacher preference, and student preference is what happens outside of the classroom.

The students were able to clearly articulate their perception of the power of music education to include and exclude. They had all observed this power in action. This is an important message for teachers to listen to and act on and to critically consider whether it is acceptable within an increasingly diverse society to present one music history, potentially invalidating the musical heritages of students and denying them opportunities to experience the rich multiplicity of music making and knowing. The students identified a gap in their experience of music education that needs to be addressed in the interests of social justice and the expansion of understanding and appreciation for music as it is practised by diverse peoples and cultures. With this goal in mind, New Zealand researcher Janet Mansfield (2002) proposes the "differencing" of music education. She is concerned about the privileged position of the Western musical canon and the associated "rules" and concepts of music making. According to Mansfield, music education that is underpinned by an "aesthetics of difference" (2002, p. 190) would allow the repositioning of previously marginalized or excluded musics and would challenge Western values and narratives regarding musical definition and meaning.

Similarly, the concept of the "decolonized" curriculum is an important central idea for those confronting the marginalization of groups within education, the privileging of Western ways of knowing, and, in particular, educational practices that disadvantage or alienate indigenous peoples (Bradley, 2006; Smith, 1999). Similarly, American researchers Kramer and Arnold (2010) propose that students are encouraged to think about music in terms of the shared ways people engage with music rather than in terms of Western musicological categories. This approach avoids the privileging of any particular musical tradition and characterises music as a "fundamental mode of expression of all people" (p. 1).

Critical discussion in the context of a curriculum that is informed by the cultural knowledge and musical identities of the students is an important aspect of culturally responsive, inclusive music teaching. According to Greene (1995), teachers need to be aware of the ways that classroom music-making requirements and experiences may align with or be in conflict with the musical self-images and multiple musical identities that students adhere to: "Teachers can only benefit from being aware of the complex web of musical meanings with which we all negotiate, and of the intrinsic relationships between students' social groups, their musical practices, and their overall musical experiences" (p. 46).

All the students interviewed were curious and open regarding cultural diversity in music education. They want to know about the many musics of the world, and they want to know about the multiple musical identities and interests of the students who share their classroom.

Active engagement with student voice could positively influence the quality and responsiveness of music education programs, with the potential to create stronger links between music program content, pedagogy, the cultural knowledge and multiple musical identities of students, and the rich musical diversity of the wider world. Researchers and educators are increasingly aware that music education cannot continue to tell only one story in a world of many musics, by the ongoing privileging of Western ways of knowing about and making music (Drummond, 2005). Conversations with this group of students have highlighted the need for music educators to foster a more critical approach that includes some explicit teaching of culturally inclusive values, operationalized through culturally informed and responsive, co-constructed pedagogical practices. Music educators and students are in a unique position to contribute collaboratively to quality music education framed by the ideals of social justice.

## Reflection Questions

What barriers and opportunities for culturally responsive and inclusive music education are identified in the chapter?

What teacher practices help to ensure that students are active participants within a co-constructed, responsive and inclusive context for learning?

As a teacher, is there a gap between the inclusive values that I hold and the reality of my language, actions, and practices?

## Note

1. The term *musics* is used deliberately here and elsewhere in this chapter to highlight the multiple, diverse nature of musical expression.

## References

Bradley, D. (2006). Music education, multiculturalism, and anti-racism: Can we talk? *Action, Criticism, and Theory for Music Education, 5*(2), 2–30.

Bishop, R., & Glynn, T. (1999). *Culture counts: Changing power relations in education.* Palmerston North, New Zealand: Dunmore Press.

Drummond, J. (2005). Cultural diversity in music education: Why bother? In P. S. Campbell, J. Drummond, P. Dunbar-Hall, K. Howard, H. Schippers, & T. Wiggins (Eds.), *Cultural diversity in music education: Directions and challenges for the 21st century* (pp. 1–12). Brisbane: Australian Academic Press.

Gay, G. (2000). *Culturally responsive teaching. Theory, research, and practice.* New York, NY: Teachers College Press.

Green, L. (2002). Research in the sociology of music education: Some introductory concepts. In G. Spruce (Ed.), *Aspects of teaching secondary music. Perspectives on practice* (pp. 66–78). London, England: Routledge Falmer.

Greene, M. (1995). *Releasing the imagination: Essays on education, the arts, and social change.* San Francisco, CA: Jossey-Bass.

Kramer, J., & Arnold, A. (2010, January). *MUS 00 "Understanding music": A culturally diverse curriculum for general students.* Paper presented at the Tenth International Conference on Cultural Diversity in Music Education, University of Sydney, Australia.

Lamont, A., Hargreaves, D., Marshall, N., & Tarrant, M. (2003). Young people's music in and out of school. *British Journal of Music Education, 20*(3) 229–241.

Mansfield, J. (2002). Differencing music education. *British Journal of Music Education, 19*(2), 189–202.

North, A., Hargreaves, D. J., & O'Neill, S. (2000). The importance of music to adolescents. *British Journal of Educational Psychology, 70*, 255–272.

Podsiadlowski, A., & Fox, S. (2011). Collectivist value orientations among four ethnic groups: Collectivism in the New Zealand context. *New Zealand Journal of Psychology, 40*(1), 5–18.

Rohan, T. J. (2011). *Teaching music, learning culture: The challenge of culturally responsive music education* (Unpublished doctoral dissertation). University of Otago, Dunedin, New Zealand.

Smith, L. (1999). *Decolonizing methodologies: Research and indigenous peoples.* London, England: Zed Books.

Thorsen, S. (2002). Addressing cultural identity in music education. *Talking Drum, 84*, 1–7.

Tiatia, J. (2008). *Pacific cultural competencies: A literature review.* Wellington, New Zealand: Ministry of Health.

ELEVEN

# "People Don't Understand": Children Learning Through Drama as a Way to Develop Student Voice

*Delia Baskerville and Dayle Anderson*

> We have to try and inspire people to stop using vehicles that make gas. (Year 4/5 student)
>
> Climate change is the reason that floods are happening. (Year 5/6 student)
>
> We need to plant more trees . . . so erosion can't happen. (Year 5/6 student)
>
> People don't understand! They need to understand to help them to be prepared for when it does happen. (Year 4/5 student)

CHILDREN VOICED THESE IDEAS ABOUT climate change as an outcome of a drama for learning process. Their words indicate the urgency they felt about climate change as a result of their engagement in this process. They perceived climate change to be an important issue about which people need to be educated and prepared. This chapter describes how children in-role as environmental scientists were supported to develop and voice their ideas.

Enactment, experiencing someone else's perspective, is a core component of drama in education. When children have an opportunity to represent another person and see experiences from multiple perspectives, they develop their ability to discover new viewpoints, reconsider usual responses, and solve studied problematic circumstances (Gundogan, Ari, & Gonen, 2013). Wells and Sandretto (2017) posit that being in-role in a fictional world allows children to participate in a learning process in order to examine and understand a human dilemma. Through drama, children have the opportunity to collaborate, problem-solve, develop empathy and reflexivity, and explore cultural assumptions and social dilemmas relating to their own issues (Bolton, 1984; Ewing, 2010; Miller & Saxton, 2004; Neelands, 1992).

The Mantle of the Expert (MotE) is a theatrical system of teaching that positions children in-role as experts in an inquiry process (Heathcote, 1984; Heathcote & Bolton, 1994). As Aitken (2013) explains, MotE means that children and their teacher work in a particular context, the "frame" (p. 43), which includes crucial aspects of the situation in which the drama will unfold. Learners receive a "commission" (Aitkens, 2013, p. 44): the task or enterprise that they undertake as a company for a "client" (p. 45), and act on their client's behalf. When adopting these key elements of the MotE approach, children "see" themselves as someone else, become immersed in the frame, and engage and work on the commission to achieve an outcome for the client (Heathcote, 1984). The MotE creates opportunities to explore curriculum through meaningful contexts (Baskerville & Anderson, 2015) and integrates learning across subjects. As science and drama researchers and teacher educators, we were interested in using aspects of MotE to investigate ways for children to learn about and respond to climate change. It is important to note that the research project described in this chapter did not involve a "pure" MotE approach as the learning did not extend to all curriculum areas and occurred over a short period (Heathcote, 1984). We used drama conventions as described in the Ministry of Education's *New Zealand Curriculum* (2007), to shape a process of learning science through drama. Conventions are "established ways of working in drama . . . that explore meaning, or deepen understanding" (Ministry of Education, 2000, p. 48). By carefully positioning these drama conventions, we hoped to create a drama for learning process that supported children to learn about the nature of science and the work that scientists do.

We knew from previous studies that this way of working can support learners to experience and rehearse scientific practices and help them begin to understand and appreciate the nature of science in ways useful for citizenship (Anderson & Baskerville, 2016; Baskerville & Anderson, 2015). Learning about the nature of science and developing scientific thinking and practice is now a common requirement in many curricula internationally, but supporting such learning has been shown to be difficult (e.g., Khishfe & Abd-El-Khalick, 2002; Lederman & Lederman, 2014). Some curricula, like New Zealand's, expect that students use their growing understanding of and about science to bring a scientific perspective to decisions and actions as appropriate (Ministry of Education, 2007). Allchin (2011) argues that students need practice to develop the skills necessary for science-informed decision-making and action. Considering evidence and using it to develop and voice an informed opinion can be seen as one such skill. Drama offers a pedagogy that has the potential to be useful in developing this, drawing on students' affective and cognitive engagement.

In this chapter, we focus on one drama convention (conscience alley) used as part of a drama process for learning science in two different classes working at two different levels of the curriculum. We identify what this convention contributed to the learning process in terms of supporting development of student voice in relation to a socio-scientific issue. We consider how being-in-role transforms children's social realities and supports them to become agents of change speaking to a world preparing to live with climate change. Data gathered during this convention provide student voice examples for this chapter. Data for this qualitative study included audio recordings of all lessons, student work samples (e.g., presentations, maps, and notes), individual student interviews (before, during, and post-process), and field notes from teacher educator/researchers' observations. Data were coded to identify emerging themes, using a process of constant comparison (Merriam, 2001).

## Setting the Scene for Developing Student Voice

In one New Zealand school, two different classes (Year 4–5, ages 6–8, and Year 5–6, ages 9–11), each with 24 to 26 children, engaged in separate but related processes which positioned them as environmental scientists. The classroom teachers worked with two teacher educators, Delia (a drama specialist) and Dayle (a science specialist), to design and implement the two processes. Selected conventions from the MotE approach provided the children with the opportunity to work-in-role as a scientist, with a goal of supporting them to be agentive, make decisions, and act upon them. Within this frame, children worked in-role as individual scientists who belonged to a company that was expert in aspects of climate change. They entered a constructed world of would-be-scientists with multiple possibilities for engaging in and contributing to a collective outcome. Teacher educators and teachers took various roles within the drama process, guiding and facilitating it.

The process in each class consisted of opportunities to build belief in and inform children's role as scientists through a series of drama conventions: hot-seating, staff noticeboard, commission letters, and conscience alley. Use of specific conventions at specific times in the process was designed for a specific purpose. "Hot-seating" meant that a teacher was in-role playing an environmental scientist. Students asked questions to find out the kind of work she did and how she felt about it. During this time, the scientist used scientific language to inform children's acquisition of accurate scientific language that they could use when writing in-role as scientists later in the process. Introduction of a noticeboard for the company activated the drama and opened possibilities for children to be informed about the nature of environmental scientists and their work.

The staff noticeboard contained photos and written information about the nature of scientists' work for the company and presented them as real people with birthdays, families, and interests. Students studied the noticeboard to learn about the company, the people who worked for it, the kind of work they did, and what they valued. Discussion around who the people were in this place and the nature of their work provided opportunities for children to understand scientists' behaviors, the nature of an ethical company, and an opportunity to develop a shared view of the work of scientists. Children then contributed to the noticeboard, adding a drawing of an object they wanted to have in their staffroom, which provided an opportunity for them to invest emotionally in the drama and created a connection to the imaginary world.

Each class received its own commission letter designed to present a different but related learning opportunity. The younger class learned about climate change. Their company's commission was to design a presentation for the local council to help their community understand climate change and its causes. The older class's commission focused on adapting to climate change. Their company was required to design a presentation to inform the local population about likely regional impacts of climate change and suggest ways to prepare for them.

Working collaboratively in teams in-role as scientists, both classes carried out practical investigations using models and examined relevant data, graphs, and diagrams. For instance, the older class considered different aspects of the catchment of *Joylantus* (their fictional context) and investigated the impact severe rainfall would have on them. Aspects of the context explored, although fictional, were intentionally similar to the geography of the school's locality. Students examined maps showing current and projected rainfall for New Zealand under global warming conditions and (out-of-role) explored their school environment to ascertain the reality of severe rainfall. Teams in both classes worked to develop presentations for the commissioning agency.

Dramatic tension was raised by a threatened withdrawal of local council funds for these presentations. At the conclusion of the drama, the children, in-role as scientists, were required to formally defend to a councilor (principal in-role) the need for their presentation to go ahead. We introduced the convention of "conscience alley" prior to students presenting their formal defense to the councilor. It was a way for students to develop and rehearse voicing their views concerning the need to understand global warming and actions needed to adapt to it. The children were purposefully scaffolded to participate in conscience alley. They first wrote-in-role from an environmental scientist's perspective and chose their main idea before voicing their advice during the conscience alley. The combined use of two conventions—writing-in-role and conscience alley—supported children to explore the dilemma of climate change and provided opportunities to voice what was important to them. At the end of the process, parents were invited into the classrooms to view and discuss the learning with their children.

## Staging Student Voice Through Conscience Alley

The following section presents ideas that children selected and spoke during conscience alley. An expectation was set that all children would contribute their selected idea. To participate in this conscience alley convention, children formed two lines facing one other. As she walked between the lines, each child spoke out advice to Delia (drama specialist in-role as a council member willing to advocate for them to the council prior to the formal meeting about removing funding). When she reached the end of the alley, having heard students' voices, Delia made her decision about advice to take to the council, turned, and shared it with the children. An audio recording was made as she, in-role as the councilor, walked between the two rows of environmental scientists.

Being in-role as environmental scientists and participating in purposefully designed activities that utilized specific drama conventions supported children to think about climate change, problem-solve, and create as-if worlds in their classrooms that fostered learning in authentic contexts. We present these themes in Table 11.1.

**Table 11.1.** Analysis of student responses spoken aloud during conscience alley

| **Aspects of student voice** | **Year 4–5: understanding climate change** | **Year 5–6: adapting to climate change** |
|---|---|---|
| Understanding the problem | The sun is heating up the water.<br>The Earth will keep getting hotter and hotter.<br>There's more danger, like, like more storms.<br>Antarctica and the Arctic will get melted because we need to use the train or the bus | Climate change is the reason floods are happening.<br>It's [climate change] causing a lot of floods.<br>There would be more water and soon Joylantus would be under water.<br>Joylantus will get full of water. |
| Recognizing risks | Ice will be in danger; animals will be in danger.<br>Countries will heat up and we will have nowhere to go in the world.<br>When global warming gets bigger, the Earth will get too hot and will kill animals and humans.<br>People in the Arctic need to know that they're getting hotter because they might get home and their home's under water. | You probably would get injured.<br>People might drown.<br>Instead of people stop drowning, people could drown.<br>So, because people probably might drown. |
| Understanding gives people agency | If people don't know about global warming the sea levels will get higher and higher and higher and cities and neighborhoods will flood.<br>It is important that people know what will happen so they will help us stop global warming so the world doesn't heat up.<br>If people learn how to stop global warming in the presentations, if we don't stop the global warming, the Earth will get dry. | So people can prepare, so they don't drown.<br>So they know what to do.<br>So they're aware of climate change.<br>So they know what do in a drought or a big landslide.<br>[So they know] what they can do to help the climate change. |
| Personal agency in helping address the problem | [We need] to let people know that the Earth is warming up.<br>We need to stop global warming because of the Arctic heating up.<br>… all of us can learn what we can do to slow down global warming. | Then we can get ready for what is coming.<br>So we can, so we can know that you use the water in any way.<br>[we need the presentations] so that they can prepare for it. |
| Knowing ways to fix the problem | The town people stop using cars and motorbikes to stop Antarctic melting | [If we prepare], it will save money on repairs.<br>[If we prepare], it'll help make Joylantus a safer place.<br>Forests wouldn't get broken as much.<br>Joylantus is safe from floods.<br>[If we prepare we could] keep the environment in Joylantus healthy. |

Table 11.1 indicates that children were able to speak out about climate change, its causes, and its impact. The conscience alley convention supported students to voice their understanding of climate change and therefore gain agency and capability to express their new knowledge to others. Students argued why presentations needed to go ahead during a meeting with the councilor in charge of funding, a role taken by the principal who had not previously been part of the drama process. During this time, children made informed decisions, prioritized knowledge, and gave voice to a particular idea relevant to the problem. Some were able to offer advice about an action to take.

The drama for learning process created a need for students to know about climate change, appreciate its consequences, and consider solutions and actions to address the issue. Children used a collaborative company voice ("we") to acknowledge their need to educate the community, suggesting that they understood the collaborative nature of scientists' work. They understood climate change is occurring, that it is dangerous to both human and nonhuman species, and acknowledged their responsibility and the importance of educating others about climate change.

## Learning From the Drama Process

Allchin (2011) suggests that students need to rehearse the kinds of actions needed for using science in citizenship. This drama for learning process provided such opportunities. Children were supported to be present in the moment as an expert speaking with authority, using their developing science knowledge to inform opinions and identify possible actions through the experience and rehearsal opportunities provided by drama conventions. During a meeting with the principal in-role as a councilor in charge of funding, children rationalized the need for presentations to still go ahead. This experience prepared the children to educate their families and community and to be agentic citizens who understand and can voice actions necessary to live with climate change.

Being-in-role as "expert" environmental scientists provided opportunities for children to develop and express authoritative voices speaking to the problem of climate change. The way the drama process was structured permitted children to advise the councilor, an adult with power. Rehearsal and scaffolding through drama conventions—writing-in-role and conscience alley—developed their confidence in doing so. The experience of conscience alley was a supportive rehearsal. Students stood close together and shared their ideas quietly, one after the other, as the adult moved past them. The adult's positioning helped too. She sought students' advice, contributing to shared power. She privileged student voice, listening carefully and respectfully, and she took on their advice, deciding to appeal on their behalf to the council. This convention prepared students for the more demanding situation of their defense and debate with the councilor deciding about the funding. Having rehearsed voicing their ideas, children were more experienced in stating informed opinions, using accurate scientific language, and positioning themselves in regard to climate change when they came to speak to an adult outsider. They voiced their opinions confidently and passionately.

## Conclusion

Specific drama conventions provided scaffolding for science learning. Being in-role as scientists—along with purposeful use and well-considered timing of conventions—supported children to understand the role of scientists, and the nature of their work, in relation to climate change. Working collaboratively in teams and contributing to a collective company outcome supported children to learn about the collaborative nature of scientists' work, to invest emotionally in the imaginary context, and to develop a shared view of the work of scientists. Rehearsal regarding the formation of ideas and expression of opinions scaffolded and supported children to a point where they were able to give voice to their learning about climate change and offer passionate justifications about the importance of knowing about climate change and the significance of consequences if they did not act. Researcher expert knowledge contributed to the structure of this drama inquiry process that supported learning about climate change.

## Informing Future Practice

In order to support and develop students' voices regarding an issue of concern through an innovative drama process, teachers may consider

- developing an authentic company context in the imaginary world,
- using drama conventions through which students can learn about the real-world issue within the imaginary context,
- providing opportunities for students to collaborate and work as a company team member to complete a commission, and
- scaffolding learning as a planned sequence to allow students to develop, rehearse, and refine their voice and perspectives.

## Reflection Questions

How might you apply the students being "in-role" as an expert approach in your classroom?

What is the purpose or function of the drama conventions "writing-in-role" and "conscience alley" in developing perspectives for students to voice?

In what ways could you use the drama conventions "writing-in-role" and "conscience alley" to support students to respond to an issue of concern?

## References

Aitken, V. (2013). Dorothy Heathcote's Mantle of the Expert approach to teaching and learning: A brief introduction. In D. Fraser, V. Aitken, & B. Whyte (Eds.), *Connecting curriculum, linking learning* (pp. 34–56). Wellington, NZ: NZCER.

Allchin, D. (2011). Evaluating knowledge of the nature of (whole) science. *Science Education, 95*(3), 518–542.

Anderson, D., & Baskerville, D. (2016). Developing science capabilities through drama: Learning about the nature of science through a guided drama–science inquiry process. *set: Research Information for Teachers, 1*, 17–23.

Baskerville, D., & Anderson, D. (2015). Investing in the pretend: A drama inquiry process to support learning about the nature of science, *set: Research Information for Teachers, 1*, 50–57.

Bolton, G. (1984). *Drama as education: An argument for placing drama at the centre of the curriculum.* London, England: Longman.

Ewing, R. (2010). *The arts and Australian education: Realising potential.* Victoria: Australian Council for Educational Research.

Gundogan, A., Ari, M., & Gonen, M. (2013). The effect of drama on the creative imagination of children in different age groups. *Journal of Education, 28*(2), 206–220.

Heathcote, D. (1984) Dorothy Heathcote's notes. In L. Johnson & C. O'Neill (Eds.), *Dorothy Heathcote: Collected writings on education and drama* (pp. 202–210). London, England: Hutchinson.

Heathcote, D., & Bolton, G. (1994). *Drama for learning: Dorothy Heathcote's Mantle of the Expert approach to education*. Portsmouth, NH: Heinemann.

Khishfe, R., & Abd-El-Khalick, F. (2002). Influence of explicit and reflective versus implicit inquiry-oriented instruction on sixth graders' views of nature of science. *Journal of Research in Science Teaching, 39*(7), 551–578.

Lederman, N. G., & Lederman, J. S. (2014). Research on teaching and learning of nature of science. In N. G. Lederman & S. K. Abell (Eds.), *Handbook of research on science education* (Vol. 2, pp. 600–620). Abingdon, England: Routledge.

Merriam, S. B. (2001). *Qualitative research and case study applications in education*. San Francisco, CA: Jossey-Bass.

Miller, C., & Saxton, J. (2004). *Into the story: Language in action through drama*. Portsmouth, NH: Heinemann.

Ministry of Education. (2000). *The arts in the New Zealand curriculum*. Wellington, New Zealand: Learning Media.

Ministry of Education. (2007). *The New Zealand curriculum*. Wellington, New Zealand: Learning Media.

Neelands, J. (1992). *Learning through imagined experience: The role of drama in the national curriculum*. London, England: Hodder & Stoughton.

Wells, T., & Sandretto, S. (2017). "I'm on a journey I never thought I'd be on": Using process drama pedagogy for the literacy programme. *Pedagogies: An International Journal, 12*(2), 180–195.

TWELVE

#  Student Voices in the Digital Hubbub

*Chris Proctor and Antero Garcia*

As critical educators, our goal is to support students in understanding their worlds—the nature of power and their possibilities for action—and working together to build more just and peaceful futures. In this chapter, we argue that dialogic student voice, authentic to students' sense of self but also strategically seeking ways to be heard and understood, is central to these goals. Our society's increasing reliance on digital media and computational technologies has transformed our worlds, the working of power within them, and opportunities for student voice. We explore how interactive storytelling, a hybrid of prose writing and computer programming, can be used pedagogically to support critical computational literacies.

In the following sections, we look broadly at the relational and pedagogical possibilities of interactive storytelling. We first provide an introduction to a free open-source web application and programming language students used to write interactive stories, and then we analyze a case study from a workshop which took place over 2 weeks in a high school's English and sociology classes. As part of a broader design-based research project to develop tools and pedagogy for literacy-based computer science education, this case study applies a reader-response lens to analyze how one student developed voice through her interactive story. We focus on three pedagogical challenges particular to supporting student voice in digital literacy spaces: *authoring identities, channeling voices*, and *developing critical awareness.*

## Interactive Storytelling

The interactive stories we discuss in this chapter are single-player, text-based games in which the player chooses paths through a nonlinear story. Interactive stories can model in-person or online discourse, allowing otherwise-ephemeral phenomena to be experienced, studied, and discussed. In previous school-based interactive fiction writing workshops (Proctor & Blikstein, 2019), students used interactive stories to model subtle uses of power such as flirting, persuasion, microaggressions, and ambivalence about self-disclosure or willingness to challenge social norms.

Rhetorical choices involved in writing interactive stories are complex. In addition to traditional literary rhetorical choices, authors script the player's interaction with the story. The author decides when to allow the player choices and the effect choices will have on story flow. By structuring choices in particular ways, authors can grant or withhold agency, force the player to become implicated in a story's action (for example, as a witness or a perpetrator), allow the player to invest in her in-game identity, or induce alienation from the story's world.

To support writer's workshop–based pedagogy (Dorn & Soffos, 2001), Proctor and Blikstein (2019) worked with secondary students at several U.S. schools to design and develop a web application called Unfold Studio, which allows users to read and write interactive stories. In Unfold Studio, interactive stories are written using a programming language called Ink (Inkle, 2016), which was designed to feel as much like writing prose as possible. The narrative is divided into knots, containing anywhere from a phrase to several paragraphs of prose. Typically, a knot ends with several options to be presented to the player, where each choice causes the story to divert to another knot. For example, Figure 12.1 shows the beginning of a playthrough of "High School Kickback," the student-authored story we analyze in this chapter. The unfolding story is on the right. Its source code (always available to players) is on the left.

The first ten lines of code in Figure 12.1 illustrate the basics of Ink syntax. The first line (-> First) is a divert, instructing the story to continue at a knot called "First." This knot is defined starting on line 3 (=== First ===). When the story reaches "First," the player sees the text, "It's 9:30PM on a Saturday night. You get a snap [Snapchat message]. Jack is typing . . . ", and is then presented with two options. If the player clicks "Open it in two minutes," the story will divert to "Hey" (which is defined on line 12). If the player instead decides to wait an hour, the story also diverts to "Hey." The player would perceive a choice, but the story proceeds the same way regardless of what she chooses. The Ink language contains additional syntax, but this is enough to follow the story presented here.

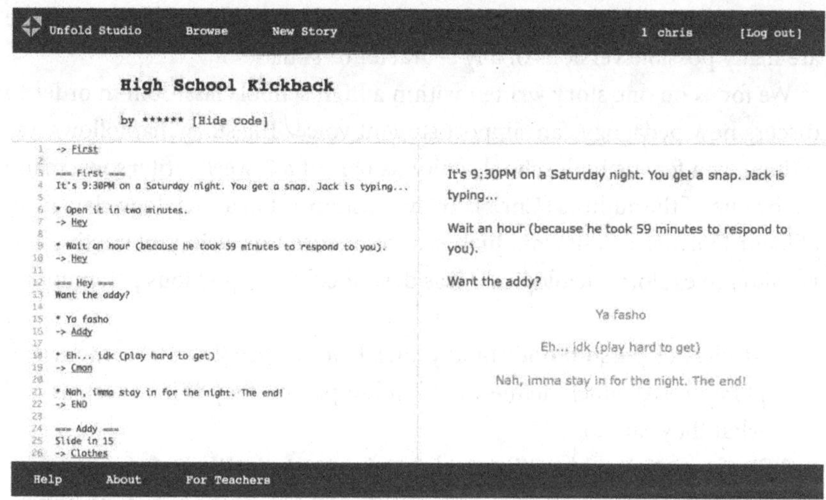


**Figure 12.1.** The beginning of a story playthrough on Unfold Studio.

## Authoring Identities

The broader theme of this book, student voice, has been an important concept in our analysis of critical pedagogy within interactive fiction, naming qualities of presence, power, and agency we seek to support in students (Cook-Sather, 2006). However, some calls for student voice are critiqued for implying that each student has a stable, authentic self, so that the teacher's role is encouraging students to share (Kamler, 2003; Lensmire, 1998). If we overemphasize sharing authentic experiences through writing, we risk creating inequities related to which experiences we value and which students feel safe sharing their experiences (Grumet, 1990). Instead, we understand identity to be something performed in social context, existing at the intersection of ideas we have about ourselves and possible selves made available by the social and cultural context (e.g. Holland, Lachicotte, Skinner, & Cain, 2001; Moje & Luke, 2009; Wertsch, 2009). This tension between how we see ourselves and who we can be in social context is particularly important in today's world of digital media, where we might be simultaneously performing different identities for family members in the same room, friends on a group text, and another public on Twitter. Because it is nonlinear, interactive fiction creates ambiguity useful for exploring these kinds of identities. There are many possible versions of any character or situation.

We focus on one story written within a high school classroom in order to discuss how pedagogy can support student voice. The story that follows was written by a female high school senior as part of a 2-week writer's workshop led by one of the authors (Chris). The workshop, set in a sociology class in an affluent Northern California high school, focused on using interactive storytelling to explore sociological ideas described in the previous paragraph:

1. **Models of personhood:** In any social world, people inhabit models of personhood which define what kind of person they will be seen as and what they can do.
2. **Performativity:** Identities are dynamic, not static. We perform our identities, bounded by models of personhood but possibly also redefining models of personhood.

After discussing these ideas, we explored them through optional story prompts such as "Create an oppressive social world where the possibilities of speech are limited for the main character" and "Create a world where the main character subverts a model of personhood s/he is assigned." The story we analyze consists of 131 lines of code, not including blank lines. We focus on three excerpts to ground how this student builds voice, empathy, and a sense of agency in her reader. We focus primarily on talk turns, which are the text in knots and choices presented to the player. Names and other identifiable details have been changed. The full story can be played on Unfold Studio at https://research.unfold.studio/stories/1207.

High School Kickback (lines 1–36)

```
-> First

=== First ===
It's 9:30PM on a Saturday night. You get a snap. Jack is typing ...
* Open it in two minutes.
    -> Hey
* Wait an hour (because he took 59 minutes to respond to you).
    -> Hey
```

```
[10] === Hey ===
Want the addy?
* Ya fasho
    -> Addy
* Eh ... idk (play hard to get)
[15]     -> Cmon
* Nah, imma stay in for the night. The end!
    -> END

=== Addy ===
[20] Slide in 15
    -> Clothes

=== Cmon ===
C'mon I really wanna see u;)
[25]     -> Clothes

=== Clothes ===
You open your closet and immediately regret saying you'd go out
bc you have nothing to wear.
[30] * Boyfriend jeans (bc girl, that's the only bf u can get), your dad's
t-shirt, and white converse
    -> Uber
* Black, deep-v bodysuit, two sizes too small jeans, black velvet choker,
and those cute new booties you just bought
[35]     -> Uber
```

The story begins by setting the scene: "It's 9:30PM on a Saturday night" (line 4). The player gets a snap (Snapchat message) from Jack inviting her (we presume) to a party. Writing in second person, the author positions the player as someone having an experience and (her)self as someone who is controlling the experience. Figure 12.2 shows possible story flows in lines 1 through 36. The choices in this excerpt do not affect where the story goes; rather, they are about letting the player craft her in-game identity, particularly how she positions herself with respect to Jack. Jack apparently took a long time to write back. Should you respond immediately (positioning yourself as available and interested, possibly vulnerable) or should you wait the same amount of time that he took to write back to you? Power is at stake here, in ways that will develop significantly later in the story.

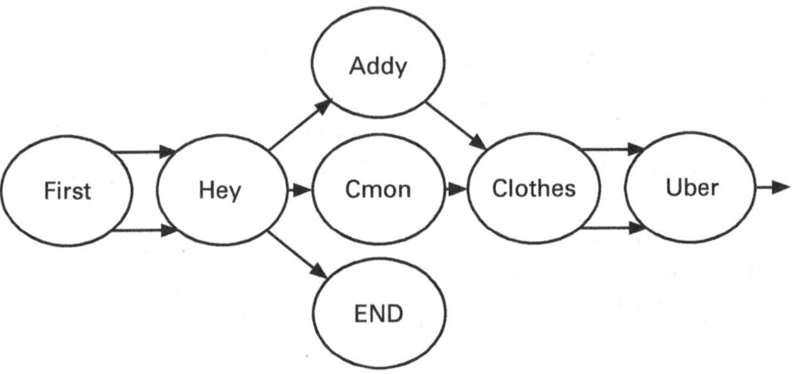


**Figure 12.2.** Story flow diagram for Kickback, lines 1–36.

After Jack offers to send the address of a party ("Want the addy?" [line 11]), the player again gets to choose enthusiasm, standoffishness, or to decline altogether. This third option immediately ends the story, though the player can immediately replay and make a more productive choice. Even though there is no real option to avoid going to the party, forcing the choice positions the player as having affirmatively chosen to attend, structurally echoing "fear of missing out" social pressure. The choices rejoin at "Clothes" (line 27), where the player chooses her self-presentation. Should you dress in "Boyfriend jeans, . . . your dad's t-shirt, and white converse" or "Black deep-v bodysuit, two sizes too small jeans, black velvet choker, and those cute new booties you just bought"?

The primary effect of interactivity in this excerpt is not to affect the outcome of events but to allow the player to experience the internal thought process that accompanies external actions—actions that some readers (classmates) might not have realized were intentional acts of identity authorship. Within the context of a classroom writer's workshop, this dynamic can be extremely productive. It allows authors to represent vulnerable situations from multiple perspectives while preserving ambiguity about their relationship to lived experience. Players take active steps to build identities within the story, which potentially humanizes characters they encounter and offers a template for enacting similar empathy-building steps in real life.

## Channeling Voices

If we are thinking of identity as authored and performed in sociocultural context, then voice must be more than disclosure of a preexisting identity. The words and actions with which we author our identities are not ours; they already have meanings and histories. Voice—getting heard and understood—becomes a process of assembling identities from meanings around us, hopefully recognizing voices already present in words we use.

This idea of voice-as-dialogue is a feature of writing generally (Ivanič, 1998), but its workings are made explicit and visible in interactive storytelling. Most of the first excerpt of "High School Kickback" (lines 1–36, earlier) is told as the player's internal monologue. But in "Clothes" (line 28), the internal monologue begins to speak in (or ventriloquize) a judgmental external voice. If the player chooses to wear "Boyfriend jeans," a casual outfit, this voice interjects, "(bc girl, that's the only bf u can get)." Speaking in this voice implies accepting its logic: wearing boyfriend jeans (as opposed to the seductive alternative) means presenting yourself as nonsexualized and unavailable. Regardless of what the player chooses to wear, voicing such a self-aware description of these choices testifies to an understanding of what kinds of clothes might be worn to such a party and what they would signify. This fluency marks the author, character, and player's in-game identity as belonging to the community of partygoers. The author's weaving-together of voices intensifies in the second story excerpt.

High School Kickback (lines 37–70)

```
[37]  === Uber ===
      You think about it ... Do you wanna drive or get a little crazy tn?
      * Drive yourself
[40]      -> Chill
      * Order an Uber
          -> Cray

      === Chill ===
[45]  John Mayer is bumping as you pull up to the func. You can't drink you
      dummy. You have a sad night because happiness is contingent on
      alcohol consumption. The end!
      -> END
```

```
[50] === Cray ===
     Javier is two minutes away. You get into the car and adjust your choker
         -> House

     === House ===
[55] You have finally arrived. Do you ...

     * text Jack that you've arrived
         -> Less
     * walk in with confidence
[60]     -> More

     === Less ===
     Jack comes outside ... "hey, you're a little early." He leads you inside.
         -> People
[65]
     === More ===
     You barge in the door and it's just Jack and some underclassmen boys
     sitting on the couch playing FIFA. They all stare at you.
         -> People
[70]
```

In "Uber" (line 37), the player contemplates whether to "drive or get a little crazy tn," referring to drinking or drugs. Choosing to drive is a dead end: "You can't drink you dummy. You have a sad night because happiness is contingent on alcohol consumption. The end!" (lines 45–47). Which voices are speaking here? The narrating voice separates itself from the player's inner thoughts, chiding the player for a mistake. It is as if the narrator were ending the story to go to the party, leaving the player behind. Is there also an ironic overtone mocking the claim that "happiness is contingent on alcohol consumption"? The prominence of drinking and driving as a non-option can be read as addressed to the school norms generally and the teacher specifically, positioning the author as a good student having the courage to address real issues.

What does it mean for a high school senior to talk about these topics in her sociology class? It puts her at risk of school-based discipline while also possibly allowing her to share important personal experiences and bolster her social standing as a risk-taker. She can shield herself from possible disciplinary consequences related to drinking by harnessing the classroom's legitimization of lived experience and possibly also existing expectations about the privileged status of self-disclosure in a creative writing context. At the same time, the narrating voice clearly presumes that drinking and driving is not an option. For the "official" classroom community—one of this story's audiences—this is a laudable stance. It would be possible to bring up similar topics with traditional creative writing, but there is more space within interactive storytelling to call up voices without necessarily attaching them to the author's in-classroom identity.

## Developing Critical Awareness

Ultimately, the goal of critical literacy pedagogy is to help students understand the world around them and their place in it so they can participate in building shared futures. The final excerpt from the student's story shows how interactive storytelling can support this goal. As the story unfolds, the character—but also possibly the player—builds an identity in a process scripted by the author. Playing and replaying a story can be seen as guided practice for developing the same understandings in real life. In the final excerpt, the player is touched inappropriately by a boy at the party and must confront both the uses of power that makes the violation possible and think through possible responses.

High School Kickback (lines 71–107)

=== People ===
People begin to file in and it becomes v lit. Colin, the boy you've been friends with forever comes up to you to chat. He's very drunk and begins to grab your ass.
* You let it slide. He's like your brother and it's happened before and you've mentioned something, but nothing's changed.
    -> Notice
* You've mentioned this to him before and he still hasn't done anything to change. You're annoyed so you go off at him and make a scene. You head
over to the couch to cool off.
    -> Comfort

```
      === Notice ===
      Other guys notice how he's acting towards you and realize they can do
[85]  the same. Even though you know it won't escalate to anything more if
      you don't want it to, it's pretty disgusting. You move to the couch to try
      to get away.
          -> Comfort
[90]
      === Comfort ===
      Steph comes over to join you on the couch. She's being super nice to
      you and you have a pleasant conversation. She notices that you're still
      super tense from before so she offers you to hit this joint.
[95]  * Hit it and trust this girl. It's probably just weed.
          -> Done
      * Ask her what's in it.
          -> Answer
      * Say thanks, but no thanks.
[100]     -> Explore

      === Answer ===
      She says it's Angel Dust. You're not quite sure what that is ...
      * You decide to smoke it anyways. F*** it!
[105]     -> Done
      * Eh, it's probably best if you don't.
          -> Explore
```

The main conflict of the story takes place in "People" (line 71), as Colin, an intoxicated friend, touches the player inappropriately. The player must make a choice. Should she "let it slide," voicing excuses that Colin is "like a brother" and, pragmatically, that previous attempts to get him to stop have been ineffective? Or should she "go off at him and make a scene?" Each alternative contemplates authoring an identity, partly voicing an internal justification for the choice and partly imagining its social reception.

The significance of this scene, and of the story, depends on the player's agency in a way that is distinct from standard narrative writing. What choices are available to the player, and will they have any impact on the outcome? The answer is ambivalent. On one hand, saying nothing allows other boys to construe the inaction as permissiveness: "Other guys notice how he's acting towards you and realize they can do the same. Even though you know it won't escalate to anything more if you don't want it to, it's pretty disgusting" (lines 84–86). On the other hand, the player's choice does not affect how the story ends. Both choices lead to "Comfort" (line 91), a de-escalation of the immediate situation but without any structural change. Importantly, these meanings are shaped by authorial choices. It could be that denying a player agency within a story contributes to a transformative experience for real-world readers. See Proctor and Blikstein (2019) for an example of how a student used this effect to contest her teacher's racist interpretation of a joke.

Several pedagogical strategies shaped the conditions which made this storytelling possible. First, the writer's workshop format centered student reading and writing, enabled by Unfold Studio's affordances for writing, sharing, playing, and remixing stories. Within this space, we observed (and actively encouraged) diverse literacy practices. Some students spent hours playing stories before deciding what they wanted to write about. Some students wrote in pairs. Some sat with groups of friends playing and discussing their stories or asked for feedback from specific peers. Because stories were published to the web, some students shared their stories with people beyond the classroom.

Within this space, the teachers cultivated and reinforced norms, invited students to mini-lessons on particular topics (for example, more advanced programming), and met with students individually. It was particularly helpful to explicitly discuss sociological ideas first and to explore their dynamics in concrete everyday situations. For example, there was an extended discussion of various ways parents sometimes impose identities on their children. These familiar experiences provided footing to consider how they were affected by formations such as gender, sexuality, race, and social class. Many students wrote about how they developed stories as illustrations of ideas that came up in discussion. The distance between authors and voices they brought together in stories made it easier to model and share personal experiences. The availability and replayability of stories made them potentially transformative experiences for their players.

## Conclusion

Youth today are growing up in complex literacy spaces in which communication is regularly mediated by multilayered digital media. We are more connected than ever, but we have very little control over meaning-making processes at work. Instagram, Snapchat, Twitter, and the like have full control over how (and whether) our content is presented, to whom, and in what context. The issues we have addressed in this chapter, authoring identities, channeling voices, and developing critical awareness, are more challenging and more important in the landscape of digital media. We have found that interactive storytelling can open productive spaces for modeling, understanding, sharing, and acting on digitally mediated experiences. We invite you to join us in exploring the possibilities of supporting student voice through interactive storytelling.

## Reflection Questions

In your worlds (e.g., work, family, social media), how do you author different identities?

How does social media change the way we channel voices? For example, people often speak by recontextualizing content created by others.

As our literacies shift from print to digital, what opportunities and challenges exist for critical understanding and social change?

## Recommended Resources

Unfold Studio, free open-source web application (https://unfold.studio)

Unfold Studio documentation and curriculum, including a full curriculum unit (http://docs.unfold.studio)

## References

Cook-Sather, A. (2006). Sound, presence, and power: "Student voice" in educational research and reform. *Curriculum Inquiry, 36*(4), 359–390.

Dorn, L. J., & Soffos, C. (2001). *Scaffolding young writers: A writer's workshop approach.* Portland, ME: Stenhouse.

Grumet, M. R. (1990). Voice: The search for a feminist rhetoric for educational studies. *Cambridge Journal of Education, 20*(3), 277–282.

Holland, D., Lachicotte, W., Skinner, D., & Cain, C. (2001). *Identity and agency in cultural worlds*. Cambridge, MA: Harvard University Press.

Inkle. (2016). *Ink*. [Computer software]. Retrieved from https://github.com/inkle/ink

Ivanič, R. (1998). *Writing and identity: The discoursal construction of identity in academic contexts*. Amsterdam, The Netherlands: John Benjamins.

Kamler, B. (2003). Relocating the writer's voice: From voice to story and beyond. *English in Australia, 138*(Spring), 34–40.

Lensmire, T. J. (1998). Rewriting student voice. *Journal of Curriculum Studies, 30*(3), 261–291.

Moje, E. B., & Luke, A. (2009). Literacy and identity: Examining the metaphors in history and contemporary research. *Reading Research Quarterly, 44*(4), 415–437.

Proctor, C., & Blikstein, P. (2019). Unfold Studio: Supporting critical literacies of text and code. *Information and Learning Sciences, 20*(5/6), 285–307.

Wertsch, J. V. (2009). *Voices of the mind: Sociocultural approach to mediated action*. Cambridge, MA: Harvard University Press.

THIRTEEN

# "Multiple Perspectives and Many Connections": Systems Thinking and Student Voice

*Amy Lassiter Ardell and Margaret Sauceda Curwen*

STUDENT VOICE, PARTICIPATION, AND AGENCY are increasingly recognized as vital (e.g., Gonzalez, Hernandez-Saca, & Artilles, 2017; Quaglia & Fox, 2018). In two U.S. elementary schools, teachers used an innovative systems thinking approach, which encouraged instructional practices that drew out student voice. This included listening to children's developing understandings, lived experiences, and interests.

Teachers welcomed students' offerings to co-construct a dynamic and relational curriculum. Classrooms were enlivened with mutual questioning, examining, debating, exploring, and investigating. This account captures how educators opened up spaces and meaningfully drew upon the voices of young learners in the context of developing the classroom as a collective consciousness and repositioning students as agents of change attuned to the social good (Davis, Sumara, & Luce-Kapler, 2015).

## A Glance Into the Context

### *The Schools*

Two schools partnered for this project through a common, teacher-driven interest to develop pedagogical techniques grounded in systems thinking. In observing their work, we learned about the value of centralizing student voices in learning. One school was an independent school with a mostly White, upper-middle class community. The other was a public school, comprised primarily immigrant families from Latin America, the Middle East, and Southeast Asia, with more than 50% of students living below the poverty line. In total, eight educators, representing kindergarten (6-year-olds) through fifth grade (10- to 11-year-olds), and 70 students collaborated on this project.

We gathered data using field observations and attended professional development sessions. We collected student work and conducted interviews and focus groups with teachers, students, and administrators. While the project did not start specifically as a student voice initiative, classroom teachers quickly realized that children's voices were instrumental in guiding, contributing, and leading the direction of classroom projects.

### *What Is Systems Thinking?*

Systems thinking posits that the natural and social worlds are best understood as living systems, which are interrelated and interconnected (F. Capra & Luisi, 2014). For example, a tree is more than discrete components of roots, trunk, branches, and leaves. It is its own distinct system that has patterned changes in relationship to seasonal cycles and serves as an animal habitat (B. Capra, 1990). This holistic perspective prompts inquiry into the nature of underlying relationships and networks, and it contrasts with more reductionist thinking often characteristic of U.S. schools (Bowers, 2010). Students become aware of the larger picture, identify components of a system, and then look for points of leverage to impact that system to sustain, enhance, or interrupt it (Senge et al., 2012). As complex issues like climate change come into classroom spaces, an ability to "think in systems" (Meadows, 2008) potentially can offer a way of conceptualizing and considering solutions to intractable problems. This perspective accepts change as the norm and sees responsibility as integral to societal and environmental harmony (Liu & Hanauer, 2011).

In these two schools, teachers sought out ways to pursue topics that could spark and/or incorporate student interest linked to school, state, and national standards. Curriculum projects exploring natural and social systems included exploring systems of kindness, researching urban animals' habitats, and disrupting modern-day slavery (Curwen, Ardell, & MacGillivray, 2019). A systems view is part of the recently adopted U.S. national science curriculum standards and is increasingly used in education, particularly in science (Yoon, Goh, & Park, 2017), ecojustice, and sustainability education (Cassell & Wilson, 2010).

## Systems Thinking, Student Voice, and the Classroom as a Collective Consciousness

Cultivating a systems thinking perspective is considered critical to developing global citizens who can address complex social and environmental concerns (Bowers 2010; F. Capra & Luisi, 2014). As Davis, Sumara, and Luce-Kapler (2015) note, conceptualizing global citizenship through a systemic sustainability education (SSE) lens "extends the notion of democratic citizenship to include an ethical sensitivity to issues and phenomena that exceed the human [world], coupled to a heightened awareness that one's actions make a difference" (p. 185). SSE reconceptualizes classroom teaching as enlarging consciousness of the classroom collective through transphenomenal complexity. The classroom collective is defined as a coherent group of teacher(s) and students that has its own evolving identity in the context of a particular classroom space. Simultaneously, this group is part of broader and ever-changing sociocultural and sociohistorical circumstances. Transphenomenal complexity is understood as interdisciplinary learning that is explored from multiple perspectives ranging from the personal to the global. Teachers and students co-learn through dialogic and cooperative learning practices that engage the collective's ideas and contributions.

In an SSE-informed classroom, the teacher's role is "orienting attentions, offering viable interpretations, and selecting among the options that arise in the collective" (Davis et al., 2015, p. 217). This charge means that student voice is essential. Generating many ideas is critical as SSE assumes that knowing stems from the intersection of diverse perspectives. This does not mean that traditional academic knowledge (e.g., the water cycle) needs to be "reinvented" by students. Instead, children would, for example, discuss, identify, and develop myriad solutions around how a current statewide drought could be mitigated in their personal, school, and community lives (Curwen, Ardell, MacGillivray, & Lambert, 2018). SSE conceptualizes learners as agents of change, mindful of the common good, and able to transform the world.

Systems thinking focuses on fostering agency, acknowledging, understanding, generating different perspectives, identifying leverage points to alter systems, and developing solutions. We argue that engaging students in systems thinking, grounded in an SSE approach, invites and nurtures their voices to flourish. It promotes student agency because it offers an opportunity to (1) democratize classrooms, (2) develop a holistic worldview, and (3) increase connections between academic learning and the broader world. Although these themes are inherently linked, we discuss them separately in the following sections.

## Democratizing Classrooms

Learning and interacting with others were key to democratizing the classrooms as teachers and students engaged in systems thinking. By democratizing, we assert that the presence of multilayered student voices provides opportunities for peers to draw upon various perspectives in their effort to become flexible thinkers and problem-solvers. Some teachers created learning activities and pose questions that deliberately invited students' perspectives and ideas. For example, a second-grade teacher, Jasmine, wanted her students to create an ABC wall chart to reflect concepts related to their yearlong study of kindness. She scripted open questions such as "What systems build my capacity to demonstrate kindness?" and "What systems need to be in place for me to demonstrate kindness?" to launch meaningful discussion. Student contributions included "U: Understanding shows kindness because you believe what someone is saying" and "W: Waiting shows kindness by if someone says, 'Wait for me,' wait for them. It might be a nice thing to do to them. It also makes them happy." Responding to open-ended questions, students developed their own ideas on how to act conscientiously and mindfully toward others.

In a K–1 classroom, teachers gathered students for a prewriting discussion to guide children in selecting which "broken system" they might choose to write about. In the following vignette, one child suggested a topic linked to a recent local news story of endangered animal life. The teacher accepted the child's offering as peers built upon her ideas. When one 5-year-old described a concept but not the vocabulary term, the teacher scaffolded the children with the vocabulary needed to better express their ideas:

> Child 10: The seal system. They are coming up on land and dying.
>
> Teacher 1: Is a single seal a system? A seal by itself. I bet that's connected to a lot of things. What's the system behind the seal?
>
> Child 4: The glacier. The smell and gas are interfering with the glaciers.

Teacher 1: I'm thinking of a vocabulary word, takes in smog, litter. [She pauses and waits.] It begins with a [the letter] "p."

Child 5: Pollution.

Teacher 1: How many of you think pollution is the system?

Inviting students to identify their interests was an important step in helping them link their lives to the consequences of human activity taking place in the broader natural and social world.

Opportunities for student voice communicated a value for sharing varied perspectives (Cabrera & Cabrera, 2015). These classroom spaces fostered rich thinking and promoted a safe environment (Ferguson, Phillips, Rowley, & Friedlander, 2015). Children combined their thoughts to create larger understandings. For example, during an integrated science and language arts lesson in a first-grade classroom, students collectively generated a list of animals that lived in their city. They then split up into partners to think more about relationships that might exist between animals. This activity utilized principles of dialogic learning (Phillipson & Wegerif, 2017), which effectively brought out student voice. Two students, who had decided that their categories would be "land, sea, and sky," collaborated in the following way:

Student 2: Where are we doing birds? [Student 1 writes "brids."]

Student 2: That's not how—it's i, r, d, s. [He corrects the letter sequence on paper.]

. . .

Student 2: I know . . . hamster. [Acts out hamster moves.] It's going to make a little more sense [draws a line and then a cave underneath]. It doesn't have any tracks. It's going to fall into the ocean, so we need a raft. [Draws this scene.]

Student 1: [Crosses it out.] Stop!

Student 2: I know what we can do.

Student 1: Please stop drawing stuff that isn't about this. [Student 2 goes back to drawing clouds.]

. . .

Student 2: I know another one, a spider. Some spiders can be on water and sometimes swim in sea.

Student 1: They catch food on the water.

Student 2: How about a whale shark?

Student 1: Whale shark, great! (Gives him a hug.)

Student 2: That's not how you spell whale!

Student 1: I'm doing my best, I'm doing my best!

Their dialogue zigzagged as the two youngsters cajoled, reminded, reprimanded, and even hugged one another as they aimed to complete their goal of categorizing animals. Conversational turns revealed children's interdependence, joint accountability to the learning goal, and sharing of quality ideas, consistent with key principles of cooperative learning (Gillies, 2016). Each student recognized that they had a contribution to make and their knowledge was validated. They drew upon each other's strengths. The teacher created a context for successful cooperative engagement vis-à-vis the nature of the task, small group structure, and promoting effective talking and reasoning (Gillies, 2016). Students' self-direction, self-organizing, and self-monitoring took place without constant teacher oversight. As Wegerif (2013) notes, dialogue allows individuals opportunities to hear themselves talk. Collaborative dialogue within a cooperative task drew out student voice, triggering reflection and refinement of ideas and self-awareness of one's own interests and beliefs.

With a focus on dialogic and cooperative activities, these classrooms became spaces where every voice was invited and valued. Teachers' conscious planning of questions elicited multiple perspectives and encouraged children's voices (Quiglia & Fox, 2018). An expectation that all children could contribute from their unique viewpoints cultivated vibrant learning exchanges (Ferguson et al., 2015) where creativity could thrive. Because children were steeped in an environment that assumed and valued diverse thinking and perspectives, the potential for students to gradually develop a flexible worldview was increased (Cabrera & Cabrera, 2015; F. Capra & Luisi, 2014).

## Developing a Holistic Worldview

Coming to understand the world as inherently complex and interdependent (F. Capra & Luisi, 2014) was cognitively demanding. Children noted that a systems thinking perspective "helps you understand something [a topic/concept] better" and "helps you think about hard problems." One second grader argued for the importance of systems thinking, noting, "Because if you didn't know about systems, how would you know about all things in the world?" These children expressed confidence in having a strategy to make sense of social and natural phenomena. Furthermore, in these specific classroom spaces, they were able to develop understandings through meaningful talk and actions.

Students' ideas were centralized in multiple ways. First, teachers and students kept records of their conversations. These documents were added to over time to show evolution of thinking. Second, while teachers framed the content area or project in their respective classrooms, the students guided how it was interpreted and enacted. For example, in a second-grade classroom, students designed their ideal school playground as part of a geometry unit. On one student's mapping of social systems, shown in Figure 13.1, lines drawn between real-world networks such as the "friendly system," "safety system," and "rules system" indicated a perspective that good design had to go beyond utility and provide for community harmony.

Student voice was invited via multiple modes of communication, and both oral and written evidence of what students knew and expressed were available as class resources. Whole-class and small-group discussions allowed students to verbally communicate and be mutually accountable. Drawings and systems maps offered interpretations, visual evidence, and records of those conversations. For example, one fifth-grade social studies teacher augmented a historical timeline from 1000 BC to the present with a "chalk talk" technique. She posted sheets of black butcher paper in a corner with two overarching, open-ended critical thinking questions: "How did these systems begin?" and "How have these systems changed?" prompting students to contemplate patterns of human actions and relationships throughout history as they wrote to each other over time. The opportunity for students to contribute ideas without instantaneous teacher evaluation fostered a safe space to contribute and negotiate. This silent written exchange provided an alternative space for students' voluntary expressions of ideas, incipient questions, and

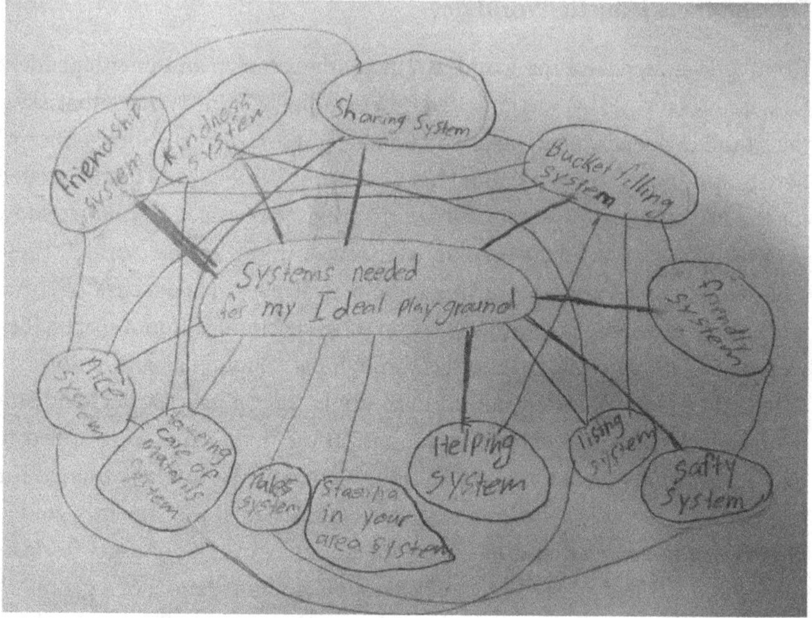


**Figure 13.1.** Child's conceptual ideal playground depicting interrelationships to other social systems.

peer interactions. These documents remained on display, indicating student voice as an instrumental and valid resource.

Through continual experiences with systems thinking, children noted they could think both widely and deeply about a variety of topics and issues as interrelated and interdependent (F. Capra & Luisi, 2014). For example, one fifth grader noted how the holistic nature of systems thinking broadened his learning "because it allows me to think from a new aspect . . . that instead of just thinking as one thing, just one-sided, there are multiple perspectives and many connections." He elaborated further on how it transcended surface observations:

> Let's say you're taking a hike outside and let's say you see a lizard . . . And if you were never exposed to systems thinking, then you're just like, "Oh, it's a lizard. Cool." . . . But if you were exposed to systems thinking, you would say, "Oh, a lizard. Well, why is it here?" You would ask a bunch of questions.

Children's observations highlighted their evolving recognition of the world's complexity, thus igniting curiosity.

The dynamic and recursive nature of a systems thinking–based curriculum allowed for "investigation, problem-solving, interdependent action, mutual respect and systems-based approaches to life" (Cassell & Wilson, 2010, p. 187). Continual emphasis on making connections and exploring interrelationships accelerated students' abilities to develop and grasp new ideas and gain an understanding of varied societal and environmental issues.

## Interacting With the World

Classroom dialogue around systems thinking encouraged children to be engaged in purposeful action beyond their classrooms. These included intentional choices students made in their individual actions, such as expressions of kindness. It also reflected a desire to share their knowledge with peers, family, and community, thus promoting global citizenship (Davis et al., 2015). Students shared about bringing some of their school learning home. One first grader noted that he took the initiative to create his own at-home learning project. His intention was to draw "all the connections I can" between systems in his bathroom, including the sink, toilet, and shower. After multiple trips to buy more chart paper, and even engaging the use of a ladder after his systems map got really big, he commented, "I'm basically making plans like [his teacher's name] for systems, so I can like get smarter and smarter at home and smarter, and smarter, and smarter." It was evident that his classroom experience, which documented his voice, fueled his sense of empowerment.

Communication beyond classrooms also took place through formal school presentations. One fifth-grade class shared their interdisciplinary project on the inequity of modern-day slavery in a local community space. It was a yearlong curricular research integrating social studies, language arts, and math to explore parallels between slavery in the United States from the 1700s to present-day experiences of marginalized individuals. Students created multimodal projects including posters, perspective-taking poems, graphical representations, and laser-designed lamps designed for a culminating art installation. They invited their families and others in the school community to visit the display. Almost in awe at its unanticipated impact and reach, a student commented:

> It was a very detailed project that I didn't know was going to be as big as it was . . . in all the other [previous] grades, if we did something like that, only parents and maybe like on rare occasions relatives would come. And I was completely wrong because a whole bunch of people came. People invited people, who invited people, who invited people. It's like a system . . . And it took a long time, but all of that time was worth it, and it took a lot of effort, which was also worth it.

Students recognized their authority and potential to "help adults learn."

Developing systemic understanding of social happenings helped students formulate specific ways they could choose to amplify, interrupt, and/or impact a system. They developed the "capacity and propensity to take purposeful initiative" (Ferguson et al., 2015). Students' extension of learning beyond school was evident in their desire to communicate their learning with others. Reaching out beyond their classrooms and sharing new knowledge with others raised students' awareness of their own agency. It heightened their sense of possibility and responsibility. They could use their voices to promote the common good.

## How Collaborative Systems Thinking Made a Difference

Teachers encouraged an enactment of systems thinking that was inherently collaborative. As a result, students' voices, participation, and agency were fostered both inside classrooms and beyond. Instructional approaches opened up classroom spaces for dialogue and perspective-taking. As such practices became expected, learners gained confidence in contributing their knowledge and considered others' imaginative ideas in problem-solving and building new knowledge. With this validation of voice, they could conceive of a role and interrelationship with their immediate and broader social world and exercised their agency. Ultimately, these contexts produced a potentially transformative experience for children. The teachers' approach nurtured teacher–student collaboration and suggests ways educators and students can feel empowered. A systems thinking perspective develops students' conception of themselves as interconnected within multiple systems and thus fosters current and future orientation of responsibility toward creation of a more just and equitable society and sustenance of the natural world (F. Capra & Luisi, 2014; Liu & Hanauer, 2011).

## Reflection Questions

How might engagement of student voice reframe what counts as knowledge?
What did the teachers need to believe and know to develop students' voice?
What academic and social trajectories do you imagine for these students?

## References

Bowers, C. A. (2010). Educational reforms that foster ecological intelligence. *Teacher Education Quarterly, 37*(4), 9–31.

Cabrera, D., & Cabrera, L. (2015). *Systems thinking made simple: New hope for solving wicked problems*. Ithaca, NY: Odyssean Press.

Capra, B. (Director). (1990). *Mindwalk* [Film]. United States: Atlas Production Company.

Capra, F., & Luisi, P. L. (2014). *The systems view of life*. Cambridge, MA: Cambridge University Press.

Cassell, J., & Wilson, T. (2010). Visions lost and dreams forgotten: Environmental education, systems thinking, and possible futures in American public schools. *Teacher Education Quarterly, 37*(4), 179–197.

Curwen, M., Ardell, A., & MacGillivray, L. (2019). Hopeful discourse: Elementary children's activist responses to modern-day slavery grounded in systems thinking. *Literacy Research: Theory, Method, and Practice, 68*(1), 139–161. doi:10.1177/2381336919870284

Curwen, M. S., Ardell, A., MacGillivray, L., & Lambert, R. (2018). Systems thinking in a second grade curriculum: Students engaged to address a statewide drought. *Frontiers in Education*, 3, 90. doi:10.3389/feduc.2018.00090

Davis, B., Sumara, D., & Luce-Kapler, R. (2015). *Engaging minds: Cultures of education and practices of teaching*. New York, NY: Routledge.

Ferguson, R., Phillips, S., Rowley, J. & Friedlander, J. (October 2015). *The influence of teaching: Beyond standardized test scores: Engagement, mindsets, and agency*. Seattle, WA: The Raikes Foundation.

Gillies, R. M. (2016). Cooperative learning: Review of research and practice. *Australian Journal of Teacher Education, 41*(3), 39–54. doi:10.14221/ajte.2016v41n3

Gonzalez, T., Hernandez-Saca, D., & Artilles, A. (2017). In search of voice: Theory and methods in K–12 student voice research in the US, 1990–2010. *Educational Review, 69*(4), 451–473.

Liu, E., & Hanauer, N. (2011). *The gardens of democracy: A new American story of citizenship, economics and the role of government*. Seattle, WA: Sasquatch Books.

Meadows, D. H. (2008). *Thinking in systems: A primer.* White River Junction, VT: Chelsea Green Publishing.

Phillipson, N., & Wegerif, R. (2017). *Dialogic education.* New York, NY: Routledge.

Quaglia, R., & Fox, K. (2018). Student voice: A way of being. *Australian Educational Leader, 40*(1), 14–18.

Senge, P., Cambron-McCabe, N., Lucas, T., Smith, B., Dutton, J., & Kleiner, A. (2012). *Schools that learn: A fifth discipline fieldbook for educators, parents, and everyone who cares about education.* New York:, NY Crown Business.

Wegerif, R. (2013). *Dialogic: Education for the Internet age.* London, England: Routledge.

Yoon, S. A., Goh, S.-E., & Park, M. (2017). Teaching and learning about complex systems in K–12 science education: A review of empirical studies 1995–2015. *Review of Educational Research, 88*(2), 285–325.

FOURTEEN

# Finding Hope Through Dystopian Novels

*Christopher Lewis*

Have you ever had the moment or that feeling, it's like, it's not a feeling, it's that moment you realize that you are not the center of the universe? (Azalea)

TODAY'S CLASSROOMS SOMETIMES FEEL LIKE a dystopian nightmare. Students, identified by their six-digit number, are like empty receptacles to be filled with information by the teacher. Paulo Freire (1970/2000), who called this kind of learning the *banking method*, argued that this form of schooling is like a factory where students leave as products of their manufacturer. They sit passively in neatly aligned rows, taking copious notes and regurgitating information. Knowledge is maintained and controlled by mandated curriculum, pedagogy, and institutional policy. As an educator feeling stuck in this dehumanizing system, I continually seek ways to challenge the status quo, and I do this by listening to my students. Azalea's question at the beginning of this chapter exemplifies the importance of student voice and how it can affect a teacher's pedagogy. Azalea, one of my former students, reminds me that while I sometimes feel trapped in a dystopian nightmare, youth provide hope that our world can be reimagined.

I have always loved reading dystopian fiction. In recent decades, there has been a tremendous increase in dystopian novels for young adults (YAs). The story always begins *in media res*, where some travesty, disease, war, or alien invasion necessitated a political regime change. In the characters' world, they are taught to function as members of society without question and without memory of how things came to be. They know the rules of society, but the reader does not. In dystopian novels written for a YA audience, a young hero or heroine never fits in and cannot find the comfort of community. This uneasy feeling leads the main character and trusty companions to rebel.

## Student Voices in a Dystopian Fiction Book Club

In 2015, I formed a book club with 11 high school seniors where we read seven YA dystopian novels.[1] This project, the focus of my doctoral dissertation (Lewis, 2016), began because I saw how voraciously the students read and asked me for book recommendations. They were students in my Advanced Placement U.S. History class the prior year, and I watched them grow as thinkers, regularly asking critical questions about the world in which we live and systems of oppression that affect us daily. I wondered about ways in which dystopian thinking influences our understanding of concepts like identity, power, and resistance. While I was a participant in the book club, students led our discussions about novels they selected. We met after school and on several occasions our meeting lasted a few hours. Their insights shaped my belief that educators are responsible for helping students view themselves as reflective change agents who name and resist dominant ideologies (Darder, 1991; Delpit, 1998; Freire, 1970/2000; Giroux, 1997; McLaren, 2007).

As a result of our book club meetings, I learned about the importance of utopian thinking as a pedagogical choice. We must believe that education inspires youth to ask questions and imagine new solutions for social problems. However, schooling has not always effectively prepared youth for civic engagement. YA dystopian novels, often directly connected to contemporary events, allow readers to see characters question systemic inequality and resist oppression. YA dystopian novels offer youth an experiment in understanding the relationship between the individual and society (Hintz, 2002; McCallum, 2013; Trites, 2000). When heroes and heroines are youth, "the confrontation with the realities of the adult world may lead to a standoff between adolescents and adults that empowers young people to turn against the system as it stands and change the world in ways adults cannot" (Basu, Broad, & Hintz, 2013, p. 7). In this chapter, I examine how students in our book club reacted to dystopian philosophy and its relationship to activism and resistance. Then, I explain how educators need to challenge youth to envision new societal structures based on democratic principles, developing what Giroux (2013) calls the "radical civic imagination." While difficult, adults must be willing to let youth be a part of building the world they too inhabit.

## Dystopian Resistance

During our discussions, the students explained that reading dystopian novels inspired a sense of fear—they were afraid that authors' predictions might actually come true. We constantly came back to these questions of purpose: Why do authors write dystopian fiction, and what is their message for readers? Student responses caused me to consider the philosophical importance of utopian and dystopian constructs and their impact on our world view. Angelina, giving her opinion about the dystopian genre, explained that she liked "the parts where we compare it to our world. Like we can see the similarities between what we are going through and what the people in the book are going through." Emma explained that most readers of dystopian fiction keep reading because "it can actually happen." Stacy argued that an author's purpose was connected to the message of the novel:

> But it's like this book is kind of a message. Most of us were like, why didn't anybody ever tell us that there's something wrong? And here, somebody did, but he didn't do anything about it. It's kind of like us when we were all like, you didn't tell us, and then it's kind of saying, we did tell you, you just didn't pay attention. Like there's, he's kind of like saying there's signs everywhere, but we're too like blindfolded, hypnotized, whatever word you wanna use. That we don't realize what's right in front of us.

Dystopian literature has the power to open readers' eyes to situations or conditions overlooked and ignored. Stacy's question, "Why didn't anybody ever tell us there's something wrong?" places responsibility for uncovering societal problems on someone besides the reader. People are "blindfolded" or "hypnotized" and fail to see "what's right in front of us." Emma responded to Stacy, "Or we're just too scared to do anything about it. So, might as well stay back in the shadows," meaning sometimes people are aware but choose to do nothing.

The students also commented on the way dystopian fiction inspires readers through its representation of social change and political activism. Angelina explained,

> I like dystopia in a way that it, there's always a revolt and I always relate to that because I am always trying to like do stuff for the better. I want to make a change in this world too. So, whenever I hear like, in the last book, that she joined the

> movement, I want to be her . . . I want to be part of a movement and change stuff for the better too. I like it in that sense I guess.

The students yearned to find a cause or a movement in which to participate. However, in making connections between dystopian worlds and our own, the students realized they were not ready to be fully engaged as activists:

> Azalea: I always wanna be like the characters . . .
>
> Francesca: Why would you wanna be anyone from this novel? They're all pretty bad people.
>
> Azalea: Not in this book exactly. But like the other ones where they're the heroes and they make a change. I wanna do that, but I know I can't, but not right now.
>
> Bambi: I wanna be able to have that sort of independence and say I don't even care what you guys think and like . . .
>
> Stacy: You want to stand out.
>
> Bambi: Yeah. I want to be able to stand out, but like at the same time, it's so not realistic. I mean I could stand outside but . . . [laughing] . . . I'm outstanding. [laughing]

Bambi, always playing with words and laughing at her own jokes, described the trouble with finding one's uniqueness. Azalea wanted to be heroic and Bambi wanted independence. But they shared an underlying fear that standing out would bring negative consequences. Their commentary on schooling indicated that opportunities to think about contemporary problems with a critical lens or solution-oriented framework were rare. Too much focus was placed on the past in history class and on texts in language arts. Teachers never asked students to imagine how the world could be different or how they would contribute to that change.

Our book club occurred when political protest was on every front page and social media feed. The students made connections between the dystopian novels and contemporary events like the riots in Ferguson, Missouri, and the #BlackLivesMatter movement on Twitter. Azalea talked about an image she saw posted, a quote from Collins's (2008) *The Hunger Games*, "If we burn, you burn with us," spray-painted on a monument in St. Louis, Missouri. She commented:

> I've noticed that a lot of people do get into it. Like I see on Tumblr, like the recent Ferguson thing. People bring it up and . . . are really actively blogging about it . . . they are like spreading information. And the next day, it's like back to normal, pretty pictures . . . No, we can't let this die. It's actually really important. It's not gone. Racism still exists.

This question about political resistance and agency caused others to ask why more people do not stand up for causes which they support:

> Francesca: But it's like when you see someone getting bullied in front of you and no one is sticking up for that person. And so you're like okay, they'll get over it. But when you see two or three people going up and being like that's not cool and then a group gets bigger and bigger and bigger cuz when you see someone else do it and someone else fight. It kind of gives you courage to do it too. I feel like everyone is waiting for someone else to do it.
>
> Bambi: Well if you keep waiting, what if you are the person that's meant to start it? So it's that point, who's brave enough to be the first person because I feel like everyone can be the first person to start something, it's just deciding if you're brave enough or like committed, or if you really want to start something. It's not just an idea, you're like you know what, I am gonna do it. I don't care if I am gonna win or lose. I'm just gonna go for it.

Francesca realized that dystopian worlds mirror today's society because we see inequity and discrimination but do not act. As Bambi said, individuals are often waiting for someone else to act, to be courageous, to be the first voice.

Because of the political nature of YA dystopian novels, readers might experience a kind of awakening or feel moved to participate in resistance efforts (Basu et al., 2013; Hintz, 2002; Mallan, 2004; Ventura, 2011). Will agency given to young fictional characters inspire youth readers to think and act similarly? Reading dystopian fiction "may be a small step in the direction of engaging students in social justice issues, and perhaps, sparking more overt political action" (Ames, 2013, p. 2). Youth today are at the center of political activism. School shootings in Parkland, Florida, resulted in a mass youth movement across the United States to challenge gun control laws. The #NeverAgain movement and subsequent March for Our Lives exemplify the power of social media and youth voice (Witt, 2018). Was there a direct link between dystopian fiction and the protests? No, but the contexts allowed me to connect history, literature, and contemporary events in the classroom. Simply asking students *what if* might inspire creative ideas about social change. During book club, students led the discussions with their own commentary. However, in Table 14.1, I list some possible questions that might help youth clearly name systems of oppression as they are represented in fiction and in our study of history. In my study, similar questions were provided to students in case they needed a starting place for discussions.

**Table 14.1.** Potential questions for analysis

| Theme | Questions |
|---|---|
| Power | Who is in power and how does the person/group maintain control?<br>How did that person/group/organization gain power?<br>Who is excluded from power?<br>What rights are stated/implied/ignored? |
| Knowledge | Whose knowledge is privileged?<br>What knowledge is preserved or destroyed? How is knowledge commodified?<br>What value is placed on freedom of thought and independent thinking?<br>What role does media play in regulating/mediating information? |
| Surveillance culture | What tools are used to gather information about people?<br>What information is considered most valuable?<br>What rights to people have to privacy? |
| Codification and Discrimination | How are people groups or labelled, and are groups treated differently?<br>Who decides on the labels?<br>How are accepted identities reinforced and unacceptable identities ostracized or closeted?<br>How are groups represented/excluded? How are those stances reinforced through behavior and cultural knowledge? |

Analyzing dystopian worlds, not too different from our own, encourages readers to use imagination and interact with possibility. And while most dystopian novels exhibit radical social criticism, most stop short of reinterpreting our world and conclude with the ouster of villains. Few dystopian novels go beyond the fall of totalitarianism and experiment with rebuilding foundations of democracy. Nicole Mirra (2018) discusses an approach to literary analysis where students use fiction as cultural artefacts to examine contemporary issues:

> Literary texts, through their creative forms, draw students into compelling narrative worlds. These imaginative worlds hold up a mirror so that students can analyze the real world in which they live. This analysis helps them think about social problems and gives them creative license to think about changing the world for the better. (p. 32)

Wondering what happens after the revolution potentially challenges readers with a new type of historical and philosophical thinking. Giroux (2014) argues that the integration of education and democracy are essential, where "cultivating the radical imagination, civic education and engaged and critical modes of literacy and agency are central to producing an informed citizenry, but even more so to constituting any viable notion of politics" (para. 24). Challenging students to imagine different and seemingly impossible worlds allows them to reconstitute what is happening now with what can be. Learning history as a static subject removes the unfinished nature of humanity. Integrating the past, present, and future reveals the power of possibility (Giroux & McLaren, 1987).

## Hope

In onc of our final discussions, Azalca made some profound suggestions about agency in our seemingly dystopian world:

> You said, should I be hopeless? But it's like utopia shouldn't be your ultimate goal. You shouldn't be hopeless just because we can't reach utopia or can't have world peace. You shouldn't feel hopeless, but you should be happy with what you can do while you are alive. You are going to go through a bunch of shit, it's natural. But I mean in the end, it doesn't really matter as long as you are happy with what you have done or what you are doing. You don't need utopia because in a sense you can make your own.

If we resign ourselves to the oppressive and sometimes depressing effects of schooling, then we will remain in dystopian classrooms. The infusion of a utopian impulse highlights Paulo Freire's (1998) point that all people are constantly in the process of becoming. We resist the perception that schooling is static and unchanging. The utopian impulse inspires me to rethink the purpose of education and who is part of that dialogue. Inclusion of student perspectives requires that they see themselves as equal contributors to classroom and school environments. Youth will continue to disassociate themselves from learning, questioning, and dreaming if teachers correct or silence their opinions. Expression of voice is not just about youth feeling right. More important, it is about youth feeling respected. Young people cannot be excluded from conversations about school reform because this would mean they are being treated as products of the system rather than stakeholders (Mitra, 2005, 2006). Teachers and students who want to start having discussions about power and resistance can start with YA dystopian fiction, which presents a unique challenge and opportunity to readers. As Antero Garcia (2013) argues,

> adults cannot rectify the past nor can they correct the future. It is up to the students in our classrooms—the students reading these books—to transform society for the better. YA, then, if we are to look for a unifying message *across* the books, it's about teaching youth how to grow up and own the future. (p. 133)

The utopian impulse propels our thoughts and actions toward constructing a better world. The inclusion of youth voices is necessary so they can enact their unique interpretations while reading the word and reading the world.

## Reflection Questions

How can dystopian fiction engage students in critical discussions about identity, power, and resistance?

How can educators create spaces for youth to explore contemporary issues that affect their daily lives and empower them to offer viable solutions?

What learning experiences could you intentionally design for students in your classroom to practice Giroux's idea of "radical imagination" and participate in civic processes?

## Note

1. All names are pseudonyms, chosen by the student participants. The students selected the novels we read, which included *Feed* by M. T. Anderson (2002), the *Matched* series by Ally Condie (2010, 2011, 2013), and the *Article 5* series by Kristen Simmons (2012, 2013, 2014).

## References

Ames, M. (2013). Engaging "apolitical" adolescents: Analyzing the popularity and educational potential of dystopian literature post-9/11. *The High School Journal, 97*(1), 3–20.

Anderson, M. T. (2002). *Feed.* Somerville, MA: Candlewick Press.

Basu, B., Broad, K. R., & Hintz, C. (2013). Introduction. In B. Basu, K. R. Broad, & C. Hintz (Eds.), *Contemporary dystopian fiction for young adults: Brave new teenagers* (pp. 1–15). New York, NY: Routledge.

Collins, S. (2008). *The hunger games.* New York, NY: Scholastic Press.

Condie, A. (2010). *Matched.* New York, NY: Speak.

Condie, A. (2011). *Crossed.* New York, NY: Speak.

Condie, A. (2013). *Reached.* New York, NY: Speak.

Darder, A. (1991). *Culture and power in the classroom: A critical foundation for bicultural education.* New York, NY: Bergin & Garvey.

Delpit, L. (1998). The silenced dialogue: Power and pedagogy in educating other people's children. *Harvard Educational Review, 58*(3), 280–298.

Freire, P. (2000). *Pedagogy of the oppressed* (M. B. Ramos, Trans.). New York, NY: Continuum. (Original work published 1970)

Freire, P. (1998). *Pedagogy of freedom: Ethics, democracy, and civic courage.* Lanham, MD: Rowan & Littlefield.

Garcia, A. (2013). *Critical foundations in young adult literature: Challenging genres.* Rotterdam, The Netherlands: Sense.

Giroux, H. A. (1997). *Pedagogy and the politics of hope: Theory, culture, and schooling: A critical reader.* Boulder, CO: Westview.

Giroux, H. A. (2013). Beyond dystopian education in a neoliberal society. *Fast Capitalism.* Retrieved from: http://www.uta.edu/huma/agger/fastcapitalism/10_1/giroux10_1.html

Giroux, H. A. (2014, January 13). Reclaiming the radical imagination: Challenging the casino capitalism's punishing factories. *Truthout.* Retrieved from http://truthout.org

Giroux, H. A., & McLaren, P. (1987). Teacher education as a counterpublic sphere: Radical pedagogy as a form of cultural politics. *Philosophy & Social Criticism, 12*(1), 51–69.

Hintz, C. (April 2002). Monica Hughes, Lois Lowery, and young adult dystopias. *The Lion and the Unicorn, 26*(2), 254–264.

Lewis. C. (2016). *The spaces between dystopia and utopia: Youth perspectives on identity, education, and resistance* (Unpublished doctoral dissertation). Chapman University, California, USA.

Mallan, K. (2004). Changing world orders and children's fiction: Constructing communities of critical or compliant readers. In J. Bales, & K. Bonanno (Eds.), *Proceedings Constructing Communities of Learning and Literacy* (ASLA Online 1 Conference Proceedings, pp. 100–105). Retrieved from https://eprints.qut.edu.au/4047/1/4047_1.pdf

McCallum, R. (2013). *Ideologies of identity in adolescent fiction: The dialogic construction of subjectivity.* New York, NY: Routledge.

McLaren, P. (2007). *Life in schools: An introduction to critical pedagogy in the foundations of education* (5th ed.). Boston, MA: Pearson.

Mirra, N. (2018). *Educating for empathy: Literacy learning and civic engagement.* New York, NY: Teacher's College Press.

Mitra, D. L. (2005). Adults advising youth: Leading while getting out of the way. *Educational Administration Quarterly, 41*(3), 520–553.

Mitra, D. L. (2006). Student voice from the inside and outside: The positioning of challengers. *International Journal of Leadership in Education, 9*(4), 315–328.

Simmons, K. (2012). *Article 5.* New York, NY: Tor Teen.

Simmons, K. (2013). *Breaking point.* New York, NY: Tor Teen.

Simmons, K. (2014). *Three.* New York, NY: Tor Teen.

Trites, R. (2000). *Disturbing the universe: Power and repression in adolescent literature.* Iowa City: University of Iowa Press.

Ventura, A. (2011). Predicting a better situation? Three young adult speculative fiction texts and the possibilities for social change. *Children's Literature Association Quarterly, 36*(1), 89–103.

Witt, E. (2018, February). How the survivors of Parkland began the never again movement. *The New Yorker.* Retrieved from https://www.newyorker.com/news/news-desk/how-the-survivors-of-parkland-began-the-never-again-movement

PART III

# THE YOUTH–ADULT PARTNERSHIPS GALLERY

FIFTEEN

# The Youth–Adult Partnerships Gallery

*Kevin Stockbridge*

WELCOME TO THE YOUTH–ADULT PARTNERSHIPS Gallery. This collection portrays education as enacted partnership among teachers, administrators, and students. Here, chapters reimagine teaching and learning. Teachers are typically cast in the role of educational protagonist. Students are, at best, compliant supporting characters. At worst, they are resistant antagonists. The rituals of traditional schooling pit each group against the other (McLaren, 1985). Freire (1970/2000) problematized this relationship by insisting that "education must begin with the solution of the teacher-student contradiction" (p. 72). What possibilities arise when teachers and students no longer play adversarial or opposing roles in education?

In this gallery, students, teachers, and administrators engage in education together, embodying the process of knowing. "Student voice initiatives should be *dialogic, intergenerational, collective and inclusive* and *transgressive*" (Pearce & Wood, 2016, p. 11). Education and agency intermingle in action. Together, students and teachers become agents of change, transforming the world around them—the dojo, school structures, businesses, and social spaces. In these vignettes, schooling is recast as an act of "with-ness." It invites us to ask: What in our practice resists the possibility of education as partnership? How might these vignettes help us to reenvision our classrooms and student-driven initiatives? How can we work alongside students as agents of change? What can we know and be when we work with students as co-teachers, co-learners, and co-creators?

## References

Freire, P. (2000). *Pedagogy of the oppressed* (M. B. Ramos, Trans.). New York, NY: Continuum. (Original work published 1970)

McLaren, P. (1985). *Schooling as a ritual performance: Towards a political economy of educational symbols and gestures*. London, England: Routledge & Kegan Paul.

Pearce, T. C., & Wood, B. E. (2016). Education for transformation: An evaluative framework to guide student voice work in schools. *Critical Studies in Education*. Advance online publication. doi:10.1080/17508487.2016.1219959

SIXTEEN

# We're the Bosses: Youth Action Council Designs an Equitable Makerspace

*Day Greenberg, Micaela Balzar, Angela Calabrese Barton, Edna Tan, and YAC Youth*

I want Think Tank to be a place I cannot imagine yet. (Amara, 15, female, Youth Action Council [YAC] member)

MAKERSPACES HAVE BEEN VIEWED AS a new way to support historically marginalized youth in their science, technology, engineering, and math (STEM) engagements—young people of color and kids from low-income communities who have limited access to STEM. Touted as the next panacea to "democratize" STEM education, makerspaces have proliferated in public libraries, science museums, and after-school clubs. Upon its creation at our local science museum, one of the YAC's first activities as a group was to critically discuss already-existing makerspaces and maker media. As researchers and YAC adult facilitators, we wanted to invite youth voices to collaboratively make sense of what a youth-focused makerspace should or could look like. YAC members repeatedly pointed out how the makerspaces they had seen in person or online and in magazines had "really been more about people a lot older and Whiter than us—usually White, middle-class, male adults . . . We don't think this is fair. Everybody should have the chance to make something cool, and there should be people and tools to help every kid build things and take things apart. How else will kids want to become engineers or work for NASA one day?"

Despite the increased number of makerspaces in the United States, makerspace participation and culture have been dominated by White, middle-class, male adults (Vossoughi & Bevan, 2014). Unless these spaces more fully incorporate youth of color, they will not serve this important equity goal. In this chapter, we discuss the youth's design of their makerspace and how it shaped their work there.

## Conceptual Framework

The project discussed here involves youth participatory action research (YPAR; Cammarota & Fine, 2008) with a critical justice theoretical framework (Barnett, 2005). We are concerned with expanding making and makerspaces to include voices of youth who have been largely ignored in the dominant maker discourse. Who is making, what products are made, how one accesses resources for making, and how often one is allowed in this making space, are questions too often answered using White, middle-class norms and assumptions. Makerspaces, then, can be symbolically egalitarian yet realistically oppressive. "Critical justice" challenges us to go beyond fitting youth into systems of "what is" to consider and equitably transform systems into "what can be."

## YAC

The YAC, a group of 17 youth, 9 to 14 years of age, were co-designers of the making space at their local science museum. The name of the making space is "Think Tank." The group represented the diversity of their city, including African American youth (5 girls and 1 boy), Latino (1 boy), Indian American (1 girl), and White (4 girls, 5 boys). All youth entered with prior making experiences, whether at home or in a community makerspace. The youth met every month at the science center.

The goals of the YAC were twofold. First, YAC members were involved in co-designing the actual *physical space* of the Think Tank through both design activities and discussions on (a) what kinds of spaces are attractive to 8- to 14-year-olds and (b) what supports youth in feeling like they belong in the space. For example, youth sketched out ideas for a makerspace, interviewed each other on what activities would be enjoyable, rated furniture and color schemes, and critiqued the design of other spaces. They also considered what types of spaces inspire other youth and adults to take action and what would make the makerspace "really awesome and inspiring" to the community who use that space.

Second, youth were involved in designing/co-constructing the curriculum of Think Tank. YAC members considered what types of making activities would be interesting to other youth. They also considered what outcomes were important for participating in Think Tank making (i.e., to learn, play, tinker, bring something home) and how these activities related to the design of the space. Finally, they took up the question of how these activities could empower or build confidence in both the short and long term. For example, they tested out initial activities provided by YAC facilitators and modified them according to their interests. They produced short videos on how their making efforts went, what they enjoyed about them, what frustrated them, and what they would change. They completed surveys on activities related to enjoyment, time and scaffolds needed, and ideas for expansion. YAC facilitators used the "house metaphor" to help the YAC members articulate entry points, expansion points, and multiple outcomes for activities. This meant that the science center education director reminded the youth that their house should offer "low floors" to welcome in beginners and equitable activities with "high ceilings" to welcome more experienced participants with many doors and windows reflecting a wide range of possible outcomes.

In designing their makerspace—in both physical space and activities—the youth identified several key themes that drove their efforts. The youth named their primary goal as making the makerspace youth friendly. However, cutting across their ideas were clear justice-oriented concerns about (1) power and respect, (2) making a difference, and (3) empowerment.

## Power and Respect

Youth named their desire to be "positioned with power and respect" (Samuel, 14 years old). What power and respect meant to the young people was a highly layered construct that involved *how* they worked together, on *what* they worked, and how the *space* created would make these ideals possible. The major criteria the youth named for makerspace design included welcoming, collaborative, fun/playful, recognizing difficult work, values iteration, and values making a difference.

From a physical design standpoint, designing a kid-friendly making space was an issue of creating a more equitable opportunity for other youth to enter STEM areas of learning and practice. The description of friendliness was connected to opening up and democratizing access so that making and STEM learning would be welcoming, fun, and a space of practice that recognized their value as people. One youth, Ivy, explained:

> Kids should have endless possibilities . . . I think it is important for everyone to have access to engineering, and I wanted to help make that a reality. I was excited about working on building the space so that it is fit for all kids . . . There is now a place open to everyone to make things.

Additionally, constructing the space to "fit" a diverse group of young people was central to this point. They collaborated to use their different sets of perspectives, interests, skills, and experiences as shared resources for innovative space-creation together. "What could kids accomplish with YAC? A lot, because we all think differently," stated one youth, "But we are all creative and good thinkers. We compromise a lot so we can become a group that makes awesome things."

In a speech delivered to members of the press and supporters at the grand opening of Think Tank, 10-year-old Jay announced:

> The YAC is a group of kids who want to inspire other kids on making. We are a group of 9-year-olds and up. We had many meetings to help design activities and give feedback. We also gave ideas for what the space needed to look like—VERY COLORFUL! We designed the room to be a place where we can be inspired and have fun. When we started this off this was just a room full of dust. We built the space for other kids to innovate and be creative.

From a maker curricular standpoint, similar themes were echoed about power and respect. Ivy stated, "[We want] activities that can let us be who we are. I want to do things that let me be me. In school sometimes, it's hard to be me." Megan pushed on how respect meant not essentializing youth:

> We want to see activities that are not traditionally feminine or masculine or that split us up because of who we are. We think that the best activities can let you use your interests to make that activity better . . . these activities allow for different interests. It makes it easier for us to work with others, and to spend a lot more time on our project, taking it to new levels.

Power and respect in activities also reflected the youth's desires to do things that mattered to them and their communities. Abby had prototyped a "justice box" as part of her initial making activities: a small box constructed by Abby and her friend, which contained items that had different justice-oriented messages. They included a blindfold to ask users to imagine a world they could not see. They also included a mask so that people could not immediately judge someone as male or female, racially, or otherwise. As Abby stated, they wanted their projects to make things that mattered to others: "I hope our box of justice impacts how some people think of the issues in things we used. The things we made is like kind of metaphors . . . I care about those things."

The last aspect of this theme revolved around helping others. YAC member Megan explained the importance of activities that were not only interesting but that helped others:

> When we did paper circuits, some of us were really excited with the crafting part of the activity. But others of us really liked playing with the circuits. Some of us wanted to use our paper circuit expertise to do cool things in our community, like make paper circuit mini maker kits to give out so that other kids could learn circuits in a fun way, and like starting a greeting card collection that reflected our humor.

## Making a Difference

In the examples from both Abby and Megan, we see an orientation toward making a difference. According to YAC members, activities that matter involve a deep connection to who youth are as young people, as people growing up in particular communities, and as people with particular interests, challenges, and concerns. The youth activities that matter involve making things that address problems that (a) they care about, (b) they find interesting and (c) are highly inclusive.

For example, Fall stated that "activities that matter" are "activities that let us take action on the things we care about." Megan added:

> Whether we are making paper circuits to make a card for a friend, to make a nightlight or designing something to change the world like a jacket to prevent bullying, we want to be supported in having our concerns matter, and in being able to take action on those concerns.

Focusing on the communities where youth come from is a part of what mattered to youth.

Part of taking action for youth involved "be[ing] allowed to make changes" to planned activities "so that they can matter to us" in unique and personally meaningful ways. When YAC members and adult YAC session facilitators prototyped an activity using a stop motion animation app on iPads, youth stated, "We had fun playing around with different approaches." For example, some youth used playdough to create claymation, while other youth used whiteboards to tell a story.

> Central to "making that mattered" was being inclusive. As Jazmyn noted, it included "activities that welcome all of us, young and older kids, and kids with different knowledge or skill level. We want to make sure that no one feels turned away from an activity because 'they can't do it' or because the directions sound really complicated and boring."

Megan agreed in a presentation: "We do NOT want youth to feel 'babied' because the activity was made too easy. We want to see activities that let everyone use what they know and learn something new." It was important to the youth that various entry points and a range of final products are equally valued so as to take into account youths' varying interests and agency to pursue what mattered to them and not what the making activity may have scripted.

## Empowerment

At the Think Tank grand opening, 12-year-old Ivy stated:

> Why Think Tank? To empower youth to learn about science and how to make things! Kids sometimes at their school science programs do not always have the materials and the lessons to teach tinkering and how kids can build anything they want if they put their mind to it. Think Tank teaches kids that they can be a scientist and they can build something and have fun with it. Science can be fun and it does not just have to be like school work. It can also empower kids and no matter what, they can build things and realize that maybe they don't think they are good at science, but they can go to Think Tank and have so many different tools that they realize that they can do it and it is interesting. For example, some kids might think it's too hard to make a circuit, and then they make electric art and they realize it is easy and fun, and then they can go onto make even

> bigger things like light up bracelets. Kids can choose to put their projects in the showcase or take it home, and people will be proud of them because they made it.

As noted in Ivy's comments, YAC members described the importance of being able to represent themselves to others as capable, powerful makers. To this end, they consistently worked toward designs that would allow them to showcase their work in order to help others. YAC member Jazmyn stated:

> We want our work to be recognized by others because our work deserves a LOT of respect. We also want others to see that they can do this kind of work, too because they CAN. Projects do not have to be perfect.

One way in which this dimension of empowerment played out was in how the youth sought to design a physical space for their work to be displayed publicly at the science center. For example, youth devised a Presentation Station, which was to be a digital and physical place to hang work both inside and outside Think Tank. They also argued for a "rough draft workstation," where they could share their in-progress work in a highly visible way. As Fall stated, "Kids need to know that nothing is perfect. Nothing is done." Here, Fall meant to help others realize that the process of making involves many iterations. YAC members also noted that their new makerspace should include a glass wall so people outside could see them working inside and an opportunity for people to provide positive feedback. They wanted the public to value their work as young people. As Abby noted, "we actually don't get praise a lot from grown-ups."

Sharing ideas with each other during work sessions and being able to share both in-process and finished projects with others whenever they entered the space was important to YAC members. This was just as much about learning from each other as it was about demonstrating their expertise on a public platform.

Empowerment also meant learning critical making skills. Ivy noted, "I love crafts . . . but I kinda realized that to make my nameplate really good I had to know more . . . like how to use these tools and stuff." Other youth noted similar points around the importance of making technical tools and skills easily accessible but on a timeline that made sense to kids. Jay noted, "It's ok if we have to learn something, but it shouldn't be like school. Like I need to know when I need to know it."

## Looking Ahead

The YAC youth wanted a space that promoted playfulness and legitimized different forms of embodied expertise, allowed accessibility through activities that bent norms of being/becoming, shared ideas through non/traditional channels, made "rough draft work" visible, and provided opportunities for movement and voice. In short, the youth wanted a generous, empowering space where mistakes could be made, decisions changed, multiple iterations were encouraged, and efforts celebrated. They thought it key to focus on the making process and on celebrating the process rather than focusing only on a polished, completely made artifact. It was also important to the youth that making activities prioritize the interests and agency of the youth-makers. They stressed that fidelity to these was more important than fidelity to the making activity. They wanted activities that allowed them to draw on and develop their interests or to take actions on concerns they cared about.

YAC youth also wanted to be active partners in the research conducted about their ongoing efforts. YPAR approaches are useful for this goal because they position youth as researchers who can identify and frame problems, design research investigations, collect/analyze data, interpret findings, and take evidence-based actions. This challenges and inverts traditional ideas of who has the authority to produce knowledge and whose knowledge is deemed valuable. It can empower youth who have been historically excluded to deconstruct the deficient views, oppressive systems, and subjugating discourses affecting their daily lives.

We end this chapter with a collective statement from YAC members explaining why youth action councils and youth participatory action research should continue to shape making programs, makerspace design, and maker movement research:

> We are the youth that the makerspaces hope to serve, so we are key stakeholders who *should* be involved in discussing the equity issues of makerspaces. We think that is important to include young people's voices, perspectives, and experiences as critical resources in designing inclusive makerspaces for youth from diverse

> backgrounds. If the focus is to design inclusive makerspaces for all youth, then why not listen to us? We are right here! Why not give us the power to design and to develop our own makerspaces? We can help. We want to be active partners in the research and design process.

## Supporting Youth in Taking the Lead

Getting comfortable with working with youth as educational design leaders in your learning space (e.g., classroom, museum, after-school program) can start with simple steps in daily practice. Youth want to be involved in important conversations, and they have valuable knowledge and experience that could greatly enhance institutional impact. Too often, youth expertise remains an untapped resource. Tapping into that resource can begin by asking youth if and how they want to get involved as recognized leaders in your shared learning space. Presenting them with a range of options for taking on more leadership positions in curricular design and/or teaching practices can help to jump-start the conversation, but leaving room for them to define their own goals in a partnership is equally important.

## Reflection Questions

The following are three question areas to support a critical reflection of assumptions, roles, and responsibilities to enhance your institution's developmental goals through a YPAR-informed approach. With your group, consider together:

What goals do we have for this unit or project? Who developed those goals (and whose voices are currently missing from goal-setting discussions/decisions)?

Who do we want to "reach" with this unit or project, and what do we actually mean by that? How can empowering youth to co-direct/co-teach/co-design the unit or project assist us in achieving that outreach mission?

If we invite youth to join us as partners, how are we prepared to support and respect them as colleagues from start to finish? What hidden assumptions about youth capabilities would we need to address in order to make that support real in daily practice?

## Note

This work was supported by the National Science Foundation (Division of Research on Learning Award No. 1647033).

## References

Barnett, C. (2005). Ways of relating: Hospitality and the acknowledgement of otherness. *Progress in Human Geography, 29*(1), 5–21.

Cammarota, J., & Fine, M. (2008). *Revolutionizing education: Youth participatory action research in motion*. New York, NY: Routledge.

Vossoughi, S., & Bevan, B. (2014, June). *Making and tinkering: A review of the literature*. Commissioned paper for Successful Out-of-School STEM Learning: A Consensus Study, Board on Science Education, National Research Council, Washington, DC. Retrieved from http://sites.nationalacademies.org/cs/groups/dbassesite/documents/webpage/dbasse_089888.pdf

SEVENTEEN

# Repurposing the Master's Tools: Leveraging Business Education to Build a Better World

*Linda Hogg and Anne Yates*

THIS IS THE STORY OF social transformation which happened through students' development of a business for a higher purpose. As we will explain, the world of economics and business is at a watershed moment. The neoliberal premise that the profit motive ensures businesses act for the good of society has been revealed as so deeply flawed that it is instrumental in the creation of today's social and environmental crises (Raworth, 2017). *The Final Straw*, founded by students, exemplifies a new type of business model, driven not by profit but by transformative aims. The supportive partnership of teacher-mentors was instrumental to achieving the students' transformative vision in two ways. Adult teacher-mentors helped the students to focus on their passion and work in ways that were true to their values. They also ensured that the students had the knowledge and skills needed to operate their business and negotiate the business world.

This chapter reports on a purposive case study. We were inspired by the transformational vision of Jess and Rosie's business *The Final Straw* (and other youth-led businesses driven by similar goals). Our aims in conducting this research were to (1) describe a student-created and student-run business driven by ethical considerations and transformative aims in order to inspire others to develop entrepreneurial activity outside the dominant neoliberal model and (2) identify ways that teacher-mentors can support such projects.

To acknowledge their achievements, we wanted to give credit to the students and their teacher-mentors. Therefore, with institutional review board approval and agreement of all participants, we use real names in this chapter. Data were collected from two teacher-mentors and two student founders of *The Final Straw*, an award-winning Young Enterprise Scheme (YES) business. YES is a New Zealand business education program for school students. This chapter highlights the transformative potential of student voice discovered in this research. Within the framework of business education, students contributed to social transformation beyond the classroom. In this process, pedagogy became facilitation and learning became action.

## The World of Economics and Business: From Crisis to Hope

Students studying economics at universities are increasingly troubled by the disconnect between economic theories they are taught and what is happening in the world. University economics education encourages regurgitation of theory rather than critical thinking (Earle, Moran, & Ward-Perkins, 2016). Theory developed by Friedrich von Hayek, Milton Friedman, and others, popularized at the Chicago School of Economics, has dominated economics and politics since the 1980s. It forms the philosophical basis of the current neoliberal paradigm, whose language permeates discussion internationally across multiple parts of public life (Van Horn & Mirowski, 2009). Neoliberalism regards markets as efficient because, as the argument goes, self-interest will lead businesses to create desired products and jobs. However, this theory rests on flawed assumptions and blind spots (Raworth, 2017). It ignores a range of important factors, including societal and planetary contexts.

Economics students' activism has reverberated globally over the past decade. In 2010, a mass walkout of Harvard students protested the ideologically narrow economics curriculum. In Britain, student-authors Earle, Moran, and Ward-Perkins (2016) outlined their concerns in their book, *The Econocracy: The Perils of Leaving Economics to the Experts*, and inspired the network Rethinking Economics (Chakrabortty, 2017). In the United States, the Kick It Over student collective published a manifesto, declaring, "The revolution of economics has begun . . . in the months and years that follow, we will begin the work of reprogramming the doomsday machine" (2015, cited by Raworth, 2017, p. 8).

It was within this context of crisis and discontent that a new economic framework emerged. In *Doughnut Economics* (2017), Kate Raworth draws together multiple critiques of dominant economic theory, revealing its gaping inadequacies. More important, she presents a new economic model that has, at its heart, the goal of "prosperity for all, within the means of our planet" (Raworth, 2017, p. 32). Raworth explains that because there has been a focus on measuring the dollar value of gross domestic product as the sole indicator of an economy's health, this has become the de facto goal. This means that ever-growing income and production levels are regarded as "a decent proxy for ever-improving human welfare" (Raworth, 2017, p. 35). Furthermore, she demonstrates that this focus has allowed disregard for extreme poverty and wealth and for environmental degradation that, if unchecked, threatens global citizens with "planetary apocalypse" (Collins, 2010, p. 296). Raworth's model (Figure 17.1) illustrates the economy as a doughnut, because economic activity beyond the doughnut would not be possible without degrading the environment and economic activity that exists inside the doughnut represents human deprivation.

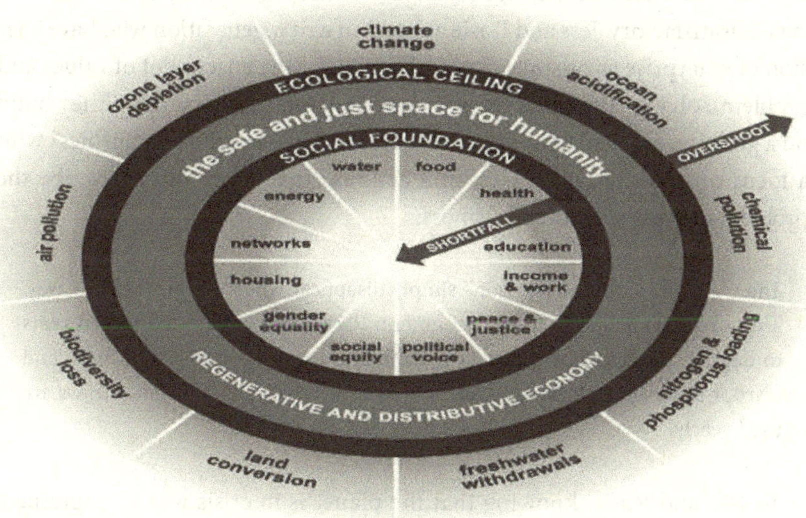


**Figure 17.1.** Doughnut economic framework. From Raworth, 2017, p. 44. Reprinted with permission.

According to Raworth (2017), "ours is the first generation to properly understand the damage we have been doing to our planetary household, and probably the last generation with the chance to do something about it" (p. 286).

## Introducing Jess and Rosie

Unaware of the turmoil in the halls of economics academia, Rosie O'Hagan and Jess Reiher hatched their own plan—their contribution to reprogramming the doomsday machine. Rosie and Jess were students in their penultimate year of high school at St Mary's College, Wellington, New Zealand. They had been friends since they were 5 years old, and part of their bond was their shared passion for the environment. They saw YES as an opportunity to create a better, more sustainable world. In YES, they would create and run a business for their transformative ends.

These two students intuitively understood key ideas from Raworth's doughnut framework for sustainability and justice, although they were unfamiliar with the theory itself. Jess said, "In high school, our eyes have been opened to the fact that there's a lot of not sustainable enterprises." They considered this very unsatisfactory. Jess and Rosie are part of a new generation who have a vision of enterprise as organization and action for the enactment of values and problem-solving. Their key value is environmental sustainability. They build on a growing movement of entrepreneurs who are repurposing business with a focus on transformative aims and actions. This is how they describe the problem addressed by their business:

> The reality is, plastic straws don't simply disappear when we throw them away. They are detrimental to the environment. Plastic straws take 200 to 400 years to degrade, are a major threat to marine life, are made from fossil fuels, and disrupt ecosystems. In New Zealand alone, over 500 million plastic straws are used yearly.

To Jess and Rosie, knowing that the planet is in crisis was so engrained, it was like knowing you need to breathe. It did not need to be argued. They saw this as common knowledge in their generation. Jess said: "What's the point in *not* being sustainable, if you can see where the world's going . . . and everyone *can* see where it's going . . . but our parents' generation are like 'who needs bamboo toothbrushes?'" At 8 years old, Jess had written a newspaper article about plastic pollution—environmental degradation was a long-held concern. On a recent family holiday in Vietnam, Rosie was distressed to see huge amounts of plastic bottles and straws littering waterways. She told us, "We saw so much pollution everywhere, even snorkeling in the sea!" For

Rosie, these scenes graphically illustrated the way the world is being trashed. She was aware that a lack of care for the environment is hurtling Earth toward catastrophe, and she knew the disastrous impacts if people are inattentive and unwilling to change. The sights in Vietnam heightened Rosie's passion and urgency to be part of the solution.

Jess and Rosie both felt a responsibility to contribute to positive change, not just in their actions but also through influencing others. As Jess said, "Both of us were like, we need to do this." They emphasized that it was important to them "not just to have a sustainable business, but to promote the message."

## *The Final Straw*

Rosie and Jess wanted to develop a YES business that helped create a better world. Their business, *The Final Straw*, was a not-for-profit. Its mission was "to raise awareness and reduce the effects of plastic waste on the environment . . . [by] form[ing] working partnerships with businesses and help[ing] them work towards a more sustainable future." They operationalized the mission by selling environmentally friendly, high-quality flexi-paper straws to cafes at an affordable price and by providing posters and brochures to their café buyers (for display in the cafes since they were "designed to raise awareness among customers about reducing the impact of plastic waste and educate and encourage them to 'do their bit'"). Jess and Rosie targeted cafes because of the number of straws they used every day—the potential impact of their resource use was much greater than that of households.

The first part of the business mission, raising awareness, was crucial in the students' minds because this meant enhancing impact through raising consciousness of the urgent need to live more sustainably. As they explained, "We supply [cafes] with eco-friendly alternatives . . . but we also really want to communicate the message . . . the message is *really* important to us." As both a morally legitimate and useful business activity, *The Final Straw* was a social enterprise (Bridge, 2015), designed according to value-driven transformational goals.

In early brainstorming in their original seven-member team about the nature of their business, Rosie told us, "I was really pushing for this, both of us were." When we met them, near the end of the life of the business as defined by the school year, there were four in the group. However, only Jess and Rosie presented on the business at the national YES awards. Gradually, The Final Straw had become Jess and Rosie's project.

## Adult Support for Students' Transformation Aims

Rosie and Jess knew that they wanted to start a business, what they wanted to achieve with their business, and why. To enact their vision, they needed adult support. Two adults played pivotal roles: Marion Myers and Gavin Millar. Marion was the teacher at their school who worked with YES students, and Gavin was the regional YES coordinator.

When we asked Jess and Rosie what their teacher-mentors did that was helpful, they told us Marion was nice and Gavin was fun. But when we probed further, both Marion and Gavin described that they had employed diverse intentional actions. When we shared what we learned about these teacher-mentors' pedagogy with Jess and Rosie, they confirmed that our description captured "perfectly" their experience. Marion's and Gavin's pedagogy supported student autonomy by

1. helping students to reach inside themselves and identify their passions and values to drive the business activity. Marion called this "feeding the flames."
2. enhancing students' skills and knowledge on an as-needed basis—learning the master's tools.

### *Feeding the Flames*

Marion accentuated to students that YES was an opportunity to do something positive in the real world, and she was not going to teach them—they would learn by developing and running their own business.

Marion told inspirational stories of YES alumni. Jess and Rosie were very impressed by businesswomen Brooke Roberts and Alexia Hilbertidou. Brooke, driven by her commitment to social equity, founded Sharesies, which offers share market access to people who want to invest as little as $5 per week. Alexia is CEO of GirlBoss New Zealand, which she started when she was 16 years old. Rosie told us excitedly that Alexia had spoken at a school event: "She said that whatever your passion is, you can turn it into a business . . . She's amazing . . . now she's got a Queen's award."

Although Marion presented role models, she encouraged students to develop businesses that were uniquely their own. She focused on supporting teams to find their passion and consider what they could do with that passion to make a difference. Jess and Rosie remembered Marion had said, "There's no point in creating a new business if it's not for a purpose, because there's so much stuff out there. If it's not going to better the world, then what's the point?" Jess and Rosie told us Marion saw what they were passionate about, and responded, "Right, what can you do with that?"

In Jess and Rosie's team, a problem was that their deep passion was not shared by all their teammates, which created an early impasse. Gavin successfully supported the students to think about their team direction. He instructed them:

> I want you to find a room and lock yourselves in. I want you to take junk food and whatever . . . take a little speaker with some loud music and have a whiteboard or something you can post stuff up or draw stuff up— . . . I don't want anyone coming in—no one is able to come into this room in this 90-minute session . . . I want a judgemental-free environment where you guys can just be crazy . . . play loud music and dance, eat food, write stuff, draw stuff . . . just go for it without the fear of anyone walking in.

Gavin stressed it was important to "let [students] do things; let them work it out . . . they might find a way of doing something new, and they do, often. They come up with ingenious things that nobody's ever thought of before."

Marion saw herself as a cheerleader. She made a point of never dismissing students' ideas, abilities or dedication. She was acutely aware of messages communicated through tone of voice. Her upbeat tone helped students respond positively to challenging questions. If she was unsure about an idea, she asked, "How will you do that?" Jess and Rosie valued being challenged "in a nice way." Jess considered, "She sat back and let us figure it out ourselves, which was really good, but when we missed something, she'd go, just look at this. How about if you look at it from this way? She's good." Marion gently challenged students to reflect on how consistent their business practices were with their values, encouraging alternative approaches to problems.

Marion's questions helped the team critically reflect on decisions and processes—they found it to be a valuable integrity check. One such positively delivered challenge helped Jess and Rosie see that their initial packaging idea was not environmentally friendly. In their final report, they proudly wrote:

> We opted for stickers made from ethically sourced and biodegradable materials, and if using paper (i.e., for flyers and posters) we ensure all paper used is FSC[1] certified, so we know it is sustainably sourced.
>
> We reuse all packaging and put them towards other purposes, which means our business produces minimal waste. We avoid all plastic packaging, and even the tape on our packaging is eco-friendly (Kraft paper tape with solvent rubber-based adhesive).

Jess and Rosie said it would have been very de-motivating if Marion had told them what to do. Marion's positivity was important. Jess and Rosie advise teacher-mentors: "If students have a passion, just foster this." Marion was deliberately positive, but she couldn't help but be enthusiastic because "I get excited by what the girls do."

Gavin had a similar philosophy. He described his role as being "the cool uncle . . . once they've had a meeting with me, they walk away going, oh okay, we've got a new lease on life, let's go." Jess and Rosie affirmed his approach. In their eyes he was "so good with teenagers." Gavin recognized that being creative is hard, that students need to learn that mistakes are normal. He told teams, "We want you to have the courage to try new things." He encouraged teams to identify what did and didn't work and to keep trying.

### *Learning the Master's Tools*

Marion and Gavin taught Rosie and Jess ways to negotiate the business world and to pursue *The Final Straw*'s higher goals. They passed on tools of business, which included the language, professional procedures, knowledge, and skills needed. This is comparable to developing the facility to code-switch for students. These weren't presented as a linear curriculum but on an as-needed basis.

Marion taught students about conflict management when they faced a challenge. Jess's passion and drive were seen by some team members as too controlling. Her perspective was that team members were not fulfilling their responsibilities. Marion saw it as her role to help develop their problem-solving skills. She chaired a team meeting and asked everyone to share their feelings about group cohesion and operation. Marion also used role-play to prepare students for difficult conversations. She played the role of a team member with whom Jess was having a conflict. They roleplayed scenarios until Jess was comfortable and confident to proceed with the conversation herself.

Students were also taught how to pitch ideas. Because they wanted to have the biggest impact they could, Jess and Rosie decided to approach the Wellington Hospitality Group. This is the biggest hospitality chain in New Zealand with 22 cafes. To prepare, they drew on their extensive research into different types of environmentally friendly straws. With Gavin's guidance, they developed a careful script to highlight advantages of their chosen straws. He provided advice on what to focus on, what to say, and what not to say. They rehearsed the pitch together. For the students, this pitch was high stakes: "It was scary, really scary . . . I didn't know I could do stuff like that . . . but our confidence has grown so much this year." To their surprise, the Wellington Hospitality Group managers were young, encouraging, and keen to buy their straws. This was the beginning of an important business relationship.

Marion taught meeting procedure to emphasise the importance of protocol: Meetings need to be chaired, have an agenda, record minutes, and conclude with delegated tasks. She stressed that work happens between meetings, and each team member should complete their tasks and report progress. Marion developed an understanding of accountability by expecting minutes to be emailed to her and by occasionally dropping in on meetings. She emphasized business-like communication and grooming as well as the importance of being proactive.

Gavin and Marion also made students aware of networking. Students were encouraged to reflect on resources they could access. Gavin invited diverse businesspeople to talk to help develop students' networks. He selected role models carefully: "We try to make them as young as possible, ex-students who've been out there maybe three to five years . . . students gravitate to them straight away . . . they go, oh you've already done it . . . they'll listen."

Pedagogy in this program had two key purposes. One was to "make room" for student agency. By "feeding the flames" and not imposing a curricular expectation, teacher-mentors used their privilege to open space for student voice and vision. They realized that students must be the decision-makers (Mitra, 2004). The other role of pedagogy was to present students with tools needed to negotiate the business world. Jess and Rosie used the master's tools, not to maximize profit but for their vision of transformation.

## Conclusion

According to the team's goals, *The Final Straw* was very successful. Over six months, they sold 36,000 bio-degradable paper straws, wildly exceeding their aims. Their modest profit was donated to Sustainable Coastlines, a New Zealand environmental charity. In December 2018, a new post on *The Final Straw* Facebook page read:

> What an incredible night at the 2018 YES National Awards!! We were so honoured to receive the BP National Excellence Award for Social Enterprise, and to be in a room full of amazing, inspiring people. We are so grateful for the opportunities YES has given us, and for everyone who has supported us to save the planet, one straw at a time!

Before winding up the business, Jess and Rosie put a plan in place to ensure that their customers could continue to purchase the straws—completing their mission for sustainable change.

In their enactment of ethical entrepreneurship, Jess and Rosie resisted prevalent profit-driven business models. Their business idea was grounded in their wish to shift the trajectory of the current environmental calamity. Their plans and actions reflected determination to meet their ethical aims. Intuitively, Jess and Rosie were a living embodiment of principles described by Raworth (2017).

For enterprise education to be experiential, transformative, and authentic (Robinson, Neergaard, Tanggaard, & Krueger, 2016), there must be solidarity between teachers and students. Although students founded and ran *The Final Straw*, teacher-mentors contributed to the ecologically conscious business. The adult–student partnership was instrumental in achieving Jess and Rosie's transformational aims. The students drove the project with their vision of the world they will inherit, and the teacher-mentors facilitated students' negotiation of the world they presently inhabit.

## Reflection Questions

What possibilities can you think of to transfer ideas from this chapter to other curriculum areas?

What opportunities exist in your teaching context to encourage students to think about futures that exist within the doughnut model?

Think about what is involved in the teacher-mentor role, in order to support student visions for transformation. How is this different or similar to the ways that you currently enact teaching? How could you prepare to take on this type of role?

## Note

1. The Forest Stewardship Council is an international non-profit, multi-stakeholder organization established in 1993 that aims to promote responsible management of the world's forests.

## References

Bridge, S. (2015). Is enterprise education relevant to social enterprise? *Education + Training, 57*(8/9), 1009–1019. doi:10.1108/ET-05-2015-0030

Chakrabortty, A. (2017, February 9). The econocracy review – how three students caused a global crisis in economics. *The Guardian*. Retrieved from https://www.theguardian.com/books/2017/feb/09/the-econocracy-review-joe-earle-cahal-moran-zach-ward-perkins

Collins, D. A. (2010). Heading for a world apocalypse? *The Journal of Social, Political, and Economic Studies, 35*(2), 269–302.

Earle, J., Moran, C., & Ward-Perkins, Z. (2016). *The econocracy: The perils of leaving economics to the experts*. Manchester, England: Manchester University Press.

Mitra, D. (2004). The significance of students: Can increasing "student voice" in schools lead to gains in youth development? *Teachers College Record, 106*(4), 651–688.

Raworth, K. (2017). *Doughnut economics: Seven ways to think like a 21st-century economist*. White River Junction, VT: Chelsea Green Publishing.

Robinson, S., Neergaard, H., Tanggaard, L., & Krueger, N.F. (2016). New horizons in entrepreneurship education: From teacher-led to student-centered learning. *Education + Training, 58*(7/8), 661–683. doi:10.1108/ET-03-2016-0048

The Final Straw. (2018, December 7). *What an incredible night at the 2018 YES National Awards!! We were so honoured to receive the BP National Excellence Award for Social Enterprise, and to be in a room full of amazing, inspiring people. We are so grateful for the opportunities YES has given us, and for everyone who has supported us to save the planet, one straw at a time!*

[Image attached] [Status update]. Facebook. Retrieved from https://www.facebook.com/thefinalstraw.yes/

Van Horn, R., & Mirowski, P. (2009). The rise of the Chicago School of Economics and the birth of neoliberalism. In P. Mirowski & D. Plehwe (Eds.), *The road from Mont Pelerin: The making of the neoliberal thought collective* (pp. 139–180). Cambridge, MA: Harvard University Press.

EIGHTEEN

# Applying Gentleness Against the Force: The Dojo as a Site of Liberation for Autistic[1] People

*Erin McCloskey*

COME WITH ME AS WE enter the dojo. The long rectangular room awaits you, filled with mats and soft coverings traveling a few feet up each wall. Sun shines through the window at the back of the room. It's 9:15 on a Saturday morning, and the room starts to come alive. Sensei Scott[2] walks the room and chats with different people. An 11-year-old autistic boy named Max runs back and forth across the mat, his hands in front of his face, his smile as wide as his lips will allow. He uses his hand as puppets and reenacts favorite segments of cartoons he has viewed multiple times. More bodies move through the door. Shoes come off and are slid into cubbies. There are rules to follow in the dojo. The first one is, before stepping onto the mat, bow to a photo framed high on the wall of educator and judo founder, Jigoro Kano.

In this room, you will find autistic and neurotypical adults in black and brown belts, teenage autistic students, and some students' autistic or neurotypical parents and siblings in white, yellow, and green belts. The room echoes with laughter and the sounds of bodies hitting the mat. One student is making animal noises. Some are staying to themselves on the edges and in the corners of the room. Steve, an autistic teenager, bites his fingers and looks around. Everyone is making the space their own, and everyone is given the space to be who they are.

Class begins and Sensei asks participants to line up. All the students drift toward each other, eventually forming a straightish line from black belts—the highest ranked players—to the white belts, all of whom have been participating for less than a year. The room becomes quiet. Everyone is kneeling. Sensei Scott faces the line; he kneels and smiles. All bow.

I became interested in looking at how autistic students learn in spaces outside of school after spending a year with parents when they attended special education meetings about their children (see McCloskey, 2016, 2018). I found that school meetings were organized to allow people to describe learning and behavior in particular ways. I have been thinking about special education for close to three decades. First, as a special education teacher, more recently, as a teacher educator/researcher at the college level, and as the parent of an autistic teenager. I chose as my next research project to look at autistic youth learning in spaces outside of school. The data from which this chapter is written come from a larger institutional review board–approved research project that captures the learning of autistic students in the dojo. In the dojo, there is a reciprocal process of learning and teaching and "voice" emerges in the movements, actions and vocalizations of autistic participants. I apply the work of Freire (1970/2000) to show how the cyclical nature of teaching/learning promotes liberation of autistic identity through not only executing of judo movements (tori) but also adjusting one's physical responses to these movements (uke). I explore pedagogical implications of becoming both the tori and the uke and contrast these ideas with pedagogical practices often used in schools to "manage" behaviors of Autistic individuals.

## The Force: Oppressing Autistic Students

Most commonly, intensive behavioral interventions such as Applied Behavior Analysis (ABA) are used in schools to manage autistic students' behaviors. Very briefly, behaviors targeted for change are carefully worded on official documents for use with personnel who come in contact with the student at school. The documents describe how to anticipate and then react to certain behaviors. Each behavior is broken down to describe what happens before the behavior takes place, how to teach alternative behaviors, and consequences for the student should they not exhibit the desired behavior (Shyman, 2015). For example, one student in judo, Isaac, has a behavioral intervention plan (BIP) that states that he will diminish his "inappropriate social boundaries." If he were to ask a peer to play and this peer said no, the appropriate response is to accept the answer and find another friend to play with. Any other response, according to Isaac's BIP, could have the consequence of staff intervention, requiring that Isaac's behavior be redirected. For example, he might be separated from other students so that a staff member can review with Isaac the rules of appropriate social boundaries.

ABA procedures require that teachers and service providers look at behaviors, but not the feelings behind them (Storey & Haymes, 2017). As a recipient of ABA in her earlier years, Sequenzia (2015) says that ABA "consists of commands an Autistic child must follow to exhaustion, responses an Autistic child must give 'correctly', even if the answers don't match the child's feelings or preferences, and the repression of movements that Autistics use to regulate their own bodies" (para. 11). In Freirean (1970/2000) terms, this system of changing behaviors is oppressive because it constructs Autistic students as people whose actions and thinking need to be controlled. The implementation of a scripted plan to change one's behavior is akin to the banking style of education (Freire, 1970/2000). Autistic students are expected to behave in ways as dictated by BIPs with little regard to context or feeling. This disconnection can be physical, where they are removed from the classroom, but also social and emotional because they are taught to believe that the reasons for their behavior are unacceptable. One day, when Isaac asked a neurotypical child to play with him, the child said no and called him "a loser." Isaac ran away from the playground. Isaac was then segregated from his peers while the adult reinforced the rules of appropriate social boundaries that were written on his BIP. Isaac was not seen as someone who could feel pain from being rejected. Isaac's feelings, and his behavior as a result of those feelings, spurred isolation and were interpreted only through the perspective of this neurotypical adult. This frames autistic people's behavior as unconnected to other people around them. The dojo, however, was different.

## Alternative Worlds: In the Dojo

As Freire notes, liberation is possible through a synthesis of critical reflection and action. He states, "The teacher-student and the students-teachers reflect simultaneously on themselves and the world without dichotomizing this reflection from action, and thus establish an authentic form of thought and action" (Freire, 1970/2000, p. 83). Yet, autistic people are given very little space or time to do either of these when ABA interventions are applied. So, we turn to a space outside of school, the dojo, where autistic people reflect, take action, and engage in ways that expand concepts of voice. It is a place where they participate as full community members and are not distilled down to a behavior plan.

### *Being Uke, Being Tori*

Kano (1986) advocates that certain lessons are to be learned in judo that apply outside the dojo. One of those maxims is to "pay close attention to the relationship between self and other" (p. 24). Biklen's (2005) work in synthesizing case studies of nonverbal autistic people also contends that successful learning happens when parents and teachers pay careful attention to and observe the actions of children and then adjust their actions in kind. The reciprocal nature of noticing and adjusting happens in the dojo when judo players take on the roles of uke and tori. The sensei pairs players together when they are practicing different movements that are critical to playing randori. In randori, the free practice of judo, judo players are required to spontaneously read the movements of each other and plan responses. It is through these roles that players show what they have learned and assist others' learning. Taking on the roles of uke and tori allows all participants to engage for a common purpose. Cooperation is essential and the autistic person's actions are necessary and valuable. Let's turn to the story of Max to see how this works.

### *Max*

Max attends a special school for autistic students. As Rachel, Max's mother describes, he often prefers to stay at home and play on his electronic devices. But judo time is different! Max enjoys the community, the socialization, and the physical feedback of judo. These same things resonate with many of the judo players, both autistic and neurotypical. Max is funny, and he enjoys making others laugh. If he notices that one of the lines from a movie is making people laugh, Max will repeat it multiple times so others can keep enjoying it. Max's parents believe that these judo experiences are excellent opportunities for him to continue to grow. They also feel it can help him connect with his sister, a wrestler who occasionally attends Saturday judo class.

Sensei Scott has been volunteering his time at the school to demonstrate judo for over 20 years, starting when his son was first enrolled there. It is clear that Max connects with Sensei Scott and Sensei Scott with Max. Sensei helps Max get ready for class by readjusting his belt. Max strokes Sensei Scott's shoulder, and he smiles out of the corner of his mouth. Sensei Scott pulls the knot in Max's belt tight, stands up, and pats his shoulder. Max takes off, dashing across the mat with a high-pitched squeal. Max seems to appreciate the humor that the Sensei brings to classes and the high standards he has for all his students. If Sensei Scott believes a student can perform better, he will let them know.

Teaching and learning in the dojo is cyclical and routinized. Each class follows the same format. The predictable routine is comforting to many of the students who do not like unexpected change. When Max first started at the dojo, hc would complete a roll or a move, lay on the ground, and then reach his arms up to the sky and try to get someone to come over and help him up. Every week, there would be a chorus of people encouraging Max to get up on his own. Other participants would shout, "It's not nap time Max," or "Come on, Grandpa, it's time to get up!" or "Good job, Max, do it again." Sensei Scott might come over to Max and say, "You're not getting any help. You can get up." Max would stay on the floor, giggle, wiggle, and eventually get himself up. While this behavior might seem disruptive or uncooperative, Sensei Scott viewed it as Max joining the community and engaging with other participants. Sensei did not encourage this behavior, nor did he admonish Max for it. Sensei found meaning in Max's behavior. As he explained to me, "Max is new to the dojo. He might get a lot of help in other areas, but he can do this. He's figuring things out."

Max was watched carefully by Sensei Scott as he inhabited uke and tori roles. Being tori requires that you execute a judo move as you've been taught. It requires that one coordinate their body while moving their partner to practice a throw or foot sweep. If too much force is used, the tori can harm the uke, who is adjusting their body and response so that the tori can be successful. It is a delicate dance. It requires that the tori take the point of view of the uke and vice versa.

In a typical class, Sensei Scott introduces the move they will learn and/or practice by providing an example as students sit or stand against the wall. He requests the help of another adult black belt, and they walk through the steps of the move, stopping in certain positions to point out where his hands and feet are in relation to his partner. Some students look away as Sensei Scott and his assistant demonstrate; others watch. Some students make vocal tics. Some students watch through the fluttering of their hands in front of their eyes. Sensei Scott continues on. He never requires that students "be" a certain way while learning because he has learned that learning doesn't look one way.

One day, Max is paired with Abe, a 26-year-old autistic brown belt. Abe instructs Max about how to execute the move that was just demonstrated. Abe talks, moves Max's hands and offers encouraging words. Sensei Scott walks over to watch. He stands back as Max and Abe work together. He watches how Max cares for Abe in the role of uke. It's important for the uke to have the tori's wellbeing in mind as they practice the moves. The tori can only execute the move with the uke's cooperation. They will practice this move 20 times, and with each repetition, Max and Abe find ways to support each other by moving their own bodies so each has good positioning. Then, they switch roles. Here, all players support each other so that each individual, and the community as a whole, can thrive.

In the beginning, Max was always paired with a student who had more experience than himself. Sensei Scott is watching and waiting for the right time for Max to take on the role of mentor. It is almost a year later when Max becomes ready to do this, right before he is awarded his yellow belt. Sensei Scott has observed Max adjusting his resistance according to who he is paired with. When Max is playing Abe, a much taller and stronger player, he provides more resistance to Abe's moves. Sensei Scott pairs Max with Carl, an older autistic teen who has been playing judo longer but who is much slighter and who stims at various times during moves, forcing his partner to wait. Max adjusts his playing to suit Carl. Sensei Scott is paying attention to Max's "voice," his movement, and his actions that display his understanding of judo concepts. Max "tells" Sensei Scott, through his patience and slower movements with Carl, that he understands the dimensions of this partnership—the change in partner has changed how he should behave. Sensei Scott observes Max incorporating this concept into his judo. Not a word is spoken.

*Michael*

It's another Saturday and a new student arrives. He enters the dojo a few minutes before class begins. He looks tentatively at his parents as they usher him into a seat by the door. He weaves his fingers together and gently rocks back and forth to a rhythm only he can hear. Isaac and another autistic man about Isaac's age, his good friend Will, walk over to the new student and say hello. Isaac says, "Welcome. You are here to play judo. You will have a fun time." Isaac sticks out his hand, and Michael, the new student, is encouraged by his mom to do the same. Will follows Isaac's lead, sticks out his hand, smiles, and looks down at his feet. They shake. Michael is 13 years old. He speaks only a little, but he smiles a lot. He is provided with a gi, the jacket worn by judo players, and a belt. He slowly walks onto the mat.

The class follows the familiar routine. It is time for all to line up and take turns rolling down the mat, two at a time. Michael gets confused about how to execute a move and starts to cry. Sensei Scott reminds him that everyone in the dojo is practicing, even the black belts. He tells Michael that he never has to worry about doing the moves perfectly and that he should just try his best. Another black belt tells Michael that he is doing great for his very first time. Max watches this interaction and walks up to Michael and says, "To infinity and beyond!" repeating a line from *Toy Story*, one of his favorite movies.

Then it is time to pair up students as uke and tori to practice moves they have learned before and a move that Sensei Scott has just demonstrated. Sensei Scott matches Max with Michael. He walks toward them and stands close by. Sensei Scott tells pairs to practice the move 10 times and then switch roles. Max starts as tori. He uses his voice the entire time he works with Michael. He squeals, laughs, recites movie lines, and hums as he carefully moves Michael's body to execute the move. He then takes his turn as tori. As Michael tries to recall how to move his body, Max moves his own body to help. Now he can complete the move. Max grunts as though he is suffering big falls so that it makes Michael look like an experienced judo player who is slaying him in competition. Sensei Scott looks on. His evaluation of these players happens in quiet observation. He can witness how his demonstrations have influenced his students' actions.

## Applied Gentleness: Liberating Autistic "Voice"

Changing narratives about autistic people's behavior requires understanding that their actions are oftentimes their voices. Honoring autistic students' voices means seeing their movements, stims, and actions as methods of communication and not isolated behaviors to be fixed. Judo means "gentleness against force" and Sensei Scott applies this idea in the dojo to not only judo moves that he teaches but also by resisting neurotypical interpretations of behavior. As an educator, he is instead applying the gentleness of observation to notice learning and to listen to his students' voices. In the dojo, autistic students learn judo and so much more. When given the space, students learn that they are in control of their bodies and that they are both teachers and learners. In turn, Sensei Scott knows he must learn from each of his students and that this learning happens when students are immersed in a community of learners who are all valued and respected. Amanda, an autistic woman who earned her black belt after over 15 years of practice, shared that, as a child, she never liked to be touched. She had difficulty socializing and was very tense. While schools looked to change her behaviors by providing goals for her obtain, it was always on their schedule. She described the dojo as a space where her autism is a part of who she is, and she is allowed to wholly be that person. Amanda stated, "Judo has helped me overcome a lot of issues. Like, it's really helped me release pent up energy, I'm much more relaxed. And it's also helped me socialize more with people. I've made a lot of friends in this." There is a lot to learn in the dojo about the reciprocal nature of teaching and learning, but you have to look for it.

## Conclusion

Myers (2019) calls for spaces where Autistic people can "resist oppression, and reframe the dialogue on autism . . . spaces for youth to form alliances, push one another, and hold another up" (p. 92). Schools can be these places. Autistic students may not always use language, but they use their voices, which are sometimes their behaviors, to express a full range of human emotions. Sometimes, paperwork created by the special education process flattens and limits our understanding of these voices. As Sensei Scott demonstrates, if we believe they are there and we observe closely, we can see and hear these voices.

## Reflection Questions

Closely observe the actions of a student or students you work with. What do their behaviors tell you? How do you see your teaching reflected in their actions?

Look carefully at your students' special education paperwork. In what ways are these representations multidimensional, and where do they become flat?

As a teacher, how do you relate to the concepts of oppression and liberation? Where do you feel oppressed in your practice? Where do you experience liberation?

## Notes

1. I use identity-first language when discussing Autistic people in general because I believe autism is an important part of someone's identity. See Brown (2011) for a full discussion about the difference between identity-first and person-first language.

2. Pseudonyms have been used to remove all identifying information about participants.

## References

Biklen, D. (2005). *Autism and the myth of the person alone*. New York, NY: New York University Press.

Brown, L. X. Z. (2011, August 4). *The significance of semantics: Person-first language: Why it matters*. Retrieved from http://www.autistichoya.com/2011/08/significance-of-semantics-person-first.html.

Freire, P. (2000). *Pedagogy of the oppressed* (M. B. Ramos, Trans.). New York, NY: Continuum. (Original work published 1970)

Kano, J. (1986). *Kodokan judo*. New York, NY: Kodansha USA, Incorporated.

McCloskey, E. (2016). To the maximum extent appropriate: Determining success and the least restrictive environment for a student with autism spectrum disorder. *International Journal of Inclusive Education, 21*(11), 1204–1222. doi:10.1080/13603116.2016.1155667

McCloskey, E. (2018). Ratio profiling: The discursive construction of the continuum of alternative placements. *Disability & Society, 33*(5), 763–782. doi:10.1080/09687599.2018.1453784

Myers, B. A. (2019). *Autobiography on the spectrum*. New York, NY: Teachers College Press.

Shyman, E. (2015). *Besieged by behavior analysis for autism spectrum disorder: A treatise for comprehensive educational approaches*. Lanham, MD: Lexington Books.

Sequenzia, A. (2015, February 11). *My thoughts on ABA*. Autistic Women & Nonbinary Network. Retrieved from https://awnnetwork.org/my-thoughts-on-aba/

Storey, K., & Haymes, L. (2017). *Case studies in Applied Behavior Analysis for students and adults with disabilities*. Springfield, IL: Charles C Thomas.

NINETEEN

# "It Was Time for Us to Take a Stand": An Ethnic Studies Classroom and the Power of Student Voice

*Jorge F. Rodriguez, Carah Reed, and Karen Garcia*

> I told myself enough is enough and it's time to do something about these issues. I gathered up people that felt the same way as me. We all agreed and made sure that we left our High School on a much better note. It was time for us to take a stand. (Janet, student activist)

In this chapter, we invite you to join us—a high school graduate, an Ethnic Studies teacher, and a university ally—as we reflect on a story of student mobilization for change. Some of us will share firsthand narratives while others, such as the university ally, will contribute an interpretive analysis. We all grew up in the region where our story takes place. This affords us a personal understanding of the cultural and political dynamics described in our story. To protect identities, we use pseudonyms for students and teachers.

This is a story about ways that students named and directly addressed issues in their school to create change. Student activist, Janet, reflects on some injustices that stirred students into action:

> I've always been passionate about making a difference. Education, to me, is very important. I believe we, as students, deserve to be treated with respect. There are students from other high schools that don't need to deal with half of the issues we face with on a daily basis. For example, our school locks the restrooms during lunch! This is an issue that shows that the way we are treated in this high school is just not fair.

This movement for change formed in the context of an Ethnic Studies classroom in a California high school. The school began offering Ethnic Studies in 2015, providing students with a more holistic understanding of racial histories within the United States. The Ethnic Studies movement gained recognition during the Civil Rights era, challenging mainstream education to include an intersectional social-historical understanding of identity within a U.S. context (Banks, 2012). This is an interdisciplinary approach to education, drawing from Critical Race Theory, Feminist Theory, Critical Studies, Cultural Studies, and others as its foundation.

## Seeing the Larger Context

To begin, we contextualize the political, cultural, racial, and educational realities of our community. The high school in reference is one of the largest in our city, with a population of 2,800 students. Almost 98% of students are Hispanic or Latinx of any race, and 92.7% are eligible for free and reduced-price lunch under the National School Lunch Program (NSLP). For most students who attend this high school, making ends meet is a struggle for their families. Often, families co-share housing due to unaffordable rents and high housing costs (González, 2017).

The economic and racial demographic struggles of the school mirror those of its city. Compared to the quality of life and education of youth within the rest of the county, students' learning and development experiences are drastically inequitable. Some adults like Mrs. Becky, the Ethnic Studies teacher, recognize the injustices of student educational experiences. Her reflections below describe what she sees:

> Being an educator at [this] High School for 19 years, I feel that sometimes students are not factored into the decisions that are made on campus. The classes are busting out at 40 students each. Students are given little consideration in how the schedule is built.
>
> Oftentimes students are not allowed to advocate for their needs. They must just take what they are given. The lunch area is packed, and students are anxious to get in line for lunch because it takes almost all lunch time to get lunch while waiting in line. Bathrooms are often locked.
>
> Rarely are students taught to think for themselves. Mostly students are given packets or worksheets to finish instead of the teacher taking time to explain and excite engagement in the classroom. Students are bored.

> And they are criminalized. Just this year, administration stopped students who were late to first period. They confiscated their phones. One young man was asked if he was on drugs. The place becomes more about order and domination than free expression and learning to lead.

Mrs. Becky's observations critique the deficit thinking and low expectations pedagogically implemented within her high school (Lacayo, 2016). She demonstrates how her school seeks to control youth. In her statement, she references the importance of student-initiated advocacy. She emphasizes the importance of providing a space for dialogue. Mrs. Becky understands the importance of "free expression" and "learning to lead." From her pedagogical perspective, this means turning over power to students. Her beliefs and her practice emphasize the importance of allowing students to fully embrace their education. It means that instead of being criminalized, youth must be perceived as smart, thoughtful, and capable.

Mrs. Becky reflected on her own educational experience, elaborating on differences between education at the high school and that within more privileged, affluent school districts:

> I know that, as a teacher, I am always thinking about how students are taught in other districts, districts with students who have more access, more privilege. I am a product of a system like that: small class sizes, trust for students, few gates, no police-officers, curriculum that inspires one to be a leader. These districts have teachers who look at the whole child and gifts they bring to the classroom. They see their students as smart and not deficient.
>
> I am always striving to put students at the center of their experience in class. I try to create meaning. I try to make stuff applicable. I see students as leaders, as smart and having capacity. I know they can become anything that they want. I want them to enjoy learning and see themselves as active participants in the process. I want them to understand their power within this system. I want them to see that they have agency.

Unfortunately, not all teachers, administrators, schools, or city officials see education and students as Mrs. Becky does. Stigma and deficit thinking about youth are prevalent throughout the region.

Students from low-income and marginalized environments understand that the school lacks resources and that their education is less than they deserve as learners. Their families also understand and feel the disparity. The high school's city is predominately Latinx, immigrant, and low income. According to Arellano (2008), "illegal immigration" has become political code justifying discrimination, demeaning attitudes, and segregation from Hispanic, Latinx, and immigrant communities. Prevailing perceptions and assumptions about the surrounding city are deficit-based, attributing negative characteristics and stereotypes to those who reside in and affiliate with the community (Lacayo, 2016). This affects education as well.

## Enough Is Enough! Student Self-Determination

Our story begins as youth in the school identify and address issues they encountered daily. Mrs. Becky's class provided a space where students discussed problems they experienced, and she provided historical examples of how other students advocated and fought for their education. The reflective process that students engaged in motivated them toward action. Janet describes their process and experience:

> The journey of this project began when we watched the movie *Walkout*. The movie was based off of Chicanas/os fighting for equality in their school in Los Angeles in the 1960s. In my Ethnic Studies class, all the students decided to make some changes in our school. We were very motivated to make change.
>
> We got into groups. Each group wrote problems they saw at school down on paper. A lot of the problems listed were about the restroom situation. We had the same situation as the kids in Los Angeles walkouts did. The administration or security would lock the restrooms during lunch, and they would leave them locked for the rest of the day, leaving about 2,800 students in our school unable to go to the restroom. The administration believed that we would get in fights or maybe even do drugs if we went to the restrooms.
>
> We are discriminated against a lot in our community just because of the color of our skin. In our school, you would see around four security guards constantly looking to get someone in trouble. The list included more than the restrooms: we had issues with lunch lines, teachers, administration, and gates.

> We felt solutions to our issues should not be too much to ask for. We wanted to feel welcome and feel like we matter.

Janet voicing out her needs, given the environment she navigated at her school, was impressive and powerful. Her narrative demonstrates her passion and commitment toward addressing long lines during lunch, access to restrooms, security guard policing, and teacher/administrator perceptions. One phrase that should be noted in Janet's statement was "We wanted to feel welcome and feel like we matter." In her book *Subtractive Schooling: U.S.-Mexican Youth and the Politics of Caring*, Dr. Angela Valenzuela discusses evidence that caring in education is vital and necessary for a more equitable learning experience for Mexican and Latinx youth (Valenzuela, 1999).

Students identified direct parallels between conditions in East Los Angeles that led to walkouts and conditions they experienced. They demonstrated their willingness to contribute and advocate for the improvement of their high school. Janet articulated the process her class embarked on and how they mobilized for action:

> We wrote on sticky notes any issue regarding counseling, bathrooms, lunch line, administration, etc. We accumulated all the responses and many of us had similar experiences and inconveniences. Then, Mrs. Becky introduced us to Youth Participation Action Research projects. It was new to most of us, however, all of us were open to learning.
>
> Our teacher shared ideas about what our education might look like if issues were addressed. Then, my team started to think about how we could bring our ideas and concerns to the administration. I personally wanted to work on this because it was very important for me to try to confront the people who have the most power in this school.
>
> We started our project by creating a survey to gather the concerns of other students in our school. Each person in the team typed up questions for our survey. We then analyzed each other's questions and voted on the ones we would use.
>
> We went around campus at lunch and even during our class to give people these surveys. The responses we got were very powerful. Students gave us their honest

> opinions about administration, teachers, counselors, and just about everything in the school.
>
> We took all the data from the surveys and wrote down the solutions students wanted and the problems that came up the most. This was all great data because now we had over 200 students that felt the same way about these issues, making our voice all the more powerful.

After collecting survey responses, Mrs. Becky's class processed the information and began to address issues reported on campus. They began to question their school culture and policy. They pushed back on normalized expectations such as locked restrooms and lunch line injustice (such as athletes cutting in line, making the lines even longer and impossible to acquire lunch). As students began addressing these issues, they witnessed changes on campus. Excitement set in. The changes affirmed the power students hold when owning, committing, and engaging with their education in critical ways. Mrs. Becky described the students' energy during this time:

> As the students began to collect responses some became excited, others overwhelmed. Two days into the data collection, athletes were no longer able to cut in the lunch lines. Victory at the gate is always inspiring. This created a spark for the rest of the class. Some students struggled to ask/give surveys, some were hustling in the early morning to get students to fill out surveys before school. Also, some groups incorporated checking locked restrooms, taking pictures of restrooms without mirrors, and such. It provided guidance to all groups.
>
> Some became overwhelmed and some loved the challenge . . . We were pushing against many pillars of the system with this project. No wonder it was so hard and will continue to be in further facilitation of this lesson. Changing perspectives, putting power into the hands of students, making the learning completely connected to what they create. It is dynamic to say the least.

Seeing change, students continued to collect information from their peers. They wanted to invite the administration to meet with the class to present their findings. They used their survey findings to develop a 10-point plan summarizing issues faced by the student body. They hoped that the administration would engage in dialogue with the class and begin to implement some attainable solutions. The plan outlined the need for the following:

- [We want] A 15-minute break between second and third period.
- We want our administration to trust us.
- We want better food that even the principal would be willing to eat.
- [We want you to] Give students privileges on dress code.
- [We want] Teachers who actually want to help us succeed in life.
- [We want you to] Let students make their own decisions.
- We deserve open/clean and fully supplied restrooms.
- We want more respect from teachers, strengthening the balance for teachers and students.
- We demand more late starts and early releases.
- We demand filtered water fountains.

Janet reflected on the power and significance of the meeting with the administration:

> On April 20, the national student walkout day, we asked the president of the school board, our principal, and all administrators to come to our 5th period class. The school board president was the only one that responded to our email. So, we thought she would be the only one coming into our classroom but everyone [school administrators] else ended up coming. I was in shock because we had everyone that we wanted to confront in our classroom.
>
> I'll certainly never forget that day. I let out everything I kept inside and confronted them with how I felt about everything in this school to the point where tears were coming down my face from the anger I felt. It was a great feeling to tell them how I felt in front of their boss. You don't really get an opportunity like that so I wanted to take advantage of it. They heard our voice that day and we let them know that we wanted change in our school. Things had to change around the campus because it was time for change.
>
> After that day we started to notice a shift between the administration and us. We noticed that they were now more open to hearing our concerns. We really appreciated that. We felt like our voice was finally being heard.

Mrs. Becky's reflection regarding that meeting further explained what occurred:

> On the National Day of Protest, we only heard word from the president of the board. No administrators had confirmed. We have one principal and four assistant principals on site. We had not practiced what they [the students] were going to say. I figured they knew their issues. Again, free expression and experience are what I lead with. I had faith in the students and what they were doing. They had their own opinions and had their surveys and areas of concern. Holistically they were ready to meet power with power. We all have to start somewhere.
>
> The students spoke. Gradually the administrators walked in. They [the students] addressed their issues to the president of the board and the administrators. Some students got emotional. "You do not listen to us." Bathrooms, and gates were discussed. One student indicated that they had results from surveys. It was apparent that the leadership was not ready for this formulation. It was a strong learning lesson. Many students were scared to speak, but the students who did speak made an impact. Real learning, real power, real protest.

The effect of this meeting continues to this day, beyond graduation of some of the youth leaders. One outcome of the work was the formation of a student council, specifically designed to enhance communication between administration and students. This council is following through on the demands of the 10-point plan proposed by the Ethnic Studies class. It is exciting to see student voice activated and students embracing their agency and self-determination. A number of student concerns are now being addressed: student lunch lines are shorter, athletes are not given priority, and students have more access to restrooms. But what is most important is that students have acquired skills and strategies such as organizing, advocacy, data collection, and the formulation of solution-based proposals, which they will use for years to come.

The youth showed determination against all odds. Their actions were particularly important given racialized perceptions of students in their community (Lacayo, 2016). The need for students to advocate for their education sheds light on limitations that afflict schools like this one that serve low income communities of color (Acosta & Mir, 2012; Ladson-Billings, 2006; Valenzuela, 1999).

Deficit limitations placed upon youth of color and marginalized identities are still the norm in our educational systems and society (Apple, 1979/2004). Because these students were in this Ethnic Studies class, they were able to work in partnership with a teacher who fostered critical and insightful curricula. These students were able to see their identities acknowledged in the classroom. The pedagogical tools used by Mrs. Becky, such as Youth Participatory Action Research (YPAR; Cammarota & Fine, 2010), ignited students' desire to ask questions and critically examine their educational environments. YPAR allowed students to interpret their realities and contextualize them within social and academic frames. It enabled them to ask important questions and address social inequalities within their own school environment. The students spoke truth to power and called out injustices in ways that were sincere, direct, and unapologetic.

## Learning From Youth Voice

As we authors met throughout the summer months preparing to tell this story, we discussed, planned, and questioned the message we wanted to relay. We reflected on the audience that would read these accounts. We wanted to be transparent and intentional. We hoped sharing this story would motivate educators and students to addressing injustice and oppressive power within their schools.

In our reflection, we came up with three key lessons of this chapter. First, classrooms can be sites where student reflection and self-motivation can be fostered. We saw this when students in our high school reflected upon their learning environments to pinpoint issues limiting their learning. Second, classrooms can be safe, youth-led spaces. The mobilization of these students was possible because they felt safe to question and act without fear of being reprimanded or controlled. Finally, classrooms can be spaces to critically examine/question expectations normalized within students' environments. Students in this Ethnic Studies course questioned everything, even mundane struggles that had become normalized in their schooling experiences.

We end with a reflection by Mrs. Becky:

> I have always thought that students should be in a classroom where they have voice. They need to be the center. Their narratives, ideas, and opinions should be the starting point of leaning.

> The Ethnic Studies curriculum is liberating and lends itself to a fuller education. The curriculum acknowledges identity and power. It returns students to themselves in every capacity.
>
> Student voices must be shared. Their hearts must be nurtured. They must find creative agency and freedom in what they decide to pursue.

May we strive endlessly to create spaces for our communities that spark creativity, critical analysis, and reflective perspectives of the world we navigate.

## Reflection Questions

What practices could you use to monitor your thinking and professional practice for bias and deficit thinking?

What can educators do to provide youth spaces where they can exercise self-determination and have a positive sense of self?

How can educators include students in determining what knowledge is important and appropriate for their learning and/or unlearning?

## Recommended Resources

### Movies

Bruce, L. (Producer), & Olmos, E. J. (Director). (2006). *Walkout* [Motion picture]. USA: HBO.

McGinnis, E. I. (Producer), & Palos, A. L. (Director). (2011). *Precious knowledge* [Motion picture]. USA: Dos Vatos Productions.

### Websites

Xicanx Institute for Teaching and Organizing (XITO): https://www.xicanoinstitute.org

Rethinking Schools: https://www.rethinkingschools.org

### Books

Cuauhtin, R. T., Zavala, M., Sleeter, C. E., & Au, W. (Eds.). (2019). *Rethinking ethnic studies*. Milwaukee, WI: Rethinking Schools Ltd.

## References

Acosta, C., & Mir, A. (2012). Empowering young people to be critical thinkers: The Mexican American studies program in Tucson. *Voices in Urban Education, 34*, 15–34.

Apple, M. W. (2004). *Ideology and curriculum*. New York, NY: Routledge. (Original work published 1979)

Arellano, G. (2008). *Orange County: A personal history*. New York, NY: Scribner.

Banks, J. A. (2012). Ethnic studies, citizenship education, and the public good. *Journal of Intercultural Education, 23*(6), 467–473.

Cammarota, J., & Fine, M. (2010). Youth participatory action research: A pedagogy for transformational resistance. In J. Cammarota & M. Fine (Eds.), *Revolutionizing education* (pp. 1–11). New York, NY: Routledge.

González, E. R. (2017). *Latino city: Urban planning, politics, and the grassroots*. New York, NY: Routledge.

Lacayo, C. (2016). Latinos need to stay in their place: Differential segregation in a multi-ethnic suburb. *Societies, 6*(3), 25. doi:10.3390/soc6030025

Ladson-Billings, G. (2006). From the achievement gap to the education debt: Understanding achievement in U.S. schools. *Educational Researcher, 35*(7), 3–12.

Valenzuela A. (1999). *Subtractive schooling: U.S.-Mexican youth and the politics of caring*. New York, NY: SUNY Press.

TWENTY

# Collaborative Leadership: A Story of Student–Principal School Transformation

*Susanne Jungersen*

I ARRIVED AT PORIRUA COLLEGE, A secondary school, at the lowest point in its history. I was to be its next principal. Porirua College is a medium-sized secondary school located in Cannons Creek, 25 kilometers from Wellington, the capital city of New Zealand. The school is made up mainly of Māori and Pasifika students, youth from historically underrepresented groups in New Zealand. Porirua is also designated as a decile 1a school. This means that schools like Porirua have the highest number of students who come from households with the lowest socioeconomic status. Nationwide, there are about 15 secondary schools in this category.

Due to some national changes, by the time I was appointed principal, enrollment had dropped to fewer than 400 students. It was under threat of closure. Parents of higher economic means began to choose other schools for their children. It was suffering from White flight during this time. The challenge before me was great. Additionally, this was my first time taking a senior management role at any school. Previously, I had worked in a middle-class girls' school with realities much different than those faced by Porirua. It was all rather a shock to me from the start.

This chapter looks at the transformative power that student voice had at Porirua College by highlighting two schoolwide projects. Because I am reflecting on these projects in retrospect as a now-retired principal, sharing processes and events, I cannot provide direct quotations from the students who were involved in the projects described in this chapter. Nonetheless, I hope to share the powerful effects that their voices had in shaping the school. I approach this chapter with a firm belief that student voice is an essential element to school transformation because I am certain that including all viewpoints of people affected by a problem brings the best results. Students have a unique perspective on their own school, and they have answers to our issues.

Listening to them gives the best chance of fully understanding the problem. If the correct problem is posed, the correct solution will be found. I am convinced that student voice should be elicited by building trust in the process. In a school change project, both staff and students need to feel assured that the best results will arrive by working together on the basis of equal rights to a voice and a place in the decision-making process. This is most likely to be the case where there are equal numbers of students and staff since no one has a deciding vote. No one faction of the school has a greater say or greater authority. Achieving consensus or a working compromise is a more likely outcome and will be done with full buy-in from all parties. I stipulate that this is a democratic process, that it works for short-term or time-bound, specific school change projects with a clear goal or goals in mind. I believe full-school transformation arises from a series of these successful school change projects.

## Project One: Eliminating Vandalism

When I arrived, the school was at a very low point and the sanitary facilities reflected that. The morale of students, support staff, and teachers was also very low. There was a problem with vandalism in the girls' restrooms. The problem had been going on for some time and was so bad that support staff had given up on it completely. Vandalism is generally hard to combat without getting the "buy-in" of a community, and I knew the challenge would be greater in a school where everyone felt so disheartened. In order to find some plausible solution, I decided to include students in the process of attempting to eliminate vandalism in the girls' toilets.

We had 200 girls in the school. But the entire bathroom facility for all of them was down to only two toilets. Neither one had a seat, just the ceramic bowl. There was also no toilet paper. One of them had no working flush mechanism. The other had no door. The rest of the facility was terrible. In the tiny space outside the stalls there was one handbasin with cold water, but there were no towels and no soap. The "mirror" was a piece of shiny tin. A couple of inches above head height was a rusty iron grid that stretched from side to side and then disappeared over a wooden partition. Girls ran away from school at odd times during the day, presumably to find functional facilities. The truancy rate of female students was up to an average of 25% a day.

I was horrified when I saw the state of these bathroom facilities. I didn't understand how this could be acceptable to anyone. When I spoke about it to other members of the staff, they didn't seem to be surprised or shocked. That in itself seemed appalling. It showed me that the school was in deep disarray. People were willing to accept an extremely low standard with regard to facilities for students. In fact, this was mirrored by low expectations in all other aspects of the school. Most staff I spoke to about the girls' bathroom facilities were adamant that the girls would trash the facilities if repaired. They saw no point in fixing the issue.

*Listening to the Girls*

It seemed that female students were trashing their toilets, so I assumed they would know why this was happening. Understanding the issue meant turning to them. Also, I believed that they should have a stake in the solution. I imagined that collaborating with students would allow aggressive kids, who perhaps felt powerless, to become young people who could be certain that they could make a difference. This project might show students that they had influence and power to make changes.

To make this happen, we formed a Reclaim the Bathroom Facilities committee. It consisted of myself, one female board member, and three senior girls. The members of the committee were selected by the student council and me. The board member, Lorna, was astonished by the existing state of the girls' facilities. She wondered if the iron grid that hung above the restrooms might be a suicide prevention strategy to stop girls getting up high and hanging themselves. She connected such structures to ones she had read about in jails. The committee had much work to do to solve this problem and make these spaces more humane.

From the beginning, it was clear that the committee was dedicated to the idea of all five members having equal status. This equality was felt in setting goals, designing a strategy, making decisions, and creating recommendations. It was important that the girls knew this wasn't just an exercise in consultation with them. This was a collaboration. School leaders should enable a form of democratic process to occur in a school setting where feasible. This shows students how democratic processes work and teaches them the kind of skills that will help them become active, aware citizens in the adult world. I was very comfortable with full student collaboration and knew we had power in the matter since I was the newly appointed principal. I was also clear that this project was also about centralizing respect for students in our school. The bathroom vandalism was a symptom of the astonishing neglect, abuse, and indifference I was finding in the entire school.

Seeking a solution, the three female students and I made official fact-finding trips to other schools, asking to see their bathroom facilities—perhaps an unusual request from principal to principal. We viewed bathroom facilities in a number of different schools. The three girls consulted with quite a large number of female students in other schools as well as our own students in hopes of finding an answer to the problem we faced. Afterward, we drew up a plan with simply expressed goals, intended outcomes and recommendations. We took this plan to the board of trustees. The students spoke at the board meeting. The board agreed to install mirrors, toilet seats, lockable doors, soap, hot water, and toilet paper. They also agreed to open another set of girls' restrooms that had been nailed shut in another part of the school. That was the easy part of undertaking this project.

*Getting to the Heart of the Problem*

After the restrooms were restored and opened, the facilities were trashed by girls a few weeks later. The three senior girls from the committee realized I needed to be told some deeper truths about the matter. They told me some girls didn't know how to use the facilities exactly. They said some girls went there to have meetings to talk about abuse happening at home. They told me girls used toilet paper strewn all over the floor to sit on while they had their meetings. Some girls went there to hide, to smoke, and to have time out. It was their only venue to give each other support and advice that provided privacy. The vandalism happened at these times by girls who were angry about things happening at home. Vandalism was a part of venting grief about ongoing abuse as well. The girls had no access to an adult with whom to share some of the problems they were facing. I was open to the idea of finding out why students do these sorts of things. It is not a positive step to default to the assumption this is just bad behavior, something that needs to be punished.

To combat continuing vandalism and other student issues that the senior girls told us about, we had a girls' assembly. It was led by the three senior girls.

It was actually fun! We all laughed as I explained how to use the facilities properly. The senior girls spoke to their peers about getting a place for girls to talk. We knew from the reaction of the girls in the assembly and continuing conversations others had with the committee, that the school needed other additional resources—a nurse, a female guidance counselor, and a female doctor. These things took time, but we got most of them in the end. The vandalism of the girls' bathroom facilities lessened and then stopped completely. Over time, we also added a social worker, dental services, and community liaison officers to our campus resources.

## Project Two: Student Appointments Panel

Students can be trusted to make good decisions if the adults in a school recognize their voices as equal and afford them equal power to make decisions. Setting clear structures for projects engaging student voice is also important. In fact, I found little success in developing student voice where the goals, structures, outlines of desired outcomes, or rationale for a project were ill-defined. For example, our student council was not effective. It had no clear definition of what it could or could not do. While leadership expected it would help inform the board of trustees with student voice and perspectives, it didn't do that. Students are not confident. Their "default setting" was to defer to adults and their demands in all important things. The student council was not able to form opinions on many matters to do with changes in the school, nor were they able to provide ideas of new directions we could take to solve some of the intractable problems we had, both in our community and in our school, as long as they were given no structure. We found the key to successful use of student voice was in having defined projects with a clear start and end point.

### *Students in Hiring*

The most successful use of student voice came about when we had to appoint someone to upper management such as a deputy or assistant principal. We would set up two separate appointments panels—one for students and one for adults. The adult panel would consist of the usual board of trustee members, the principal, parent representatives, and a staff representative. The student panel would be made up of student leaders, a student representative from the board of trustees, and two or three others chosen by the student council. The two panels were given the exact same information when reviewing an applicant.

In setting up interviews, we rented a couple of rooms at a local venue. Each candidate had two separate interviews with the two panels. The student panel developed their own set of questions to ask candidates. The feedback we often had from candidates was that the students asked the more searching questions and that the more difficult interviews were with the students. Once interviews were over, both panels convened in the conference room and discussed who were preferred candidates. Students had an equal say in the conversation. It was usual that we would make the appointments in that room, together.

Students developed questions that reflected their concerns and their ideas for change needed in the school. Students asked about uniforms, teaching styles, practice, and experience. In other words, they asked the same kind of questions as the adult panel did, but they had a keen eye for inauthentic answers or for candidates that condescended to them. For instance, students were unhappy with how the school was perceived. It had a poor reputation and they wanted to know how candidates would go about changing that. They were also interested in matters of discipline and guidance. They wanted to know how candidates related to Māori and Pasifika students and what experience they had with working with students from these backgrounds. They developed some case studies and asked candidates how they would deal with the issues they outlined.

I believe the members of the adult interview panels were always extremely impressed with the caliber of the questions developed by the student panel and the quality of their reflections. On at least one occasion, a candidate did not proceed further through the appointments process because they made the mistake of not taking the student panel seriously. They answered in a way that the students did not think was professional or positive. One student panel suggested that a candidate be knocked out of the running because they were concerned at his response to a student question. The question asked was, What would he do if he caught a student with marijuana in his backpack and it was a first offense, would he contact the parents? The candidate apparently said no, he would not contact the parents. The student explained to us that they were concerned about that because they felt it was a health and safety matter. They also took issue with his body language. He was "laid-back," as though he wasn't respecting the status of the student panel within the process. He was not appointed.

When it came time to decide who to appoint, the number of times we all agreed by consensus was very high. The 12 or so of us from both panels would have productive, serious, and genuine debate. In my view, the exercise was a complete success. The students on the panel were held in high regard by the rest of the student body. It made things easier for the newly appointed senior staff members to be accepted by the students. The whole thing taught us to respect the sense and capability in the voices of the students.

## What I Learned in These Projects

Engaging student voice with students as co-constructors for change, I learned a number of lessons. In dealing with the problem of the restrooms, I learned what lay behind a difficult problem. Students revealed that the underlying issue was a deficit of support for a range of issues that our girls faced on a day-to-day basis. I learned that vandalism in the girls' bathroom facilities was not a disciplinary matter. It had never been simply about bad behavior. By working with students as collaborative agents of change, we set a standard of respect between adults and youth in our school. Student trust was gained when they saw we were sincere in our determination to include student voice in our work to improve the school. They saw results. Such a standard of trust and respect proved to be critical in a journey to make positive changes. We continued to build on a mutual understanding of equality. Equality in having a say and in decision-making was possible in specific, time-bound change projects. Anything less than equality would not have enabled our students to feel they had power and agency in the matter. It would not have changed their depressed outlook on themselves or the school to the same extent.

I also learned much from the hiring projects we did with students. The experience of having a separate student appointments panel helped me to realize that senior school managers can trust students to be fully involved in decision-making. They should be part of the continuing journey to improve the school. The clarity with which student panels were able to make their views known and point out important realities for effective leadership appointments forms a lesson for administrators. Sometimes, students know best, or at least have separate and valid views which are hidden to adults. It's a lesson about the need to build trust between school leaders and students. Only by doing this can the hidden but important narratives of student lives come to play in making informed and effective decisions.

I learned that the best way to promote an authentic, ongoing student voice in the school was with a series of change projects that took the school forward. Schools are naturally hierarchical places. Such structures can facilitate the smooth running of routine processes. However, school change projects might best be framed with an ethic of equality. This means finding room for everyone's voices, ideas, ideals, issues, and hopes to be brought together in conversation in the act of decision-making. Students and staff in my school needed to know working in this equitable way was real, sustainable, and effective. Once this was established, working together democratically became more the norm in other aspects of the school. I believe that democracy can work in this way in a school with any students.

One further point must be made. Students' self-esteem was hugely impacted by these projects. Having been equal partners in creating positive, successful change within their school changed how they saw themselves in a wider context. They felt less shame about their school. They no longer felt powerless to improve things in their communities. They were affirmed as equal to their teachers in their ability to participate and meaningfully contribute for the good of their school. Students became more aspirational, seeing tertiary education as a possible destination after school. Respect for themselves, their families, and their school grew, as did positive school results in academic terms. Not surprisingly, we also had better outcomes for every key performance indicator set for our school.

## Conclusion

The power of engaging students as co-constructors in collaboration with adults is immensely effective. It is respectful of their intellects and dignity. It models for them how collaboration brings results and how teamwork happens effectively. The further lesson for me, as the leader of the school, was that I did not know everything about the students. Having gained the trust of the students through working together, I was enlightened! I was able to make better decisions because it was done with them. School leaders should understand how student voice can help in making positive changes in schools. It is done by respecting students' active contributions in an equal partnership usually, at least initially, within well-defined and time-limited projects.

## Reflection Questions

Drawing from the ideas in this chapter, how might a teacher construct spaces for democratic exercises and practices in their classroom and curriculum?

In constructing these curricular democratic spaces, is it possible to focus on processes that have "real world" outcomes/impacts/results? Why would this be important?

School staff may have entrenched ideas about how students should be positioned in relation to decision-making that affects the whole school. How could democratically minded teachers best argue that collaborating with students about important decisions brings the best outcomes for all concerned?

TWENTY-ONE

# Angeles Workshop School: An Experiment in Student Voice

*Ndindi Kitonga*

> Education is at its best when all participants are a community. However, a baseline cohesion is useless without trust and respect between all participating members: students and teachers alike. At Angeles Workshop School we do everything as a cohesive unit. Everyone's voice is heard and acknowledged as valuable. Everyday tasks require teamwork between all members of the school.
>
> A place like this is not just a school. It's a thriving, loving group where we hold similar values, respect each other, and know that our interactions are just as important as the academics. (Joe Hempelmann)

THE OPENING WORDS WERE WRITTEN by Angeles Workshop School (AWS) 2018 alumni Joe Hempelmann for his college freshman English composition class in 2019.

## Introduction and Theoretical Framework

AWS is a Grade 6–12 microschool in Los Angeles, California that I (Ndindi Kitonga) co-founded with Scott Stubbe in 2014. We exist to co-manifest a learning environment that emboldens active participants in our world and fosters analytical, self-motivated learners who love and appreciate their local and global community. We describe our school as "revolutionary" (Stubbe & Kitonga, 2013). We offer a student-led, application-based curriculum rooted in authentic interaction with the community for about 25 students (ages 11–18).

We describe our school community as "city-as-classroom," denoting the importance of our families and local community members as an extension of the school. To us, city-as-classroom means maintaining dialogue between students and local community in order to disrupt the culture of silence around important issues that are rarely part of the standard curriculum yet permeate students' lives (Freire, 1970/2000). The city-as-classroom structures we created (and continue to co-create with community) are designed to get students to name their worlds and offer them the tools to be community problem-solvers. We have three main city-as-classroom structures. The first is schoolwide family participation in decision-making around issues. The second is engaging our civic community where it thrives on weekly Thursday field trips (dubbed city-days). We might tour a local factory, go to a city hall meeting, or create art with an artist at their studio. The third is to invite local community members to host discussion and help us learn about how we can best contribute to our city in a weekly experts-and-enthusiasts program. Parents and extended families often participate and offer great insights.

Our impetus in designing this school is informed by critical and humanist educational philosophies. We believe that education is inherently political and that students should be involved in addressing rich, moral and socio-political questions (Freire, 1970/2000; McLaren, 1994). We founded AWS after feeling frustrated and voiceless in a progressive school environment that we considered stifling for ourselves and families. Educators and families could have input on surface matters but never on curriculum or learning experiences. The deep philosophical and pragmatic questions that ultimately led to our founding of AWS were "How/why do schools with progressive visions struggle to embrace student and educator agency and fall into traditional product-oriented education models?" and "What would it mean to create an environment that nurtured community building, authentic student voice, and a love of learning?" As you will see, AWS is a source of celebration, insight, and challenges.

Table 21.1 shows key principles of humanistic and critical educational theories. Alongside critical theory, we considered humanist models that center learners and advocate self-directed learning, experiential pedagogies, and dialogical problem-solving with peers. However, we wanted learners to be able to not only focus on but also move beyond their individual interests and explore greater sociocultural questions. AWS aspires to create a challenging problem-posing curriculum that relates to students' knowledges and invites them to be active participants in their worlds. Student choice is a fundamental principle at AWS, but it is tempered by educators' recommendations of fundamental skills, content, concepts, and values. While we desire for students to be fully immersed in curriculum that is interest-based, practical, engaging, and critical, we want students to have the tools necessary to navigate both mainstream and alternative schooling worlds. This is both a practical and a philosophical concern. We understand that most of our students will matriculate into learning environments dominated by hierarchical, standardized curricula. Over 50% of our students are people of color from working-class backgrounds whose ability to apply foundational skills and navigate dominant White middle-class culture will greatly affect their future educational and career plans as they do not have generational resources to fall back on. Scholars like Delpit (2012) warn us about the inherent injustice in not teaching basic skills and explicitly decoding dominant cultural forms (language, ways of communicating, etc.) to students, particularly those from marginalized backgrounds. While we do not subscribe to top-down curricula, we emphasize certain skill building and literacy acquisition. It is our hope students use those foundational concepts to navigate new learning environments and to problematize the structures of mainstream schooling they encounter.

**Table 21.1.** Theoretical frameworks informing Angeles Workshop School practices

| Theoretical frameworks | Principles |
|---|---|
| Humanist Education (Glasser, 1998; Rogers, 1995) | *Choice and Control:* Emphasis on student choice<br>*Students' Felt Concern:* Affective learning: impetus for learning lies in students' concerns and interests<br>*The Whole Person:* Students interact with ideas and content cognitively, affectively, and physically.<br>*Self-Evaluation:* Emphasis on self-assessment that develops and activates internal student voice<br>*Teacher as Facilitator:* Teacher is an unobtrusive resource who is available for students, at most a guide<br>*No Mandated Assignments:* Homework is optional. |
| Critical pedagogy (Freire, 1970/2000; McLaren, 1994; Sehr, 1997) | *Student-based curriculum:* Exploration of sociopolitical questions relevant to students' lives<br>*Nonlinear, Interconnected Core Content Education:* Topics/units/subjects are linked through thematic lenses that ask critical questions about our culture and values.<br>*Democratic student participation:* Student involvement in decisions about issues concerning the school community |

This chapter examines some ways that student voice is enacted within AWS. I specifically focus on our attempts to develop structures with students that promote democracy and the collective good while honoring individual student concerns and inherent tensions.

## Student Voice as Political Participation

With our eclectic approach to education, is it possible to nurture a schooling environment in which students can experience "radical collegiality" (Fielding, 2012, p. 15), where participatory forms of engagement and decision-making are occurring? We begin every morning at AWS with a 5- to 10-minute practice of mindfulness and a daily forum meeting. For our mindfulness practice, a teacher or student guides the group through a breathing and/or visualization exercise. Daily forum was conceived by our student, Conor, in early 2014. After each mindfulness session, practiced since our inception, students discussed their experiences at home or school, asked questions about the world, or simply sat and shared with friends before the first academic class. After several weeks of these informal meetings, Conor wondered aloud, "Why don't we just make this a thing? We sit here for about 30 minutes after mindfulness every day and discuss issues. Why can't this be part of the official school day?" The other students enthusiastically agreed, and we have honoured our daily forum routine ever since. The following vignette is a comprehensive description of this student-generated tradition.

Researcher and educator, Roy Danovitch, completed a yearlong study at AWS for his dissertation, *Powerful Voicings: Agency and Identity at a Humanistic-Inspired Alternative School* (2019). In the description that follows, Danovitch captures the introspection, thinking, feeling, and talking together that goes into our daily forum decision-making processes:

> There are no bells marking the beginning of the session, and judging by where students take their seats, no rigid grouping or seating plans either. Twenty-five students of different age levels (11-17) sit together, alongside their teachers, who, outside of their size, blend in seamlessly. With an inquisitive and casual tone, Scott, asks the group, "So, how's everyone feeling? What's on your mind?" With these simple questions—an inquiry into what students were feeling and thinking—Daily Forum is officially underway. After a brief silence, students give brief reports on how they spent their weekends, interesting things they watched on television, things on their minds. After some sharing, Nick, an 8thh grader, gestures that he has something to say. He is frustrated that Angeles students aren't respecting the ban on sugary soft drinks. "We made an agreement, and no one's really listening, so we need to do better." Most students agree; they

> had raised the issue several times before, and even discussed research on the addictive qualities of soda during Science class.
>
> But a few other students disagreed, in particular, Yalda, an 8th grader:
>
> "That's so hard core, when I drink the soda I'm not harming anyone else, and even if some people think it's unhealthy, then why should it be banned? We ban things like racism and bullying, not like my preference for Pepsi, I actually came here so I could drink soda at school!"
>
> The students listened, and a few people appeared to agree. Ndindi asks students what they feel is the difference is between norms, values, and rules. Suddenly, the tenor of the dialogue turns more reflective.
>
> What immediately becomes clear is that there is no prescriptive plan for this meeting; there are agenda items to cover—a proposal from the students to change the location of one of their "City Days Exploration" trips, an Eco-Activist set to visit on Thursday, a guided session focusing on coding—but what seems to take precedence is an open-ended dialogue about school agreements, current events, and community values that generates a wide range of perspectives and reflections. The give and take—interspersed with playful jokes and spontaneous references—infuses the community with a transgressive but fundamental reflective quality, as if it were authoring its identity without concern for traditional boundaries and roles. (Danovitch, 2019, p. 59)

For the remainder of the school week, we engaged in deep conversations on this issue. To prepare students for effective and respectful discussion and debate, Scott and I begin every school year with a whole-school conversation we call "Talking About How We Talk to Each Other." Using resources from fields in restorative justice and peaceful parenting/teaching, we share simple procedures for respectful communication. While we employ many tools, here I want to highlight I-statements and limit-setting, both nonjudgmental approaches to communicating with others. To facilitate learning, we often role play scenarios that young people might encounter (e.g., struggling to be honest with a friend, negotiating a limit with a parent). With these techniques, students can recognize how conflicts are natural aspects of life that they can address and learn from without losing integrity (Bippus & Young, 2005).

In this particular conflict, Yalda continued to advocate for herself at almost every daily forum meeting for a week while other students continued to challenge her views. Yalda used I-statements like "When I am told that I can't have soda, I feel that those around me do not trust my ability to make my own choices." Other students responded with statements like "I hear you and want to support your choices but I think we should create some limits around the amount of time and space we engage with this issue because I know others have other concerns that I want to address." Our role as facilitators was to rely on previously agreed-upon communication norms and encourage students to create solutions together. After five years of using these tools, students are better able to express themselves and listen to each other more effectively. While these tools work well in our school community, they are often tweaked and renegotiated based on specific conflicts and students.

Our agreed-upon norms on sugary drinks emerged from discussions we had engaged in with the community (teachers, students, and parents) the previous year. As a new student, Yalda and her parents were not a part of our previous decision-making. Integrating new students and their families as full participating members of the AWS community is an ongoing challenge because our community is reconstituted constantly. Ultimately, we collectively decided to keep our sugary drink restrictions in place as a way to promote both individual and communal health. We (teachers and students alike) usually vote on decisions like this. However, in this case, Yalda had an obvious minority position, and we typically avoid putting students on the spot in such situations.

The related issues of sugar intake, food, and wellbeing have been addressed in many AWS daily forum meetings, city-days, experts-and-enthusiasts programs and other curricular programs. For instance, experts and enthusiasts who spoke at AWS on various food-related issues included a local dietician, a local food vendor, and an epidemiologist. Students invited their parents to cook with us and discuss how their family came to healthy food practices. Our local grocer was very up front about food labels and the big-food business. Students in my science classes wrote several papers on topics like food deserts and the soft drink industry. Students in a literacy class created a healthy cookbook. We explored the intersections of food, health, and religion when students noted relationships they have to food based on their faith-based practices. Students identified a Diwali event they wanted to participate in and a Coptic Orthodox Ethiopian community to visit and learn with. Our nonlinear, yearlong exploration of this theme allowed us to co-create curriculum and consider how food decisions are made, not only in our families but also in our greater local community. We now have a small community garden and "giving board" at the front of the school that provide produce and clothing for the local unhoused community.

This simple vignette reveals an important tension in our work with students. We are attempting to foster a learning community where oppressive attitudes and values in our lifeworlds are revealed and can be addressed (Darder, 2018). On one hand, we claim to embrace student voice and freedoms. On the other hand, we espouse a values-based curriculum, one that is explicit in our commitment to collective decision-making and certain understandings about social justice. Can student voice be truly realized under these confines? As we engage dialogically as a school community with issues of politics, curriculum, society, and our inner lives, how can individual wants or even needs all be met?

First, we eschew top-down democratic models, and, in line with Dewey's (1939/1976) ideas, consider democracy to be something we must "practice" every day because it relates to specific attitudes, character development, and purpose. Second, we believe that students are unique individuals who should learn in the most noncoercive, democratic, and safe environment possible. Quite simply, students can exercise their rights in our community in safe and responsible ways as long as they are not interfering with the freedoms of others (Jones & Welch, 2010). For example, students can choose to skip classes in lieu of other activities. They cannot, however, hinder other students from participating in a class by choosing an activity in the same space that is disruptive to the collective. We also acknowledge students' rights to learn as they go, change their minds, try activities over and over, and fail safely. For us, the major role of teachers is to not only nurture individual self-expression but also facilitate ways for the school community to engage with minority views seriously and with responsible consideration. So, even if a student like Yalda "got her way" with sodas at school, our focus as a learning community is not only on what Yalda the individual gets but also the process we engaged in to reach those decisions. Dewey (1939/1976) warned us not to "fixate [on] what has been gained instead of using it to open the road and point the way to new and better experiences" (p. 229). Toward that end, we spend a lot of time reflecting on past-made decisions and posing questions that tap into how students with opposing positions are viewed by the group and how they view themselves. We also have ongoing conversations on how to engage in decision-making without imposing conformity culture on each other. What we have found is that through the continual small exercises in "democracy," students begin to practice listening to each other's ideas as well as bravely presenting their own.

While our daily forum focuses on school-related matters, it is more often than not an important space for dialogue on greater political and social issues. Over the years, students have become concerned about issues like police brutality, mass incarceration, environmental justice, and homelessness in our community. Students will often raise these issues here. When we notice gaps in students' understanding and see widespread interest in a political topic, we suspend morning agenda items and host a quick teach-in. Because critical pedagogy is at the heart of our mission, there is an expectation that students will participate in these discussions, although they are not forced to if they are uninterested. A teach-in is an informal political educational forum that is supposed to be participatory in nature. This educational model is associated with anti-war radical activism in the 1960s (Phillips,1965). In many ways, the teach-in is our attempt at a Freirean problem-posing approach to political questions (Freire, 1970/2000). While the teach-in in itself does not constitute praxis as Freire conceived it, the students' ability to ask uninhibited questions, find and share relevant resources in their investigation of the issue, provide their own critical insights, and display willingness to reevaluate their positions makes teach-ins an effective primer for issues-based engagement with our community.

## Student Voice and Curriculum

We consider that rejecting a traditional banking model (Freire, 1970/2000) means democratizing the curriculum design process. Humanistic education models do not impose any curriculum on learners and rely on students to guide their own inquiry (Rogers, 1995). Our model is different because, although we believe in students' rights to choose what they want to learn, we also acknowledge their right to a high-level critical curriculum and to explore topics that they have not even considered yet. What that means is that we have "traditional" curricular subjects taught in the mornings and entirely student-led projects in the afternoons. Morning class sessions are co-created with students. At the beginning of the school year, students express their interests and types of activities they would like to be involved in. The teacher will then pose curricular goals for students. The curriculum is co-created from there. For example, last year, I taught a high school chemistry class. The students expressed a desire to learn more about cooking, food sustainability, nutrition, and the environment. They also wanted to cook, design foods, do some writing, and make some cross-cultural connections with students in other countries. During our early class meetings, we co-designed a food chemistry course. The course not only "covered" content that is taught in standard chemistry classes but also was richer because it deeply explored questions designed by students. We view this dialogical process where students can move individual felt-concerns into the realm of collective action to be what Fielding describes as "democratic fellowship" over one of "atomistic individualism" (Fielding, 2011, p. 66), and we look forward to working with students to develop these capacities by continuing these established practices.

At the end of the quarter, each student completed a project that was meaningful for them. One student developed a sustainable food, priced it, and wrote a research paper along with a public access article for it. Another student designed a food photo journal that described recipes and chemical reactions associated with creation of the food. Yet another student recreated food from the 1930s' Depression in an attempt to understand how families survive during difficult economic times. We had also agreed on several tasks that students would complete, including writing an in-depth research paper, weekly quizzes, and lab reports. Surprisingly, students wanted quizzes because they thought that these would be valuable in advancing their knowledge.

I have described curriculum co-construction in a way that suggests that students are always amenable to this process and that educators' and students' visions always align. This is sometimes not the case. Recently, Jasper, a middle school student, presented us with an interesting challenge. His peers all agreed on a long-term writing assignment in my science class and noted their chosen areas of growth for the term. Jasper (a new student) felt that his choice not to do any writing should be honored. He was open and eager to learn about "Cells, Human Societies and Public Health"—the agreed topic—but not to do any written assignment. According to Jasper,

> All my life, I have been made to write about things that are boring, and I don't care about. I know this is a chance for me to write about something I like but I'm just tired of writing. I will be taking this quarter off from writing.

For me as an educator, this declaration presented a conundrum. I understand gains and benefits that happen when students continuously practice and improve their writing. I consider giving students access and opportunities to a strong academic foundation to be a matter of justice. It is with these tools that students can "name their world" and even change it. If students are to be active agents in their education, student–teacher co-generation of curriculum must be a reflective process and continually renegotiated. How can we listen to Jasper and suspend our own agendas as teachers while ensuring he receives everything he deserves as our student? We continue to struggle with this question in active dialogue with Jasper.

Despite these challenges, we consider our curriculum creation process to be important in offering experiential and flexible learning opportunities while promoting true ownership of the learning process and responsibility toward others.

## Final Thoughts

Angeles Workshop School is an ongoing experiment built on the radical notion that young people should and can be free, and their voices are vital, not only in classrooms but in larger sociopolitical contexts. We embrace the challenges of co-creating structures with students that honor students' identities and experiences to foster greater sociopolitical agency. We continue to joyfully work, play and learn as we strive to provide "practical incantations of lived alternatives" (Fielding, 2012, p. 17) and an "anticipatory image of broader transformations" (p. 19). We welcome all fellow, like-minded educators to join us in the struggle to realize worlds where young people are democratic participants in their communities.

## Reflection Questions

How do these ideas relate to your teaching or schooling context? What similarities and differences do you notice?

Fielding (2001) invites us to "construct new practices and create new public spaces (physical and metaphorical)" (p. 106) if we are to develop communities of practice beyond traditional school models. What ideas for new practices, spaces, and frameworks to nurture student voice will you take from this chapter?

## Recommended Resources

### Democratic School Projects

Angeles Workshop School: www.angelesworkshopschool.com
The Selby Project: https://www.selbyproject.org/

### Respectful Communication

Restorative Practice Resource Project: https://www.restorative.ca
The Peaceful Parent: https://www.peacefulparent.com/

## References

Bippus, A. M., & Young, S. L. (2005). Owning your emotions: Reactions to expressions of self- versus other-attributed positive and negative emotions. *Journal of Applied Communication Research, 33*(1), 26–45.

Danovitch, R. (2019). *Powerful voicings: Agency and identity at a humanistic-inspired alternative school* (Unpublished doctoral dissertation). Columbia University, New York, NY.

Darder, A. (2018). *The student guide to Freire's "Pedagogy of the Oppressed."* London, England: Bloomsbury Academic.

Delpit, L. (2012). *"Multiplication is for White people": Raising expectations for other people's children*. New York, NY: New Press.

Dewey, John (1976). Creative democracy: The task before us. In J. Boydston (Ed.), *John Dewey: The Later Works, 1925–1953. Volume 14: 1939–1941, essays, reviews, and miscellany* (pp. 224–230). Carbondale: Southern Illinois University Press. (Original work published 1939)

Fielding, M. (2001). Beyond the rhetoric of student voice: New departures or new constraints in the transformation of 21st century schooling. *Forum, 43*(2), 100–110.

Fielding, M. (2011). Patterns of partnership: Student voice, intergenerational learning and democratic fellowship. In N. Mockler & J. Sachs (Eds.), *Rethinking educational practice through reflexive inquiry* (pp. 61–75). Dordrecht: Springer.

Fielding, M. (2012). From student voice to democratic community: New beginnings, radical continuities. In B. J. McMahon & J. Portelli (Eds.), *Student engagement in urban schools: Beyond neoliberal discourses* (pp. 11–28). Charlotte, NC: Information Age Publishing.

Freire, P. (2000). *Pedagogy of the oppressed* (M. B. Ramos, Trans.). New York, NY: Continuum. (Work originally published 1970)

Glasser, W. (1998). *Choice theory: a new psychology of personal freedom*. New York, NY: Harper Collins.

Jones, P., & Welch, S. (2010). *Rethinking children's rights: Attitudes in contemporary society*. New York, NY: Continuum.

McLaren, P. (1994). *Life in schools: An introduction to critical pedagogy in the foundations of education*. New York, NY: Longman.

Phillips, M. (1965, March 27). Now the teach-in: U.S. policy in Vietnam criticized all night. *The New York Times*. Retrieved from https://www.nytimes.com/1965/03/27/archives/now-the-teachin-us-policy-in-vietnam-criticized-all-night.html

Rogers, C. R. (1982). *On becoming a person: A therapist's view of psychotherapy*. Boston, MA: Houghton Mifflin.

Sehr, D. (1997). *Education for public democracy*. New York, NY: SUNY Press.

Stubbe, S., & Kitonga, N. (2013). *Angeles Workshop School: A revolutionary education*. Retrieved from http://www.angelesworkshop.com/home.html

PART IV

# PEDAGOGIES OF WITH-NESS

TWENTY-TWO

# Pedagogies of With-ness: Reflecting on and Beyond the Exhibition

*Linda Hogg (with) Charlotte Achieng-Evensen (with) Kevin Stockbridge (with) Suzanne SooHoo*

## Coming to the Idea of With-ness

We conceived of this book as an exhibition gathering together the work of scholars, teachers, students, and teacher educators who articulate a collective vision. We believe in the importance of educators coming alongside students and working with them to elevate voice and agency. As a writing community, this shared ethic united many from the United States and across the Pacific Ocean to New Zealand. While the authors have been refining their work, we, as editors, have been curating the collection. We have been closely examining the art pieces, gazing for long hours at the diverse canvases and reflecting on the fresh insights that each offers to our espoused ethic.

Having assembled this collection, we now gather outside the galleries, reflecting on how this art has influenced our knowing. From our privileged, intimate view, we discuss a shared quality, the essential thread at the heart of these pieces. We identify it as an ethic of with-ness. In this discussion, we came to realize the importance of with-ness for us, too, as the editorial team. With-ness was the glue that kept us together through challenges of geography, time zones, and editing responsibilities.

In this concluding chapter, we interrogate with-ness both as our new learning and as encountered pedagogies. Then, we leave you with a found poem selected from students' quotes. We hold that students have the final words. What happens next, dear readers, we leave to your possibility-posing and creativity.

## Defining With-ness

With-ness is an ethical concept imbued with psychological, social, political, and epistemological elements/facets. It is lived experience, enacted in mutuality and reciprocity. With-ness requires collective responsibility to move back and forth as we listen, seek, ponder, engage, reflect and perhaps reengage. With-ness is whole-bodied, and it demands active participation. Therefore, we utilize a call-and-response format, not only to define with-ness but also to enact it with you. We are not seeking answers but a way to engage with you as you ponder.

*With-ness Is . . . Shaping Group Identity*

Philosophers Heidegger (1990/2011), the Dali Lama and Desmond Tutu (Dalai Lama, Tutu, & Abrams, 2016), and Freire (1970/2000) believe that being in-the-world means being with people. Classroom cultures that embrace a concept of with-ness naturally move from "I" to "We" characterizations (Freire, 1970/2000).
**How does the concept of *with* change the relationship between teachers and students? Between students and students?**

*With-ness Is . . . Perceiving Each Other*

Former president Obama argues, "We can understand each other, and we all have a common set of hopes and dreams and impulses we can recognize in each other. And our survival depends on that" (2019, cited by Paul, 2019). He invites us to break through self-affirming cocoons, which would lead to, in Nick Hopkins's words, "a fundamental shift from seeing people as *other* to seeing them as intimate" (cited by Spinney, 2014, p. 130). We are alone no more and less likely to see classmates and teachers as Other.
**What happens when students and educators discover that they have allies in the classroom?**

*With-ness Is . . . Caring*

Where teaching is an act of love (Darder, 2002), an ethos of caring flourishes. With-ness is nurturing our humanity in educational settings. In with-ness, we cultivate authentic relationships.
**What does it mean when young people say, "I never felt like I belonged in school?"**

*With-ness Is . . . Embracing Imperfection*

Real connection involves being really seen and feeling secure in the knowledge that our imperfect self is worthy (B. Brown, 2012). Students and educators can bring their unfinishedness into classrooms without shame or guilt. They can grow and make mistakes as well as bring and express their identities without fear.

**How might embracing perceived imperfections be essential for the development of human potential in our learning spaces?**

*With-ness Is . . . Leveling Power*

Power is redistributed as we recognize multiple sources of knowledge in learning environments. Students and teachers bring expertise and values into the curriculum. Teaching and learning are co-generative.

**Whose knowledge is represented in classrooms? For whose benefit?**

*With-ness Is . . . Collaborating in Learning*

Harnessing the power of dialogic teaching (Littleton & Mercer, 2013; Wegerif, 2014) and cooperative learning (D. Brown & Thomson, 2002) involves a diversity of voices. By creating polyphonic learning spaces, we enact respect and support.

**How do we raise up and honor multiple voices and forms of expression?**

*With-ness Is . . . Engaging Synergy*

With-ness is organic and dynamic. When students and educators work together, their synergy catalyzes transformation, engendering ways to engage in new realities, new kinds of solidarity in action.

**What possibilities do we limit by resisting synergy in our classrooms?**

*With-ness Is . . . Expanding Knowledges and Worldview*

How we come to know, our epistemologies, can alter the way we view the world. Shifting our disposition from "I learn" and "I teach" to "we learn" and "we teach" inspires and emboldens students and educators. We move beyond worldviews that are individualistic to embrace a more collective, interconnected vision.

**How does one's worldview change when seen through collective lenses?**

## Pedagogies of With-ness

Looking closely at the word *pedagogy*, as through a kaleidoscope, we can shift our lens to include multiple ways of understanding. In an instrumentalist view of pedagogy, the art of teaching merely focuses on teaching models and strategies as approaches teachers must learn to step through and perform each stage correctly. This prescriptive perspective encourages the pedagogue to view their art as akin to mastery of different artistic techniques and processes to be effectively applied. Shifting our kaleidoscope lens reunites us with pedagogy's original meaning. As SooHoo and Wilson (2015) note, "the etymology of the word *pedagogy* comes from the Greek word paidagogos, which means a slave who escorted children to school (www. Merriam-webster.com/dictionary/pedagogy)" (p. xv). This lens allows us to consider *actors involved in the pedagogical act* as well as the action of pedagogy. To escort is to walk with. Thus, we view pedagogy as the study of educator–student with-ness. Both adult and student are involved. Pedagogy becomes relational, purposeful, and protective.

With-ness as pedagogy means that the art of teaching is interpersonal. Who we teach is as important as the subject. We see students "reality, history and perspectives" as having a central place, to humanize pedagogy (Bartolome, 1994, p. 173). Therefore, the calls and responses and meditations from the earlier section of this chapter can be used to interrogate and inform pedagogy.

## Closing Thoughts

By nature, an exhibition of work problematizes life's phenomena (Freire, 1970/2000). It evokes viewers' imagination, sentiment, or curiosity to identify codes and symbols by which society perpetuates its rules for social relations. Inherently, art poses questions that agitate consciousness. Art invites engagement, leading both creators and viewers to examine their critical actions as subjects in their world (Freire & Freire, 1994/2014). How will you turn the dial of your kaleidoscope? What new perceptions and conversations have you gained, related to the artwork? Culture? Yourself? Students? What twist of the kaleidoscope toward with-ness could create transformational possibilities for you and your students?

## Last Words From Students

The following "found" poems are derived from direct quotations by students in our chapters. *Shadows* consists of rejections of student voice and identity whereas *Lights* illuminates students being heard. Enjoy their review before you depart our exhibition of vignettes.

### Shadows

You do not listen to us.
The way we are treated in this school is just not fair.
I just never felt like I belonged in school.
When I was new to class, classmates swore at me and called me names.
I always felt like I was the outsider, so I was by myself most of the time.
I found school depressing.
Some of the teachers don't know how to deal with the Black kids.
I felt like I wasn't good enough.
I just wanted a helping hand but I never got it.
Your hand gets tired so you just put it down and give up.
If I don't get attention, I want to leave.
The teacher was rude. Everybody hated her.
She took my hat off and never gave it back.
We deserve to be treated with respect.
We deserve open/clean and fully supplied restrooms.
Kids teased me about being girly.
Stop gendering everything!
Weird. Different. Disconnected. Distant. Other. Outsider.

### Lights

Student voice is about being heard,
about making connections

to the real world
to the teachers who helped me learn,
she who listens,
he who helps.
I call on my teacher,
she does not crack
I have always been passionate
in making a difference.
be part of a movement
be brave enough
to take action on the things we care about
Finally, doing things that let me be me
Finally, my voice being heard.

## References


Bartolome, L. (1994). Beyond a methods fetish: Towards a humanizing pedagogy. *Harvard Educational Review, 64*(2), 173–194.

Brown, B. (2012). *The power of vulnerability: Teachings on authenticity, connection, and courage.* Louisville, CO: Sounds True.

Brown, D., & Thomson, C. (2002). *Co-operative learning in New Zealand.* New Plymouth, New Zealand: Dunmore Press.

Dalai Lama, Tutu, D., & Abrams, D. C. (2016). *The book of joy.* London, England: Hutchinson.

Darder, A. (2002). *Reinventing Paulo Freire: A pedagogy of love.* Boulder, CO: Westfield Press.

Freire, P. (2000). *Pedagogy of the oppressed* (M. B. Ramos, Trans.). New York, NY: Continuum. (Original work published 1970)

Freire, P., & Freire, A. M. N. (2014). *Pedagogy of hope: Reliving pedagogy of the oppressed.* New York, NY: Bloomsbury. (Original work published 1994)

Heidegger, M. (1990/2011). *Introduction to philosophy: Thinking and poetizing.* Bloomington: Indiana University Press.

Littleton, K., & Mercer, N. (2013). *Interthinking: Putting talk to work.* Abingdon, England: Routledge.

Paul, K. (2019, September). Obama says presidents should avoid social media in apparent Trump jab. *The Guardian.* Retrieved from: https://www.theguardian.com/us-news/2019/sep/18/obama-trump-social-media-tv-twitter

Spinney, L. (2014, February). Karma of the crowd. *National Geographic, 225*(2), 120–135.

SooHoo, S., & Wilson, T. (2015). Foreword. In P. McLaren, *Life in schools (6th ed.),* xiii–xvii. Boulder, CO: Paradigm Publishers.

Wegerif, R. (2014). *Dialogic: Education for the Internet age.* London, England: Routledge.

# Contributors

**Charlotte Achieng-Evensen** is a Kenyan-American K–12 educator and academic. Her work is centered in the intersections of Indigenous philosophies and colonization, culturally responsive methodologies, and professional learning for teachers. She has been a practitioner within the K–12 system for the past 20 years.

**Quaylan Allen** is Associate Professor in the Attallah College of Educational Studies and Director of First-Generation Programs at Chapman University, Orange, California. His research addresses educational equity by critically examining implications of social and educational policy and practice on culturally diverse populations.

**Dayle Anderson** is Senior Lecturer in the School of Education at Victoria University of Wellington, New Zealand. Dayle's research interests have a sociocultural focus, including development of teacher knowledge and beliefs and primary science education. Email: dayle.anderson@vuw.ac.nz.

**Amy Lassiter Ardell** is Clinical Assistant Professor and Program Coordinator of the Master of Arts in Curriculum & Instruction program in the Attallah College of Educational Studies at Chapman University in Orange, California.

**Delia Baskerville** is Lecturer in the School of Education at Victoria University of Wellington, New Zealand. Delia's most recent work is an ethnodrama performed by student actors, which presents the experiences of young people who truant, from her PhD. Email: delia.baskerville@vuw.ac.nz.

**Micaela Balzar** is Director of Innovation and Learning at Impression 5 Science Center. She has been working in the informal science education sector for over 25 years.

**Angela Calabrese Barton** is Professor in Educational Studies at the University of Michigan. Her research focuses on teaching and learning science for critical justice.

**Margaret Sauceda Curwen** is Associate Professor in the Master of Arts in Teacher Education program in the Attallah College of Educational Studies at Chapman University in Orange, California.

**Michelle Flowers-Taylor** earned her EdD at Loyola Marymount University, California. She was founding director of the Institute of Engineering Community and Cultural Competence at the University of Southern California. Her mission is to advance diversity in STEM disciplines.

**Antero Garcia** is Assistant Professor in the Graduate School of Education, Stanford University. Email: Antero.Garcia@stanford.edu

**Karen Garcia** is a student, community organizer, poet, and artist.

**Day Greenberg** is a University of Michigan postdoctoral researcher who conducts participatory research with youth on learning and development in out-of-school STEM.

**Linda Hogg** is Senior Lecturer in the School of Education at Victoria University of Wellington, New Zealand. Linda's research explores how schools use minoritized students' strengths and skills to transform their educational experience, and teacher education for social justice aims. Email: linda.hogg@vuw.ac.nz

**The Impression 5 Science Center Youth Action Council** is a group of youth recruited from out-of-school science programs to inform institutional action.

**Susanne Jungersen** was Principal of Porirua College, a New Zealand high school, from 1997 to mid-July 2016. She is now retired. Email: Susanne.jungersen@gmail.com

**Joanna Kidman** (Ngāti Maniapoto, Ngāti Raukawa, Ngāti Toa Rangatira) is Professor of Māori education at Victoria University of Wellington in New Zealand. Her research focuses on the politics of indigeneity, Māori youth, and settler-colonial nationhood.

**Ndindi Kitonga** is Co-founder of Angeles Workshop School, a radical secondary school in Los Angeles with a focus on democratic learning. Ndindi, a Kenyan American educator and activist, is also a published scholar in the areas of critical pedagogy and democratic education.

**Christopher Lewis** has taught high school history and English since 2005. Currently, he is a Teacher on Special Assignment supporting English learners. He earned his PhD from Chapman University and his areas of interest include youth voice, dystopian fiction, and civic engagement.

**Katherine Lewis** is Assistant Professor of Education and Director of the Multiple Subject (K-8) credential program, Dominican University of California. Katherine's research centers on social and cultural elements of education, including gender-inclusive schooling and social justice leadership. Email: Katherine.lewis@dominican.edu.

**Erin McCloskey** is Associate Professor of Education at Vassar College, Poughkeepsie, New York. Erin's research interests include looking at how interactional processes around literacy contribute to what counts as ability/disability. Email: ermccloskey@vassar.edu

**Adreanne Ormond** is an indigenous Māori from the Māori nation of Rongomaiwahine who was raised on her ancestral homeland. As a senior educationist within the university sector, her work involves economic, social, and political transformation for Māori society.

**Gabrielle Popp** is a Fulbright scholar and secondary English teacher at Beacon Day Treatment, Southgate, Michigan. Email: gabrielle.popp@gmail.com.

**Chris Proctor** is a PhD candidate at the Graduate School of Education, Stanford University. Email: cproctor@stanford.edu. Website: http://chrisproctor.net.

**Carah Reed** is a 20-year veteran teacher at a local high school in Southern California. She is car-free, student-centered, and a lover of all things hip-hop.

**Jorge F. Rodriguez** is Assistant Professor in the Integrated Educational Studies program within the Attallah College of Educational Studies at Chapman University, Orange, California.

**Tracy Rohan** is Principal Learning Support Adviser in the Ministry of Education, New Zealand. Tracy, of Ngāi Tahu descent, has a special interest in music education. Her many roles in education include teacher, teacher educator, and adviser. Email: tracy.rohan22@gmail.com

**Kevin Stockbridge** is Clinical Assistant Professor of Teacher Education in the Attallah College of Educational Studies, Chapman University, Orange, California. Kevin's research focuses on the wisdom of liminality and otherness, which illuminates possibilities of community and solidarity in/through education.

**Suzanne SooHoo** is Professor Emerita at Attallah College of Educational Studies, Chapman University, Orange, California. Suzanne's research focuses on critical pedagogy and qualitative research in different contexts: China, New Zealand, and Santa Ana, California.

**Edna Tan** is Professor of Science Education at the University of North Carolina at Greensboro. She investigates justice-oriented STEM learning.

**Huia Tomlins-Jahnke** is a member of Ngāti Kahungunu iwi, New Zealand. She is Professor of Maori and Indigenous Education at Massey University, New Zealand. Email: H.T.Jahnke@massey.ac.nz

**Anne Yates** is Senior Lecturer in the School of Education at Victoria University of Wellington, New Zealand. Anne's aim with her research is to enable more equitable access to educational opportunities. Email: anne.yates@vuw.ac.nz.

# Index


#BlackLivesMatter, 132
#NeverAgain, 134

A

*A Nation at Risk*, 3
Abd-El-Khalick, F., 94
Abrams, D. C., 212
Acosta, C., 182
action, 23
action research (AR), 7
activism, 130
African American female students, 37, 45–46
  academic identity of, 37
  asset-based perspective of, 44–45
  identity and, 39
  listening to, 43–44
  multicultural worldviews, 38, 40–42
  narrative analysis of, 38
  possible/oppositional selves, 38, 42–43
  sacred space, 38–40
ageism, xviii
agency, 132, 141
agender, 18
Aitken, V., 94
Aja, A. A., 3
Alcoff, L., 2
Allchin, D., 94
Allen, Q., 55
Alter, Z., 7
American Psychological Association, 18
Ames, M., 133
Amsden, J., 76
Anderson, D., 94
Angeles Workshop School, 197–99, 206
  city-as-classroom and, 197–98
  city-days, 198
  critical pedagogy and, 204
  curriculum of, 197–98, 202–3, 204–6
  curriculum co-construction at, 204–6
  mindfulness practices at, 200
  peaceful parenting/teaching and, 201
  radical collegiality and, 200
  restorative justice and, 201
  student voice and, 200–4, 204–6
  teach in, 204
  theoretical frameworks informing practices at, 199
  top-down democratic models at, 203
  use of experts and enthusiasts at, 202–3
anti-war radical activism, 204
Apple, M. W., 4, 182
Applied Behavior Analysis (ABA), 166, 167
Ardell, A., 118, 119
Arellano, G., 178
Ari, M., 93
Arnold, A., 90
Artilles, A., 117
atomistic individualism, 205
Autistic People
  liberation of, 165–66
  oppression of, 166–67
  resisting oppression, 172
  voice and, 171–72
authoring identities, 103, 105–8

B

Baker, M., 71
Baltodano, M., 8
Banks, J. A., 176
Barnett, C., 144
Bartolome, L., 214
Baskerville, D., 94
Basu, B., 130, 133
becoming, 136
behavioral intervention plan (BIP), 166, 167
being-in-role, 99
being-in-the-world, 212
Bell, J., 33
Berryman, M., 32, 33
Bhabha, H. K., 15
biculturation, 40
Biklen, D., 168
Binder, P., 33
Bippus, A. M., 201
Bishop, R., 33, 89
Black academic failure, 50
Black males, academically successful, 49–51, 55–56
  academic tracking of, 52
  anti-intellectualism and, 50
  culturally relevant pedagogies and, 49, 51
  deficit discourses and, 50
  disproportional discipline of, 52
  high expectations for, 52–53

racial stereotyping of, 52
teacher support of, 53–54, 54–55
Blikstein, P., 103, 104, 113
Bloomfield, D. C., 3
Bolstad, R., 7
Bolton, G., 93, 94
Bonner, F. A., 50
Bowers, C. A., 118, 119
BP National Excellence Award for Social Enterprise, 162
Bradley, D., 90
Brewer, J., 7
Bridge, S., 157
Broad, K. R., 130
Broadwin, I. T., 27
Brophy, J. E., 63
Brown, B., 213
Brown, D., 213
Brown, F., 27
Brown, L. X. Z., 173
Brown, R. N., 40
Business education, xxi, 153, 154

C

Cabrera, D., 121, 122
Cabrera, L., 121, 122
Cahill, C., 6
Cain, C., 105
Cameto, R., 59
Cammarota, J., 6, 7, 144, 183
Capra, B., 118
Capra, F., 118, 119, 122, 123, 124, 127
Cassell, J., 118, 125
Cassidy, T., 71
Chakrabortty, A., 154
channeling voices, 103, 109–11
Children's Commissioner Office, 32
Christensen, J. D., 70
city-as-classroom, 197–98
city-days, 198, 201
Cofield, W. B., 39
Cohen, J., 7
collaborative company voice and, 99
collaborative dialogue, 122
collective consciousness, 117, 119–20
Collins, D. A., 155
Collins, S., 132
commission letters, 95, 96
common sense, 37
community asset mapping, 75–76
conscience alley, 95, 97–99, 101
conscientization, 44
constant comparison, 95
Cook-Sather, A., 2, 5, 7, 34, 105
cooperative learning, 122, 213
critical educational theories, 198
critical justice theoretical framework, 144
critical literacy pedagogy, 111
critical making skills, 149–50
critical pedagogy, 44, 204
Critical Race Theory, 176
Critical Studies, 176
critical theory, 198
critical thinking, 154
Cultural Studies, 176
culturally relevant pedagogies, 49, 51
teachers' use of, 51–55
Cunneen, C., 70
Curwen, M., 118, 119

D

Dalai Lama, 212
Danovitch, R., 200
Darder, A., 39, 40, 43, 44, 45, 130, 203, 212
Darling-Hammond, L., 3
Davis, B., 117, 119, 125
Davis, C. L., 51
Davis, J. E., 50
deficit discourses, 50
deficit limitations, 182
deficit thinking, xviii, 177
DeFossett, A., 28
Delpit, L., 4, 130, 198
democratic fellowship, 205
developing critical awareness, 103, 111–13
Dewey, J., 203
dialogic learning, 121
dialogic teaching, 213
dialogical problem-solving, 198
dialogue, 41
Diera, C., 8
Dimock, M., 3
dojo, 165–66
Autistic students in, 167–71
dominant cultural forms, 199
dominant economic theory, 154
Donald, D., 70
Dorn, L. J., 104
*Doughnut Economics*, 154, 155, 156
Douglas, T.-R. M., 50

drama, children learning through, 93–95
  being-in-role and, 99
  collaborative company voice and, 99
  conscience alley and, 95, 97–99
  enactment and, 93
  future practices for, 100–1
  learning from, 99–100
  Mantle of the Expert (MotE), 94
  student voice and, 95–97, 99
  writing-in-role and, 97, 99, 101
Draxton, S., 34
Drummond, J., 90
dual-subjectivity, 6
Duncan-Andrade, J., 6
dystopian novels, 129
  dystopian resistance and, 131–35
  hope and, 135–36
  as a mirror of today's society, 133
  student book club and, 130
dystopian philosophy, 130
dystopian resistance, 131–35

E
Earle, J., 154
*Econocracy, The*, 154
Economics education, 154
educational design leaders, 151
Ee, J., 50
Emdin, C., 51
emotional and behavioral disorder (EBD), 59
emotional and behavioral disorders, students with, 59–60, 61, 66–67
  Individual Education Plans (IEP) and, 66–67
  juvenile detention centers and, 59
  natural supports and, 64
  relationships and, 61–62
  restorative practices and, 63–64
  school dropout rates among, 59
  student voice and, 60–61, 63–64, 65
  in the U.S. context, 66
  wraparound services and, 60–61, 63–64
enactment, 93
Esposito, J., 51
Ethnic Studies classrooms
  10-point plan proposal by students, 181–82
  National Day of Protest and, 182
  student self-determination, 178–83
  student voice and, 175–76
Ewing, R., 93
experiential pedagogies, 198
expert knowledge, 37, 43

F
Fecho, B., 3, 4
Feminist Theory, 176
Ferguson, D. L., 34
Ferguson, Missouri, 132, 133
Ferguson, R., 121, 122, 126
Fielding, M., xix, 1, 2, 4, 5, 6, 7, 200, 205, 206, 207
Filipiak, D., 6
*Final Straw, The*, 153–54
  business mission of, 157–58
Fine, M., 6, 32, 144, 183
Fletcher, A., 2, 4–7
Ford, T., 32, 33
Forest Stewardship Council, 163
Fox, K., 117, 122
Fox, S., 85
frame, 94
Frankenberg, E., 50
Freire, A. M. N., 214
Freire, P., 2, 4, 15, 23, 130, 135, 166, 212, 214
  banking method of education, 129, 167, 204
  critical reflection and, 167
  dialogue and, 40, 44, 45
  naming the world, xviii
  oppression and, 167
  praxis and, 1
  relational solidarity, xviii
  teacher-student contradiction, 141
Friedlander, J., 121
Friedman, M., 154
friendly system, 123

G
Garcia, A., 6, 136
Gargano, J., 2
Garza, N., 59
Gase, L. N., 28, 32
Gay, G., 4, 51, 54, 89
Gaztambide-Fernandez, R., xviii, 81
Geiger, S. G., 27
gender diversity, 17–19, 19–23, 24
gender identity, 18
gender-inclusive schools, 23
gender nonconforming, 18
gendered microaggressions, 17

genderfluid, 18
genderqueer, 18
Giga, N. M., 23
Gillies, R. M., 122
GirlBoss New Zealand, 158
Giroux, H. A., 2, 3, 130
  hidden purpose of education, 4
  passive role of students, 1
  penal pedagogies, xviii
  radical imagination and, 135
  war on youth, xviii
Glynn, T., 89
Gogen, M., 93
Goh, S.-E., 118
González, E. R., 176
González, N., 51
Gonzales, T., 117
Gray, S., 3
Green, L., 84, 85
Greene, M., xviii
Gregory, A., 50, 52
Greytak, E. A., 23
Gross, S., 5
Groundwater-Smith, S., xix
Grumet, M. R., 105
Gundogan, A., 93

H
Hanauer, N., 118, 127
Hanreddy, A., 34
Hargreaves, D., 84
Hardgrove, A., 74
Harper, S. R., 50
Harry, B., 52
Hart, R., 5
Harvard University, 154
Having, B., 3
Hawk, K., 33
Haymes, L., 167
Heathcote, D., 94
Heidegger, M., 212
Hempelmann, J., 197
Hernandez-Saca, D., 117
hidden curriculum, 4
High School Kickback, 104, 106–8, 109, 111–12
high-stakes testing, 3, 54
Hilbertidou, A., 158
Hill, J., 33
Hintz, C., 130, 133
Hogan, A., 63
Hogg, D., xvii
Holland, D., 105
hooks, b., 4
Hopkins, N., 212
Horton, M., xviii
hot-seating, 95, 96
Hotter-Sorensen, N., 33
Houle, G., 37
Howard, T. C., 51
Hudley, 40
hui, 70
humanist models, 198
*Hunger Games, The*, 132
Hunter, A., 50

I
Identity and Voice Gallery, xix–xx, 15
imperfect self, 213
Individual Education Plans (IEP), 66–67
Individuals with Disabilities Education Act (IDEA), 59
Ink, 104
Inkle, 104
Intensive Wraparound Services (IWS), 60–61, 63–64
interactive storytelling, 103–4
  authoring identities and, 103, 105–8
  channeling voices and, 103, 109–11
  developing critical awareness, 103
  models of personhood and, 106
  performativity and, 106
Ivanič, R., 109

J
Jacovkis, J., 32
Jahnle, H., 74
Jones, M., 7
Jones, P., 203
*Joylantus*, 96
justice boxes, 146
juvenile detention centers, 59

K
K-12 schools, 17, 19–23
Kahn, J. H., 28
kaikōrero, 70, 71
Kamler, B., 105
Kano, J., 168
karakia, 72

Karlsson, B., 33
kaupapa-a-iwi, 71
Kawharu, M., 69
Keeter, S., 3
Khishfe, R., 94
Kick It Over, 154
Kitonga, N., 197
Klingner, J., 52
knots, 104
Kosciw, J. G., 23
Krahn, M., 70
Kramer, J., 90
Krane, V., 33
Krueger, N. F., 162
Kumashiro, K., 3
Kuo, T., 28
Kuser, W. L., 27

**L**
Lacayo, C., 177, 178, 182
Lachicotte, W., 105
Ladder of Student Involvement, 2, 4–7
Ladson-Billings, G., 51, 54, 55, 182
Lambert, R., 119
Lamont, A., 84
Lang, J. M., 45
Lederman, J. S., 94
Lederman, N. G., 94
Lee, O., 51
Lee, P. W., 6
Lensmire, T. J., 105
Levine, P., 59
Lewis, C., 130
Lewis, K. M., 17
*Lights*, 215
listening, 43–44
literacy-based computer science education, 103
literacy spaces, 114
literary texts, 135
Littleton, K., 213
Liu, E., 118, 127
Lomawaima, K. T., 70
Lopez, A. E., 51
Lozenski, B. D., 7
Luce-Kapler, R., 117, 119
Lugg, C. A., 18
Luisa, P. L., 118, 119, 122, 123, 124, 127
Luke, A., 105
Lynn, M., 51

**M**
Macedo, D., 3
MacGillivray, L., 118, 119
makerspaces, 143
    conceptual framework of, 144
    justice boxes and, 146
    key themes of, 145
    power, respect, and, 145–47
    White dominance of, 143
    Youth Action Council (YAC) and, 143, 144–45, 147–48, 150
Mallan, K., 133
Mallozzi, C. A., 3
Mansfield, J., 89
Mantle of the Expert (MotE), 94
Māori humor, 74
Māori youth, 60
marae, 70
March For Our Lives, xvii, 134
Marshall, N., 84
McCallum, R., 130
McCarthy, T., 70
McCloskey, E., 165
McDowell, L., 74
McElwee, E. W., 27
McLaren, P., 2, 4, 130, 141, 198
Meadows, D. H., 118
Mercer, N., 213
Merriam-webster.com, 214
Miguel, C., 2
Millar, G., 158–62
Miller, C., 93
Milman, O., xvii
mindfulness practices, 200
Ministry of Education, 33
Mir, A., 182
Mirowski, P., 154
Mirra, N., 6, 8, 134
Mitra, D., 162
Mitra, D. L., 1, 4, 5, 6, 7, 8, 136
models of personhood, 106
Mohr, E. S., 3
Mohr, K. A. J., 3
Moje, E. B., 105
Montes, A., 32
Moran, C., 154
multicultural worldviews, 38, 40–42, 45
Museum of New Zealand Te Papa Tongarewa, 60
museums, xiii

Musics, 86, 87, 88, 89, 90, 91
music education, 83–84
  inclusion, exclusion and, 89
  inclusive curriculum and, 88–90
  informed by culture, 85–88
  social imagination and, 85
  students and, 85
  world musics and, 86
Myers, B. A., 172
Myers, M., 158–62

N
narrative analysis, 38
National Council on Disability, 59
National Day of Protest, 182
National School Lunch Program (NSLP), 176
natural supports, 64
Neelands, J., 93
Neergaard, H., 162
neoliberalism, 7, 154
Ness, O., 33
Nevin, A., 32, 33
*New Zealand Curriculum*, 94
New Zealand Ministry of Education, 69
New Zealand Ministry of Health, 69
Newman, L., 59
Nganga, C. W., 50
Nieto, S., 4
No Child Left Behind (NCLB), 3
Noguera, P., 50
nonbinary, 18
North, A., 84
Norton, P. L., 27
Nursten, J. P., 28

O
Obama, B., 212
O'Brien, E. L., 6, 7
O'Driscoll, S. J., 63
O'Hagan, R., 156–57, 157–58, 158–62
Oldfather, P., 7
O'Neill, S., 84
Orfield, G., 50

P
Palmer, R. T., 50
Park, M., 118
Parkland, Florida, 133
participatory action research (PAR), 6
Paul, K., 212
peaceful parenting/teaching, 201
Pearce, T. C., xx, 141
pedagogy, 214
Pedagogy Gallery, xx, 81
peer relationships, 40
penal pedagogies, xviii
performativity, 106
Perkes, C., 66
Perry, R., 28
Phillips, M., 204
Phillips, S., 121
Phillipson, N., 121
Pipi, K., 71
Pivik, J. R., 75
Podsiadlowski, A., 85
political resistance, 132
Porirua College, 187–88
  Reclaim the Bathroom Facilities, 189
  student appointment panel and, 191–93
  student voice and, 187–88, 189–90, 190–91, 191–93, 194
  truancy and, 188
  vandalism and, 188–91, 193
  White flight and, 187
Porter, A. J., 63
positive problem-solving skills and behavior, 63
possible/oppositional selves, 38, 42–43, 45, 74–75
power, 213
*Powerful Voicings*, 200
pōwhiri, 70
praxis, 1
Presentation Stations, 149
Proctor, C., 103, 104, 113

Q
Quaglia, R., 117, 122

R
racial identities, 49
racial socialization, 49
radical civic imagination, 130
radical collegiality, xxi, 200
randori, 168
Rangatahi Māori youth
  communication and, 73–76
  community asset mapping and, 75–76
  global context and, 76
  Marae-based hui, 71–72

statistics about, 69–70
team building and, 72–73
Raworth, K., 153, 154, 155, 156, 162
reciprocity, xx, 7
Reclaim the Bathroom Facilities, 189
reflection, 23
relational solidarity, xviii
reductionist thinking, 118
Reiher, J., 156–57, 157–58, 158–62
resistance, 130
restorative justice, 201
Rethinking Economics, 154
Reyes, J. M., 6
Richardson, C., 33
Richman, J., 27
Roberts, B., 158
Robinson, S., 162
Rogers, C. R., 204
Rohan, T. J., 84
Romero, A., 6
Rootham, E., 74
Rowley, J., 121
Ruddick, J., 1
rules system, 123

S

sacred space, 38–40, 45
safety system, 123
Sandretto, S., 93
Saxton, J., 93
Schaeffer, J., 70
schools
gender diversity in, 17, 19–23
standardization of curriculum, 54
Schultz, K., 3
science, technology, engineering, and math (STEM), 143, 145
Selingo, J. J., 3
Senge, P., 118
Sequenzia, A., 167
*Shadows*, 215
Sharesies, 158
Shor, I., 2
Shyman, E., 166
Siegel-Hawley, G., 50
Simone, N., xvii
Skiba, R., 50
Skinner, D., 105
Sleeter, C., 3
Smith, L., 90
social imagination, 85
social systems, mapping of, 123, 124
Soffos, C., 104
SooHoo, S., 7, 32, 33, 213
Spinney, L., 212
staff noticeboard, 95, 96
Stanley, T., xix
Statistics NZ, 69
Steinberg, S. R., xviii
St. Mary's College, 156
Storey, K., 167
Stubbe, S., 197
student forums, 7
student voice, xviii–xix, 60–61, 63–64, 65
affect on teachers' pedagogy, 129
being heard, 215
being rejected, 215
Ethnic Studies classrooms. See Ethnic Studies classrooms
learning from, 183–84
systems thinking and, 119–20
*Also see* Angeles Workshop School, Porirua College
students
academic achievement and, 89
as agents of change, 117, 130, 141
dominant cultural forms and, 199
listening to, 1–2
passive role of, 1
racialized perceptions of, 182
studying economics, 154
types of contestations by, 15
walkouts and, 179–83
*Also see* drama; emotional and behavioral disorders
*Students Uniting in Love*, xvii
students-with-teachers, xvi
*Subtractive Schooling: U.S.-Mexican Youth and the Politics of Caring*, 179
Sumara, D., 117, 119
Sustainable Coastlines, 162
Swain, A. N., 51
systemic inequality, 1
systemic sustainability education (SSE), 119
systems thinking, 117
collaborative dialogue and, 122
cooperative learning and, 122
definition of, 118
democratizing classrooms with, 120–22
description of schools using, 117

dialogic learning and, 121
holistic worldview of, 123–25
making a difference using, 126–27
purposeful action beyond classrooms, 125–26
student voice and, 119–20

**T**

Tanggaard, L., 162
Tarabini, A., 32
Tarrant, M., 84
Tate, W. F., 51
Taylor, M. F., 38
Taylor, P., 3
Te Kahu Tōī, 60
Te Momo, F., 74
Te Pou o Te Whakaaro Nui, 69
teach-in, 204
think in systems, 118
Think Tank, 143
curriculum of, 144–45
empowerment and, 148–50
Presentation Stations and, 149
Thompson, C., 213
Thompson, G., 33
Thorsen, S., 84
Thunberg, G., xvii
Tiakiwai, S., 33
Tiatia, J., 85
Tilaia, O., xvii
tori, 166, 168, 169, 171
transphenomenal complexity, 119
Trask, H., 70
Trites, R., 130
truancy, 31–33
grounded theory and, 28–31
history of, 27–28
student well-being and, 33
teacher kindness and, 33
*Also see* Youth who Truant
Trustees of Boston University, 27
Tutu, D., 212

**U**

uke, 166, 168, 169, 170
Unfold Studio, 104, 106, 113
Utopia, 73
utopian thinking, 130

**V**

Van Horn, R., 154
Van Wynsberghe, R., 76
Valenzuela, A., 179, 182
value-driven transformational goals, 157
Ventura, A., 133
Villegas, C., 23
voice-as-dialogue, 109
von Hayek, F., 154

**W**

Wagner, M., 59, 60
Walker, R., 72
*Walkout*, 178
Ward-Perkins, Z., 154
Warren, C. A., 50
Wegerif, R., 121, 122, 213
Welch, S., 203
Wellington Hospitality Group, 161
Wellington, New Zealand, 187
Wells, T., 93
Wertsche, J. V., 105
White patriarchal ideological hegemony, 50
wide-awakeness, xviii
Williams, H. D., 27
Willis, G., 3
Wilson, C. M., 50
Wilson, T., 118, 125, 214
with-ness, xvi, xvii
definition, xix, 211–14
pedagogy of, xxi, 214
Witt, E., 134
Wood, B.E., xx, 141
Wood, J.L., 50
workshop-based pedagogy, 104
world musics, 86
Wright, B. L., 50
writing-in-role, 97, 99, 101

**Y**

Yonezawa, S., 7
Yoon, S. A., 118
Young Enterprise Scheme (YES), 153–54, 156–57, 158, 162
Young, S. L., 201
youth
as the abandoned generation, 2
empowerment of, 8
levels of involvement, 4–7

Youth Action Council (YAC), 143, 144–45
accomplishments of, 146
collective statement from, 150–51
members making a difference, 147–48
ongoing efforts of, 150–51
youth participatory action research (YPAR), 144, 183
Youth who Truant (YwT), 27, 28
improving teacher response to, 33
messages from, 31–33
prejudice in the classroom, 29–31
student voice and, 34–35
*Also see* truancy
Youth-Adult Partnerships Gallery, xx–xxi, 141
youth participatory action research (YPAR), 6